UNIT
731

PETER WILLIAMS
AND DAVID WALLACE

UNIT
731

*Japan's Secret Biological
Warfare in World War II*

THE FREE PRESS
A Division of Macmillan, Inc.
NEW YORK

The Free Press
A Division of Macmillan, Inc.
866 Third Avenue, New York, N.Y. 10022

First American Edition 1989

Printed in the United States of America

printing number

1   2   3   4   5   6   7   8   9   10

Library of Congress Cataloging-in-Publication Data

Williams, Peter.   22.95
    Unit 731 : Japan's secret biological warfare in World War II /
Peter Williams and David Wallace. — 1st American ed.
        p.   cm.
    Bibliography: p.
    Includes index.
    ISBN 0-02-935301-7
    1. Japan. Rikugun. Kantōgun. Butai, Dai 731—History.   2. World
War, 1939-1945—Regimental histories—Japan.   3. Biological warfare—
Japan.   I. Wallace, David.   II. Title.
D810-B3W55   1989
940.54'13'52—dc19   88-39072
                                                        CIP

CONTENTS

ILLUSTRATIONS

AUTHORS' INTRODUCTION

Porton Down, Britain's top-secret chemical defence research establishment, lies in the gently rolling landscape of Salisbury Plain, towards the western extremity of Television South's broadcasting region. Known more correctly today as the Ministry of Defence's Chemical Defence Establishment, it was during the First World War that Porton Down first began research into chemical weapons. Its responsibilities were expanded during the last war to include the closely linked subject of biological warfare. For its entire history, Porton has remained one of the country's most secretive places, although the establishment's aims have now been narrowed to the research of defences against chemical attack.

Despite the fact that Britain unilaterally dispensed with its own chemical weapons in the 1950s, and ceased research into biological weapons as the result of a multilateral treaty in the 1970s, the awesome potential of chemical and biological warfare has remained at the forefront of the military scientific agenda. As a result, the gates to Porton Down remain closed and its current activities as inscrutable as ever to public debate and inspection.

It was originally intended that TVS would undertake a trilogy of programmes about chemical and biological warfare, including one about the work of Porton Down. Only one, however, was made: *Unit 731 – Did The Emperor Know?*

It told the story of the only known major attempt to create, deploy and use biological weapons in war – the story of Unit 731 of the Japanese Imperial Army during the Second World War. Drawing on the first-hand accounts of a number of former members of the Unit, it told how prisoners of war were used in horrific "human guinea-pig" experiments at the detachment's Manchurian death camp; how and where the biological weapons were used; how the perpetrators of these crimes escaped justice by selling their scientific expertise, in return for immunity from prosecution for war crimes; and how Gen. Douglas MacArthur, the Supreme Commander of the Allied Powers in postwar Japan, had been aware of, and was a party to, that agreement.

The film, which David C. Rea directed, made an enormous impact.

It was shown all over the world, in Europe, the Far East and the Soviet Union. The crowded press conferences in London indicated the depth of concern at the high-level cover-up the film revealed. One exchange after the London press conference was at the same time sad and shrewd. "Congratulations," said the Japanese reporter who was representing the national broadcasting system, NHK. "It is a fine piece of work . . ." Pause "But it will never be shown in Japan." Alas, he was correct.

In Japan, the activities of Unit 731 remain a politically sensitive issue. Many of the detachment's former members went on to assume high positions in the Japanese scientific community, and the activities of the Unit have even cast a shadow across the Japanese Imperial Family.

In America, by contrast, the documentary precipitated a Congressional inquiry into the claims for medical compensation from American prisoners-of-war incarcerated in a camp in Mukden, Manchuria, and allegedly experimented upon by Unit 731 scientists. The Americans were held at Mukden together with servicemen from Britain, Australia and New Zealand.

David Wallace was responsible for chapters 1, 2, 3, 4, 6, 7, 8, 11, 12, 13, 14 and 15. Peter Williams for chapters 5, 9, 10 and 16. Chapter 17 was jointly written. The authors would like to thank Prof. Kei'ichi Tsuneishi of Nagasaki University for the countless hours he spent advising on the writing of the book. Special thanks are also due to Fuyuko Nishisato whose tireless and tenacious work have greatly added to the book.

Seiichi Morimura and *Akahata* reporter Masaki Shimosato kindly donated many photographs and shared the results of many years of work spent researching this subject.

Much historical and other documentary material was given by Tomiso Asano of the *Mainichi Shinbun*, Osaka, and by Prof. Kentarō Awaya of Rikkyō University, Tokyo, and Prof. Takeo Matsumura of Keiō University, Tokyo.

William Lewis of the Military Field Branch of the Washington National Archives and Norman Covert at Fort Detrick, Maryland, spent many hours searching through dozens of record groups in their archives. Other valuable evidence was also forthcoming from John Powell of San Francisco, California, Dr Joseph Needham of Gonville and Caius College, Cambridge, Peter McGill of the *Observer*, Tokyo, Robert Whymant formerly of the *Guardian*, Tokyo, Vladimir Mikheev of *Isvestia*, Moscow, Dr Stephen Endicott of York University, Canada, Dr B. J. Brennan, in New South Wales, Australia and Greg Rodriquez Jnr and his veteran colleagues in the

United States. Crucially, our thanks to the late Dr Murray Sanders, who opened his files and his heart to us, and was able to guide us with first-hand accounts and confirmation of what had happened in Japan in 1945. We are also grateful to his wife, Peggy Sanders, for her patience with our requests.

In this country, Dr Julian Perry Robinson of the Science Policy Research Unit at Sussex University and Dr Alastair Hay of the University of Leeds gave generously of their help and support; as did Major Robert Peaty, Arthur Christie and other British veterans who had been captured by the Japanese and sent to Mukden.

Our personal thanks are also due to Jo Richardson and Fran Newitt for their unstinting efforts and selflessness during the writing of the book.

Just before transmission of the television programme, we discovered that British prisoners-of-war had indeed been in the prisoner-of-war camp in Mukden visited by scientists of Unit 731 and, that their senior officer, Major Robert Peaty, was living in the cathedral city of Winchester. He had kept a diary, extracts from which appear in this book. We talked in the sun-drenched garden of his home, amid the heavy scent of his English roses, and recalled the nightmares of forty years before. The idea that had sprung from an exploration of Porton Down had circled the globe and come to rest not fifty miles away, in the memories of an eighty-three-year-old English country gentleman. It was one of the last pieces of the puzzle whose full picture portrays in all its horror one of the best-kept secrets of the Second World War. What Japanese General Shirō Ishii called his "secret of secrets . . ."

Peter Williams
David Wallace
1988

PART 1

THE SECRET

Chapter 1

A Discovery

The myriad of angled streets that cover the Kanda district of Tokyo once housed whole communities of craftsmen in the old Edo days of Japan. Situated then just outside Edo Castle this area was a centre of trade and barter catering for the needs of the castle's illustrious occupants. Later, after the devastation of the Second World War, during the days of the American Occupation it became the centre for used-kimono sales. Many GIs picked up these beautiful family treasures for a small fraction of their actual worth, when, for the Japanese, money for food was much more important than adornment. Today, Kanda is known as a student town. Its streets are lined with second-hand bookshops, welcome havens for the habitual browser or the poor student trying to save a few hundred yen on textbooks.

One of these random browsers was a postgraduate student from Tokyo's Keiō University. He discovered, one day in 1984, a musty box of papers which, judging by their contents, seemed to have belonged to an officer in the former Imperial Japanese Army; possibly an ageing widow having a clear-out of her late husband's belongings. As he flicked through the box's diverse contents two sheaves of scientific documents stood out.[1] The first sheaf had some printed sketch maps attached: features mapped out by contours, an arrow showing wind direction and an unexplained symbol scattered about. The student paused to ponder the significance of the symbol.

Attached to the other set of papers, obviously to do with medicine, were some tables. Each column was headed by a three-figure number. He cast his eyes down the tables. The categories denoted by horizontal rows seemed to show different symptoms of a human disease. The progress of these symptoms had been carefully measured at regular intervals. With medical precision the disease had been charted to the point at which the subject died.

The table headed by the number 691 showed death after five days; for 991 it had taken longer, ten days. Measurements had been made of muscle tension at various parts of the body during the disease. Spasms had been noted.

Turning to the main narrative and research protocol section of the

3

report the student learned that it concerned tetanus, an agonising disease where the victim frequently dies in violent, painful and unpredictable muscular spasms. Its author was a Lt-Col Naeo Ikeda.

Something about the report disturbed the student. It was uncannily comprehensive. The tables were too full, too detailed. They appeared to have recorded symptoms from the beginning, the very inception, of the disease right through to its fatal conclusion. How could this happen, he wondered, under normal medical circumstances? Surely victims only reported their illness *after* symptoms had begun to appear! Then, to his astonishment, the paper revealed that each subject had been deliberately infected, in one case by injection in the heel.

Unwittingly, the student had uncovered perhaps the only surviving original evidence of one of the greatest secrets of the Second World War. Locked away behind these anonymous symbols and numbers lay one of the most sinister tales of modern times.

Chapter 2

Higher Forms of Killing

The village of Kamo in Chiba Prefecture lies to the east of Tokyo, not far from the city's much-troubled Narita airport, scene of so much violence and rioting in recent years. It was in this small agricultural village that Shirō Ishii was born on June 25th, 1892, the fourth son of a rich landowning family. Throughout the nineteenth century, from the era of the Shōgun warriors through to the reintroduction of the Imperial system under the Meiji Restoration, hundreds of poor villagers paid feudal tribute to the wealthy Ishii family. A print of Ishii's grandfather's day shows the Ishii villa surrounded by an impressive assembly of outbuildings encircled by trees, an orchard and a bamboo forest. The family had its own graveyard on top of a nearby hill shaded in a grotto of trees. Today, the graves are still there, carefully tended.

Shirō was bright, easily eclipsing his three elder brothers in academic study. At school, it is said, he could memorise whole tomes of work overnight and he gained entrance to the elite Kyoto Imperial University. For a Japanese he was a giant, measuring a full 1 metre 80 cm (nearly 6 feet) in height. He bore himself well and had a booming voice. He was an individualist, his demeanour indicating high determination and arrogance.

Graduating in medicine Ishii joined the Imperial Guards as an Army Surgeon. At first he enlisted as a volunteer. A fierce nationalist by nature, he found himself at home in the military and took up a regular commission. In 1922 he was attached to the 1st Army Hospital in Tokyo. Two years later he returned to Kyoto to continue his studies as a postgraduate researching bacteriology, serology, preventive medicine and pathology.[1] That year he was sent on a project which was to affect the rest of his life.

The island of Shikoku lies south of Honshū, the main island of Japan, and north-east of the country's main southern island, Kyūshū. It was there, in the island's Kagawa district, that a highly virulent disease, a form of encephalitis, had broken out; in Japan it eventually claimed more than 3,500 lives. This great epidemic was the first in medical history to be recognised as the "Japanese B" variety of encephalitis, a disease which results in severe inflammation of the

5

brain. It was an extremely difficult disease to study. Little was known of its cause, and it was difficult to discover its method of transmission.

Mortality was running at a high rate, around 60 per cent, when the young doctor arrived. Some quick results were needed. Ishii began the difficult task of devising an effective filtration method for isolating the microscopic virus thought to be the cause of the disease.[2] It is unknown whether he was successful. But this early experience brought him into contact with two fields of scientific research, epidemic prevention and water filtration, which were to dominate the rest of his life.

In Kyoto, city of the exquisite golden temple, beautiful Kamo River and enigmatic Ryōanji Temple stone garden, Ishii married Kiyoko, the beautiful daughter of President Torasaburō Araki of his university. This marriage, it is said, made him a distant relation to General Sadao Araki, Japan's War Minister 1931–34 and Education Minister 1938–39.* Ishii was to show throughout his life an uncanny ability to find friends and patrons in high places. Among his Kyoto contemporaries he made valuable acquaintances, although he may not have been the most popular student. Graduates from the same university in Japan were frequently organised into groups called *gakubatsu*, a powerful old boys' network. Ishii and his professors, Kimura, Toda, Kiyono and Shōji were soon to put this *gakubatsu* to sinister use.

In 1927 under the supervision of bacteriology professor Ren Kimura, Ishii gained his doctorate for "Research on Gram Positive Twin Bacteria".

Kimura remembered Ishii as an audacious though often inconsiderate student.

> In a word, Ishii was flamboyant [he recalled]. At night he would use test tubes and apparatus that other students had washed clean . . . At that time there were thirty to forty research students, and they had to be careful to share the laboratory equipment because there wasn't enough to go round. He would come at night to do his work after everyone had left . . . The others would really be annoyed when they came in and found them dirty the next morning . . . He married the daughter of President Araki whose lodging was close to the laboratory, so Ishii would drop in on him. He was really cheeky, pushing his way into a place like that.[4]

* This claim is made in an American document.[3] Sadao Araki was of humble birth. The President of Kyoto Imperial University, however, was from aristocratic stock. The claim, therefore, is perhaps untrue.

Far away in Europe the Great Powers in the aftermath of the First World War had begun to debate the ethics of various forms of scientific warfare, particularly gas warfare. By 1925 the high-water mark of public hostility to chemical warfare (CW) had been reached. Military men were feeling that it might be dishonourable to resort to such a revolting form of warfare. In Geneva on June 17th that year most powers signed a protocol prohibiting the use in war of asphyxiating, poisonous or other gases and of bacteriological methods.[5] Japan and America, however, did not ratify this protocol. Attending the Japanese delegation at Geneva was a Second Class Regular Physician, Harada, from the War Ministry's Medical Bureau. Ishii, already a theorist and advocate of biological methods of warfare, reacted strongly to a report prepared by Harada on the talks. Through an intermediary Ishii had been advancing the cause of biological warfare (BW) at the War Ministry. Lt-Gen Saburō Endō, then an assistant to the chief Japanese representative at the Geneva meetings, has recalled that young Ishii's ideas had even received a hearing with the then War Minister.

"At the time," said Endō, "Ishii's face was well known around staff headquarters. He always emphasised the role of bacteriological warfare in tactical planning." But the Army Staff were as yet unreceptive to Ishii's ideas.[6]

After an attachment to the Kyoto Army Hospital, Ishii decided to settle some questions for himself. In April 1928 he left Japan for a two-year world study trip. With letters of introduction from military attachés in Japanese consulates and embassies, Ishii visited research establishments in nearly thirty countries, including Russia, America France and Germany.[7] Junior as he then was, on his return to Japan Ishii brought with him some momentous observations and recommendations.

He told his superiors, probably untruthfully, that all the most powerful Western countries were secretly researching biological warfare.[8] And he argued that the formal prohibition of "bacteriological methods" reached at Geneva in fact implied its greatest potential as a weapon. He told leading officials of the War Ministry and Army General Staff that if Japan did not follow the same course she would find herself in serious difficulties in the future.[9] With his great interest in bacteriology he may also have brought to their attention various other matters: the destructive power of epidemics; the way in which, for example, Europe had been ravaged by plague in the fourteenth, fifteenth, sixteenth and seventeenth centuries; the way in which Germany had swept aside the Hague Declarations of 1899 and 1907 banning poison gas, as it used chlorine, phosgene and mustard gas on the Allies and finally the horror with which experiment on human beings was regarded by European medical researchers, steeped in the Hippocratic Oath. He reasoned that Japan should quickly grasp the vast lead which it was now possible to gain in an entirely new form of warfare, and toyed with the thought that if human experimental data could be found, then this would give his country an unbeatable lead.

Support for his ideas came from three interesting and influential people. One was Colonel Chikahiko Koizumi, the man soon to become the Army's Surgeon General and later Japanese Health Minister; another was Colonel Tetsuzan Nagata, soon to become Chief of the War Ministry's powerful Military Affairs Bureau[10] and the third was War Minister Araki himself. Other allies were Colonel Yorimichi Suzuki, chief of the 1st Tactical Section of Army General Staff Headquarters[11] and Colonel Ryūiji Kajitsuka, chief of the Sanitation Section of the War Ministry's Medical Bureau. A bacteriologist, Kajitsuka had met and befriended Ishii when they worked together at the 1st Army Hospital in Tokyo.[12]

Koizumi, the founder of Japan's CW programme, had a special reason for supporting Ishii, rooted in a bitter experience from his past. A graduate of Tokyo Imperial University, he had been greatly interested in biochemistry, then a subject on the frontier of science. As a military doctor he had worked in preventive medicine, publishing a paper in the *Japanese Army Medical Journal*[13] on the effect of picric acid poisoning in factories, a result of studies on ordnance factory workers. As with Ishii his concern for preventive medicine had not blinded him to the thought of using toxic substances as weapons of war, and in 1911 he requested, and received, a list of such toxic chemicals from an industrial hazards committee in Germany. In 1915 the Japanese Army Committee had established a secret research project on poison gas and Koizumi had joined it.[14]

Japan and Koizumi had watched from afar on April 22nd, 1915 as Germany launched its first incredibly successful gas attack on the Western Front at Ypres. So devastating had been the effect (in the combined chlorine gas and artillery attack 5,000 Allied soldiers died and 10,000 were wounded) that the German commander was completely unable to take full advantage. Its inventor Fritz Haber had watched from behind the lines hoping a knock-out blow might end the nightmare of deadlocked trench war. Although Britain had been in a position to retaliate in kind within five months, the magnitude of Germany's early success was not lost on Koizumi. Japan's CW programme was stepped up. Koizumi had realised the weapon's unprecedented ability to produce casualties, stretching to the limit, then finally engulfing, all medical facilities. In the last six months of the war one in six casualties had been a result of CW. Such was the power of gas warfare that during the Great War it caused 91,000 fatalities and 1.3 million wounded.

In May 1918 Koizumi had been put in charge of CW protection and set to work designing early prototype gas masks. One day in a cloud of toxic chlorine he lost consciousness and nearly died. He refused to be hospitalised and lay in bed in his laboratory for two months while being treated. To queries about his health he would reply, "Just as it is the duty of soldiers to die on the battlefield, researchers die in their laboratories."[15] In 1919 he had left for a research trip to Europe and America. That year CW's inventor Fritz Haber, in front of an outraged scientific world, received the Nobel Prize for Chemistry for his work on the synthesis of ammonia. Receiving the award Haber declared, "In no future war will the military be able to ignore poison gas. It is a higher form of killing."[16] By 1919 it was forecast that chemical munitions might outrival explosives in effectiveness. Koizumi had eagerly collected research material, but when he returned to Japan he had received a great disappointment. His work had been transferred, handed over by the Army Headquarters for Technology to the Army Science Research Institute. The Army Surgeons' Corps was held in low esteem and not regarded as appropriate to carry out further research.

So in 1930 when Ishii returned from Europe proclaiming the rich promise of BW, Koizumi seized upon it, determining not to let this other opportunity slip from the grasp of the Surgeons' Corps of the Japanese Army. From his studies of gas masks Koizumi must have known it would be a difficult task. For example, bacterial and viral pathogens are so tiny that it would take field masks a million times more efficient than those for gaseous particles to filter out germs. But BW held out promise for the Surgeons' Corps. In the Japanese Army at that time, surgeons were among the most lowly ranked, principally because they had no weapon of war. The glorious infantry was ranked highest, while the department of the Surgeon General was below even the Accountant General, above only the Veterinary Corps. Koizumi saw in Ishii's ideas power for his department, thrusting it from the rear echelon to the glory of the front line.

Ishii was elevated to the rank of major in August 1930, the year he returned from Europe and went to work in the Department of Epidemic Prevention at the newly built Army Medical College in Wakamatsu-chō, Tokyo. During the day he taught students as an instructor at the college, but at night he went on with his BW researches. Soon he appealed to Koizumi for a new department to

9

study his chosen subject. He argued that the existing epidemic prevention laboratory given to him in August 1932 was already fully occupied developing vaccines to immunise troops. Now as the director of the Epidemic Prevention Department he wanted something better. With Koizumi's support, in April 1933, at the cost of 200,000 yen, construction work began on a new epidemic prevention research laboratory (*Bōeki kenkyū-shitsu*), a low-lying building not easily noticeable to passers-by. The new laboratory was completed in October 1933,[17] just after Koizumi had become dean of the College. The same month Ishii, somewhat mysteriously, was appointed to a position in the Army's Main Weapons Arsenal.

In the 1930s two major opposing groups fought for domination in the Japanese Army: the "Imperial Way" and the "Control" factions. War Minister Araki was a leader of the former, and Nagata the latter. Ishii seems to have been able to straddle this considerable divide. He cultivated Araki's friendship and patronage, and it is said that while still a relatively junior officer he made such outrageous requests as to demand to ride in the minister's car.[18]

As Araki's near dictatorial powers were eclipsed, Maj-Gen Nagata was to become Ishii's most powerful patron. In 1934 he became chief of the Military Affairs Bureau, the most influential of all sections in the War Ministry. Unlike many Army bureaucrats he possessed a considerable understanding of science and as a former military attaché in Europe during the First World War he knew from his own experiences the power of gas warfare and he could guess the power of BW. Ishii may initially have himself paid for his European trip, but it is said that this money was later refunded by Nagata.[19] A brilliant strategist, Nagata was impressed with the massive organisation needed to wage modern war and was the first to gain widespread support in Japan for the concept of a national defence mobilisation designed to put the Japanese Army and nation on a total war footing in times of national emergency. He and his pragmatic faction, however, earned the violent animosity of younger and more radical officers who believed in the importance of a more old-fashioned "spiritual training" for war. Theirs was the "Imperial Way". Later, in 1935, a member of the Imperial Way faction stabbed Nagata to death, but not before Nagata had helped set Ishii's project into action – and saved his protégé from disgrace.

During his time at the Army Medical College Ishii was to make himself famous, perhaps surprisingly, as the inventor of a water filter. This was also to give an unseen hand in raising the status of his department in the military hierarchy. He built his first successful prototype in 1931, the year after he returned from Europe. Perhaps it

10

was the encephalitis epidemic in Shikoku which had impressed him with the need for effective filtration methods. He developed a ceramic water filter, dramatically improving on existing technology. It overcame the archaic techniques of boiling water in the field, or of using unpleasant chlorine purifying compounds, as well as the slow and cumbersome equipment then in use. Inevitably, troops irritated by the nuisance of the old methods had frequently resorted to drinking water from pools or puddles contaminated with germs. Many outbreaks of diseases such as dysentery resulted. Ishii's filter machine was a revolution making safe both foul and river water.

To demonstrate the effectiveness of the "Ishii filter", Ishii urinated into it, then drank from its output. Army and Navy chiefs attending Ishii's bizarre presentation were duly impressed. Later, after a number of modifications, both services decided in 1936 to adopt the filter for field use. It was on display when the Emperor visited the Army Medical College on March 10th, 1933. It was also on board a naval ship during an Imperial inspection and the Emperor too, reportedly drank from the device.

Ishii's filters were built in many sizes, the largest being tank-sized and mounted on a truck. To meet the massive demand for his filter a company called *Nippon Tokusho Kōgyō Kabushiki Kaisha*, Tokyo, was engaged to assist in production design, and to become sole manufacturer. The company had a factory a few hundred yards from the Army Medical College and for his continued co-operation and patronage Ishii was paid handsomely, with a backhander somewhere in the region of 50,000 yen. He proceeded to spend the money in style. This flamboyant, arrogant and loud Army Surgeon was frequently seen sampling the delights of the most exclusive geisha houses in town. Ishii spent far beyond the normal means of one of his station. His antics, behind the discreet doors of the tea room, eventually came to the attention of the military police. They wondered how such a junior officer could run up such vast bills. In those days a young businessman would earn roughly 100 yen a quarter. This young Army Surgeon had thousands to spend. Ishii was detained. Arrest in pre-war Japan was tantamount to conviction. It could have been the end of his career, but it is said that his powerful patron Nagata, hearing of Ishii's plight, would not allow his brilliant protégé to languish in jail. Ishii was released.[20] Afterwards he had a bronze bust made of Nagata which was kept on his office desk in memory of his saviour.

Inside the confines of his own laboratory Ishii could now study all the most lethal germs in the world. The exact object of his research could remain secret – in a normal bacteriologist's laboratory with its test tubes, culture plates, centrifuges and the like. If asked, he was simply researching water filtration or studying vaccines. But under these twin guises, epidemic prevention and water supply, the germ of his real interest multiplied. His work had begun.

On the outside, the status of the Army's Medical Bureau was rising. Not long after March 1934, when Koizumi became the Army's Chief Surgeon, the rank held by that position was raised to Lt-Gen. Elsewhere, officers in other service branches were being indoctrinated on the importance of their medical counterparts.[21]

But Ishii had yet another project. So illegal and so important was this work that it could never have been carried out openly in mainland Japan, but was set up in conditions of the utmost secrecy thousands of miles from Tokyo in a remote part of newly occupied Manchuria.

Chapter 3

Experiments in Manchuria

Manchuria had been occupied by the Japanese Army following the "Manchurian Incident" in September 1931. Since the Russo-Japanese War of 1904–5 and particularly since the fall of China's Manchu Dynasty in 1911, Japan had held "special privileges" in Manchuria, her imperialist ambitions centring on the rich national resources of this large underpopulated land. The Chinese Nationalist government protested to the League of Nations about the occupation and Japan, rather than accepting the League's unfavourable judgment, left the League. On March 1st, 1932, Japan promulgated the new "sovereign state" of Manchukuo, ruled by a puppet Emperor. But the commander-in-chief of Japan's crack Kwantung Army in reality controlled Manchuria.

The Manchurian Incident was precipitated by a young cabal of Kwantung Army officers, notably Col Seishirō Itagaki and Lt-Col Kanji Ishiwara, who were determined to pursue a forceful forward policy to ensure Japan's pre-eminence in Manchuria. Their swift and decisive military action was supported by Ishii's patron Nagata, then chief of the Military Affairs Section of the powerful Military Affairs Bureau. Nagata secretly supplied Itagaki and Ishiwara with 24 mm howitzers.

At the time of the Manchurian Incident, Ishii's Epidemic Prevention Laboratory in Tokyo was fully occupied supplying vaccines for troops bound for Manchuria. Shortly afterwards, Ishii became personally involved with the development of "medical facilities" in this newly occupied land.

Far from mainland Japan, in total secrecy, and with the help of the brilliant and sardonic Ishiwara, Ishii began to evolve an ambitious project. Ishii's new work was perfectly camouflaged by the poor sanitary conditions prevalent in Manchuria. The *Japan Year Book* of 1935 described health standards in the country:

. . . since it is extensive, borders on Mongolia and Siberia and is inhabited by different races, many of whom lead the insanitary life of extremely primitive conditions, and especially since coolies and refugees are constantly migrating in large groups, the risk of the spread of dreadful infectious diseases is rather common. In the past 20 years, Manchuria has often been afflicted by such plagues; for instance, the pneumonic plague of 1910–11, cholera in 1919, pneumonic plague again in 1920–21, and pneumonic plague in 1927. The prevention of infectious diseases, therefore, is extremely important in Manchuria . . .[1]

A history of the Army Medical College records that Ishii was sent on an unspecified tour of duty in Manchuria the year following the outbreak of the Incident. A team of ten military physicians, including Kajitsuka and another young Kyoto Imperial University graduate, Tomosada Masuda, travelled all over the country engaged in what were described as "industrial duties".[2] It is now known that Ishii went to the northern Manchurian city of Harbin and founded a laboratory on its outskirts.

Built on the eastern banks of the Sungari River, Harbin, with its wide streets and European-style buildings, was known as the Paris of the East. The city comprised three sections: Old Harbin; the new city; and the open town. The new city housed the railway station, the offices of the North Manchurian Railway Company and a few foreign consulates. The open town was the city's commercial centre. Population statistics compiled in 1935 reveal that Harbin was inhabited by 240,000 Chinese, 81,000 Russians and 4,700 Japanese.[3]

Harbin's shifting Russian community posed a security threat to the Japanese occupying forces. Following the Russian Revolution of 1917, and particularly after the defeat of the regime headed by Admiral Kolchak and other monarchists in Siberia during 1920–22, many White Russian refugees poured into Manchuria. Some worked on the railway, others founded agricultural settlements, but many were badly exploited as labourers. A few were formed into the *Asano* Unit of the Kwantung Army. Then, in 1924, after Sino-Soviet agreements brought control of the Chinese Eastern Railway under Russian management, many Red Russians arrived in northern Manchuria. By the time of the Manchurian Incident, the Red and White Russian communities in Harbin were of roughly the same size, and there was constant trouble between them. White and Red Russians denounced each other. The Japanese, like their Chinese predecessors, were uncertain about who was pro-Soviet and who not. All Russians were therefore under suspicion. Russian firms and shops were saddled with Japanese "advisers" whose salaries they had to pay and whose limited command of the Russian language made them dangerous intermediaries in dealings with the suspicious Japanese authorities, especially the feared Japanese Special Services Agency (*Tokumu Kikan*) and the Gendarmerie (*Kenpeitai*).

Although much of the Red Russian presence withdrew in 1935 after the Soviet Union was pressurised by Japan into selling the Chinese Eastern Railway, Harbin continued as an important spy centre. Such was its importance that Harbin's Special Services Agency was later headed by Maj-Gen Shun Akikusa, founder of the Japanese Army's Nakano spy school.[4] Ishii is said to have been acquainted with him for many years.

Ishii founded his first laboratory in Manchuria in a reconditioned soy sauce distillery outside Harbin at Beiinho (Haiinga).[5] He gave it the secret codename *Tōgō*, and when travelling incognito called himself Captain Hajime Tōgō. He used the name in veneration of the famous strategist and admiral, Tōgō, who defeated the Russians in the celebrated naval battle at Tsushima in 1905. Members sent to this unit would first be assigned to the Kwantung Army's Strategic Staff in Hsinking, where they would be given an alias. An Army Medical College history records the dispatch to Manchuria in November 1933 of researchers from Ishii's Tokyo Epidemic Prevention Laboratory to "engage in special research projects".[6] Over the following two or three years Ishii's unit grew to a strength of about 300, of whom around fifty were doctors.

Initially, Tōgō Unit was put under the command of Lt-Col Kanji Ishiwara, one of the architects of the Manchurian Incident.[7] Ishiwara was later replaced by Saburō Endō, the officer who had been an assistant to the chief Japanese Army representative at the 1925 Geneva talks. Tōgō Unit's budget, roughly 200,000 yen, came out of a secret fund and was handed over in person to Ishii. The purpose of Tōgō Unit was to research offensive BW, a subject too dangerous, and politically sensitive, for experiments in Japan proper. Mystery still shrouds the early period of Tōgō Unit, but those years also saw a considerable tightening of sanitation and epidemic prevention responsibilities in Manchuria. Police attached to Japanese consulates and offices of the powerful South Manchurian Railway Company were given primary control. Foreign medical organisations were put under considerable pressure. From the autumn of 1935 Chinese Christians, including professors and doctors at the Manchurian Medical College at Mukden (Shenyang, Hōten), were subjected to arrest and torture on suspicion of anti-Manchukuoan activities.[8] A good many mission-trained Chinese doctors found it advisable to leave the country.

Some time before 1936, Tōgō Unit moved inside the city limits to a new two-storey headquarters near the Harbin military hospital and close to the city's Pinchiang railway station. By this time Ishii had built a biological bomb and tested it. Suddenly Ishii's small unit was transformed into a 1,000-strong force. Kajitsuka recalled the event:

> Detachment 731* was formed by command of the Emperor of Japan Hirohito, issued in 1936. The Emperor's command was printed and copies of it were sent to all units of the Japanese Army for the information of all the officers. I myself was shown this command and the detachment's personnel list accompanying it, and certified the fact with my private seal. After that I took part in recruiting the junior officer personnel of the detachment and in examining the list of proposed senior officers which had been sent me by the Personnel Administration of the Ministry of War. The detachment's location was determined by the Kwantung Army headquarters. Until 1941, the detachment had no number, but was called the Water Supply and Prophylaxis Administration of the Kwantung Army, and also the Ishii Detachment, because it was the custom in the Japanese Army to call Army units by the names of their commanders. The detachment was given the number 731 in 1941 by order of the Commander-in-Chief of the Kwantung Army, who gave definite numbers to all Army units and institutions.[9]

Careful planning had gone into the formation of the unit. To the outside world it had the innocuous-sounding title "Epidemic Prevention and Water Supply Unit of the Kwantung Army". But this was merely a cover for the main purpose of the unit – to forge a new and deadly weapon for the Japanese Army.

Ishii was given formal command of the unit on August 1st, 1936, and by December 5th its reorganisation was complete. Nominally, at least, Ishii was relieved of his position at the Army Medical College.

At the same time that Ishii assumed command, many military surgeons were given "attachments": Surgeon Col Takashi Murakami to the War Ministry Secretariat, Surgeon Lt-Col Motoharu Sakuyama to the 20th Engineer Regiment.

University doctors were also brought into the Unit. In 1934 at the time of the 9th Japan Medical General Meeting, a list of promising young medical scientists had been made up by Ishii's former Kyoto University mentors: Professor Shōzō Toda, president of the Medical Department, Professor of Pathology Kenji Kiyono, Professor of

---

*The unit was referred to under a number of different names at different times: "Ishii" Unit; Tōgō Unit; Kamo Unit; 731 Unit; Manchuria 25202 Unit; Kwantung Army Epidemic Prevention and Water Supply Unit.

Physiology Rinnosuke Shōji and Microbiology Professor Ren Kimura. They had drawn up a *makimono*, or scroll, listing research teams that should be formed and who should form them. It was prestigious in the nationalistic days of the 1930s for universities to have military connections. Not only would such contact offer special military research funds, but also the supply of all sorts of materials and apparatus. Kyoto University sent the "Gang of 7", most of whom had graduated in 1930 or 1931, and included a lecturer in the Faculty of Hygiene Hisato Yoshimura, Pathology lecturer Kōzō Okamoto and Assistant Professor Tachiomaru Ishikawa. Kyoto's rival, Tokyo Imperial University, had the same sort of relationship with the Manchurian Hygiene Technology Factory at Hsinking otherwise known as the Manchurian *Den-Ken* (short for *Densenbyō kenkyū-jō*, or infectious disease research institute). Personnel arriving at the Ishii Unit were gathered over a four-year period until 1938 when the process was finally completed.[10]

Far to the south Japan's war in China expanded, following the Marco Polo Bridge Incident of July 7th, 1937. A month later a severe outbreak of epidemic disease in a unit of the Shanghai Expeditionary Force gave Ishii another chance to raise the status of his epidemic prevention and water supply unit. After a unit of the expeditionary force had advanced to Go-sho at the mouth of the Yangtze River, troops had drunk from contaminated creek water. At first food poisoning was suspected, then the culprit was found to be cholera. Plans to ship fresh water from the rear were made impossible by furious fighting, and the rear echelon already had its hands full just shipping ammunition.

Accompanying the force was Enryō Hōjō from Ishii's *Bōeki kenkyū-shitsu* in Tokyo. He took photographs of the victims' plight and sent them to Tokyo along with an urgent request to dispatch a special water supply unit. Ishii took the matter up with Army General Staff Headquarters. He was given approval to form a special unit of more than 200 personnel and five Ishii-type motorised water filter machines. Operations began in September and results were dramatic.

The successful completion of the operation set the seal of victory on an internal battle which Ishii had been fighting within the Army. Originally, both the Intendance and the Engineering Corps had contended that it was their responsibility in the field to supply purified water at the battlefront. Both Corps were above the Surgeons in the Army hierarchy. But the technical superiority of Ishii's unit assured his success in the power struggle, raising the erstwhile lowly Surgeons' Corps above its two more illustrious counterparts.[11]

This decision, made in 1938, had an unseen, but highly fortuitous side effect. It paved the way for epidemic prevention and water supply units to be attached to every division of the Japanese Army. These units would have a presence in every battle zone, supplying water and dealing with epidemics. But when the time came they would also have an ideal training and the right tactical position to wage BW. One of Ishii's dreams could come true – doctors in combat alongside the glorious infantry.

It was not long before another reward was given to the newly promoted Colonel Ishii. On June 30th, 1938, the Kwantung Army began preparations to move the Ishii Unit to a new location twenty-four kilometres south of Harbin at a place called Pingfan. The unit's existing premises were now considered too small and insecure. Another Imperial order expanded the unit and put the move into force. Unit member Maj-Gen Kiyoshi Kawashima described the order:

> As far as I can recollect, the Emperor's order fixed the personnel of the detachment, together with its branches, at about 3,000 men . . . By order of the Commander-in-Chief (of the Kwantung Army), Detachment 731's site at Pingfan Station was proclaimed a special zone of the Kwantung Army. No one was allowed to reside in or near the territory of the detachment, and no unauthorized person was allowed to enter it. This was permitted only to the detachment's personnel, and other persons were allowed to enter the zone only with the permission of the Commander-in-Chief of the Kwantung Army; aircraft were forbidden to fly over the detachment's territory.[12]

In a few short years Ishii's project had hurtled from relative obscurity to one of top-secret and national importance. Set in three square kilometres of territory near the villages of Sadun, Sidun and Wudun, Pingfan's extensive military facilities were hidden behind a high wall, dry moat and high voltage wires. It took two years to construct the establishment's 150 or so buildings, which included accommodation for thousands of people, a railway siding, an incinerator and power house with tall cooling towers, an animal house, an airfield, an insectarium, a large administration building, an exercise yard and a strange forbidding square-shaped building known as Ro block. The Japanese katakana character ro is square in shape, hence the name of the building. Although Ro block looked square from the outside, hidden from view in the centre were two other buildings known as blocks 7 and 8. Ro block was the centre of bacteria production and disease research. Blocks 7 and 8 had a more sinister purpose.

A somewhat young and impressionable recruit described his first sight of Pingfan:

> . . . the central buildings towering skyward over other buildings, with all square-tiled façades, were larger than any of those I had observed on my trip over, including Osaka, Hsinking and Harbin. These buildings reflecting the sunlight glistened in brilliant white and broke into the vast sky. High earth walls were constructed with barbed wire fencing atop. It was obvious that this compound was isolated strictly from the outside world.[13]

Unit 731 was organised into eight divisions. They were: First Division, bacteriological research; Second Division, warfare research and field experiments; Third Division, water filter production; Fourth Division, bacteria mass production and storage; an Educational Division; a Supplies Division; a General Affairs Division and a Clinical Diagnosis Division. The Water Filter Division and Clinical Diagnosis Division remained in the old "South Block" in central Harbin. All other Divisions were at Pingfan.

On December 2nd, 1940, Kwantung Army Commander-in-Chief General Yoshijirō Umezu, by the Emperor's authority, ordered the construction of sub-units at Hailar, Songo, Lin-k'ou (Rinkou) and Hailin (Botanko or Mutanchiang).[14] Three, Hailar, Songo and Lin-k'ou, were strategically placed at intervals along the Soviet-Manchurian border. Built to disperse production in the event of enemy airstrike, War Minister Tōjō signed appended tables of organisation in the Imperial orders allowing each subunit up to 300 personnel. Civilians might be employed, the orders indicated, but no more than 30 per cent of the entire personnel.[15]

A vast proving ground at Anta, deep in the remote plains of Manchuria, was also attached to Unit 731 as well as to the massive South Manchurian Railway Sanitary Institute south at Dairen. This large vaccine-producing organisation, whose director was Dr Kōji Andō, was often used because of its respectability as a sort of transfer window for scientists posted from Japan to Unit 731.

Unit 731's bacteriological research division was divided into more than a dozen squads, each investigating the warfare possibility of a wide variety of diseases. Plague, anthrax, dysentery, typhoid, paratyphoid, cholera and many other exotic and unknown diseases were studied. So too were vaccines and blood sera for the prevention and treatment of diseases. Various disease vectors, mainly insect, were investigated, as were new drugs, chemical toxins and frostbite.

Every conceivable facility was given to Unit 731. So too were luxuries lavished on the lifestyle of Ishii's researchers and workers. In the remote Manchurian plain at Pingfan a whole biological township grew up. It was known as Tōgō village.

Tōgō villagers had plentiful supplies of the best foods at times when people in Tokyo were starving. Pingfan was centrally heated against the bitter sub-zero temperatures of the Manchurian winter. Naturally, it had the best sanitation, including even Western-style lavatories. Life went on as in a rich village. There was a shrine for religious worship. In summer Unit members played tug-of-war at the sports festival and wrestled in the sumo championships. For the culturally-minded there was a drama group.

Strict measures, however, were enforced to preserve Pingfan's secret identity. Movement in and out of Harbin was carefully regulated. Unit 731 members were transported into town in covered trucks. The trucks' number plates were changed frequently, and at the Unit's Harbin rendezvous point in Jilin Street, near Ishii's personal residence, members were required to change into civilian clothes so as not to arouse suspicion from Soviet and Chinese spies. Even the uniforms of Unit 731 members did not have Medical Corps insignia, just those of ordinary line soldiers. Letters home were censored to a few lines about the sender's health and the wonderful Japanese Army life. Photographs of sensitive buildings were forbidden. Meticulous sanitary precautions were in force against the ever-present danger of infection. Houses were roped off in Tōgō village if a Unit member contracted a serious disease. The inhabitants of the surrounding Manchurian villages were subjected to rigorous security checks.

Building a bacterial weapon, as Ishii found out, was not an easy task. He and his researchers faced a myriad of problems. What kind of micro-organisms would make an effective BW agent? Should it have a lethal or incapacitating effect? Could it be produced in quantities sufficient for wartime employment? Could these living organisms be kept alive and virulent through storage and shipment to their ultimate employment on the battlefield? What type of munition would be needed to deliver the agent to the target? What were the technical and military characteristics of such a weapon?

Except possibly for a few diseases, such as influenza, pneumonia or tuberculosis, which were known to be acquired through the respiratory tract, the mechanism for transmission of infection was not clearly understood in those days. There were a great many other diseases, especially those which historically had been transmitted to men by fleas, ticks, lice or mosquitoes. Could infection with their causative organisms also be induced through the respiratory system? What was the infectious dose for each disease? Of what size should the particles be to cause infection?

Ishii approached the problem by looking for weapons that could be delivered from altitude by aircraft causing massive outbreaks of epidemics. He also researched sabotage or clandestine techniques. After immense effort and many setbacks he devised a solution to the former problem. As for the latter, by the standards of the times, it was possible to achieve more extensive and positive results by dispersing intestinal pathogens in, say, water supplies than by any air dispersion techniques.

Ever since his trip to Europe plague had fascinated Ishii. He knew it would make a deadly weapon if it could be harnessed. The disease takes several forms. The "bubonic" form in humans normally results from the bite of an infected flea, which harbours the plague bacteria *Pasteurella Pestis* inside its body membrane, the fleas having become infected by feeding off the blood of diseased rats. Bubonic plague is characterised by a swelling of the lymph nodes in the armpit and groin ("buboes"). After two to three days the bacteria often invade the lungs and pneumonic plague, a far more serious form of the disease, develops. Before modern medicines the diagnosis of pneumonic plague was tantamount to a death sentence. It is highly infectious, with an incubation period of three to four days, sometimes up to a week. The onset is abrupt, with chills, high fever and extreme weakness. The eyes redden, the face becomes congested and the tongue coated. Victims can become maniacally delirious and death may be rapid, sometimes within one day. Compared with some bacterial pathogens, plague is only moderately infectious, but more virulent strains can be cultivated.[16] Plague could create casualties often out of all proportion to the number of bacteria disseminated. Ishii deduced, therefore, that it would make an efficient weapon and set about preparing the most dangerous strains. He looked to history, to the great plagues that had ravaged continents and delighted in the chaos that such a weapon would create. Medical facilities would overload and people would flee. Armies on the battlefield would be unable to deal with decontamination on a mass scale and the strict isolation required for victims.

Plague had another advantage for Ishii. Its origins could be concealed. Science had not then provided a satisfactory answer to the age-old question of why, where, for how long and how badly a plague epidemic broke out. What better cover than for it to seem merely like a natural recurrence, especially when plague was known to be endemic in many areas of Asia, India, China and Manchuria. The enemy, perhaps, might never suspect. So in conditions of the greatest secrecy Ishii set about making his plague weapon.

Roll call for Unit 731 members was at 8.30 a.m. each morning on the exercise yard. Members would then disperse for work. On most days a putrid stench hung oppressively over Pingfan. The stench emanated from the complex's inner sanctum, *Ro* block. There, on the building's first floor a vast bacteria factory was housed. This was the source of the rotting smell that tainted the air. In dimly-lit windowless corridors bacteria factory workers went about their work mass-producing deadly pathogens. Every day the squad could be seen going about their nightmarish work pushing truckloads of bacteria along narrow gauge rails from the factory to the store. Each squad member knew they laboured in an atmosphere of invisible death. Maj-Gen Kawashima and then Major Tomio Karasawa commanded the factory. Round the clock workers would prepare for work by stripping and disinfecting themselves. Then they would put on layer after layer of protective clothing. A coverall "anti-disease suit" was invented, made of lightweight rubberised silk with a zipper front and neck drawstrings. Boots and a hood of the same material and heavy rubber over-boots completed the suit. It gave the body complete coverage with good freedom of movement, but its impermeability limited the wearing to little more than a few minutes. As high work rates were needed, risks were taken by reducing protective clothing. For this extra danger workers were paid a special allowance. Dressed in rubber knee-boots, aprons and gloves, special goggles and multi-layered gauze masks, they would wade through a sterilising pool of phenol water before entering the production line. There, they would begin work with special mass cultivators designed by Ishii himself.

First, workers made a bacteria culture medium of agar-agar, or peptone and meat bouillon in special boilers. This would then be poured into the Ishii cultivators, kept in special autoclaves under high pressure. Refrigerators cooled the culture medium, after which the cultivators were carried to a special room where the bacteria were planted. With long cotton-tipped metal rods a small quantity of live plague bacteria was scraped across the gelatin base of each cultivator. Measuring about 35 by 25 by 53 centimetres, cultivators each held fifteen trays. Next, nutrients and an anti-contaminant were added. Then the cultivators were sent on a conveyor into special incubators, in which the optimum temperature and humidity conditions for growing the particular bacteria were maintained.

The production squad worked with concentration; one error could cause death. Personnel avoided inhaling any more of the deadly bacteria that floated invisibly in the air than was absolutely necessary. Communication was by hand signals. Piles of red apples were stacked in the corner of each room in the Karasawa factory. Workers would quickly take off their masks, nibble on the apples and spit the pieces out. This they hoped would absorb any live bacteria that had entered their mouths. Hours went by as they sweated under their bulky protective clothing.[17]

The deadly harvest of plague bacteria would be ready for reaping in only two days. By then it was a milky white slurry lying on top of the gelatin base. This had to be carefully skimmed off, put in bottles, and then trucked to the bacteria store. The culture base would be sent back to the giant boilers for sterilisation and recycling. It was this recycling process that caused Pingfan's distinctive stench. The production line could be used for the mass-production of many types of bacteria. Production cycles would sometimes last for weeks and months. The line never ceased.

With the Fourth Division's equipment operating at maximum capacity, and under optimum conditions, it was possible theoretically to produce in one month about 300 kilograms of plague germs.[18]

The factory's second unit was of equal size, and bacteria production was possible at some of the branch units along the Soviet border. Both the Lin-k'ou and Hailin branches mass-produced typhoid, paratyphoid, dysentery and cholera germs. Unit 731 at Pingfan ran six-month training courses for branch staff.

If the factory's output was to be preserved the bacteria were put in refrigerators. But if it was to be transported, bacteria were packed into special bottles each holding 50 grams, then crated into metal receptacles which, in turn, were placed in twos and threes in ice-filled containers.

So large was the production plant that in the heyday of Unit 731 it had the potential for creating sufficient bacteria to kill the world's population several times over.

Now that Ishii could produce plague and other virulent bacteria in sufficient quantities for warfare, his next task was to discover how he could deliver his deadly microbes to the enemy. Various methods were tried in the search for the right delivery system.

The detailed history of how Ishii discovered an acceptable weapon delivery system for plague is not totally clear. But as early as 1938 he had become convinced that plague organisms, even possibly the hardy anthrax germ which formed spores, could not be dropped in bombs or sprayed from aircraft in "bare" form.

In February 1941, Ishii wrote to his friend Kajitsuka, now Chief of the Kwantung Army's Medical Administration, to inform him of the disappointing results with "bare" germs. Kajitsuka summarised Ishii's disappointment:

> According to what Ishii said, researches carried out by the detachment had shown that the dropping of bacteria contained in aerial bombs was of little effect because, as a consequence of strong air pressure and excessively high temperature, the germs of dysentery, typhoid, paratyphoid, cholera and plague, being frail, perish almost 100 per cent.[19]

But Ishii hinted to Kajitsuka that for some time he had had his eye on a startling new solution to the problem. He considered it to be one of the greatest achievements of Unit 731.

His eye had come to rest upon the humble flea. As in nature, so too in war this minute insect could be relied upon as the carrier of pestilence. Plague bacillus is resistant to cold; cultures in an icebox retain their virulence for months, even up to ten years. But outside the body cultures are not very resistant to heat or chemicals. So Ishii sought to protect them inside the flea. More than a dozen types of flea are known to bite man, and it was among these that Ishii sought a vector for his plague cultures. At first Colonel Kiyoshi Ōta was put in charge of the project. Later he was succeeded by civilian technician Hideo Tanaka. To yield vast quantities of fleas and feed them, enormous numbers of rats had to be caught and bred. This was the job of Unit 731's animal house run by Ishii's elder brother Mitsuo.

Rats served a dual purpose in Unit 731. Not only were they used to breed fleas, it appears that these rodents were also used to maintain the strength of the plague germs. According to one worker it was erroneously felt "necessary to have the germs pass through animal bodies once a month in order to prevent the germs from losing their strength". This method of "separation culture by passing through animals" was tricky, time-consuming and dangerous, requiring that germs be removed afterwards by dissection of each animal one by one. Germs were removed from blood in the lymph glands, the spleen and the heart, and then replanted on culture media.[20] Needless to say vast numbers of rats were needed.

At times of peak production members of Ishii's force were required to dress in civilian clothes and go rat-catching. If questioned why they were trying to catch the rats alive they were told to reply, rather implausibly, that the pelts were required to make hats for airmen. Such was the scale of the work that the rat factory sometimes held tens of thousands of rodents.

A flea will normally ingest about 5,000 plague organisms at one feeding from a rat which is suffering from an average dose of the disease, its blood containing 100 million organisms per millilitre. These bacteria will multiply in the flea's digestive tract. A few days after it has fed on infected blood, under the microscope can be seen clusters of plague in the stomach. This later rises up and clogs the throat and oesophagus, which become distended. It is at this stage that the flea becomes infective with its bite. The elastic recoil of the walls of both its pharynx and gullet, when the flea stops sucking blood from its victim, may drive back into the bite wound highly infective blood. The infective flea may regurgitate as many as 10,000 to 24,000 organisms at one biting. Some of these usually enter the blood of the new host who, if susceptible, contracts bubonic or septicaemic plague.[21] Ishii found that an infective flea, with its blocked gullet, could live and carry its deadly bite for up to one month. Moreover, a single bite was found to be sufficient to cause infection.

He had found a method suitable for weapons use. Kawashima described the flea factory:

The Second Division had four special premises for the mass breeding of fleas, in which a fixed temperature of 30 deg C was maintained. Metal jars, 30 cm high and 50 cm wide, were used for the breeding of fleas. Rice husks were poured into the jars to keep the fleas in. After these preparations a few fleas were put into each jar, and also a white rat for them to feed on. The rat was fastened in such a way as not to hurt the fleas.[22]

There were more than 4,000 cultivators each capable of producing 10 to 15 grams of fleas in each production cycle.

Breeding of fleas was also carried out at 731 branches. The tiny fleas – the human variety (*pulex irritans*) – solved many problems for Ishii. In addition to storing plague organisms safely for around a month, their sturdy bodies were much more resistant to air drag. They would naturally target themselves at human beings, and if the rat population of any town became infected, epidemics could often persist. But Ishii still had to solve the problem of how to deliver them to the enemy.

At first he tried to spray them from aircraft using compressed-air containers. Testing continued over a long period of time but was not effective. To hit a target, aircraft would have to fly too low, coming into danger from enemy anti-aircraft fire. Flying higher would mean too much dispersion. Eventually in the latter half of 1943 the Kwantung Army Commander-in-Chief General Umezu banned the technique.[23] The risk was too great of it backfiring on to Japanese personnel, he observed. Ishii had probably been aware of this problem, for in June 1941, Ōta had been ordered to carry out tests with bombs. Again, however, as with "bare" germs, it was found that heat generated by the large quantities of explosive required to detonate a metal-cased bomb proved fatal to fleas.

Ishii was a nocturnal worker. One night he had a brainwave. In his excitement he immediately ordered all the Unit's officers to be woken so he could explain it. Sleepy-eyed, they heard that the bomb should not be made of metal, but of clay. Drawing from his experience in ceramics in his water filtration work, Ishii proposed that a porcelain bomb would be easier to detonate, requiring less explosive, causing less heat, and thus much safer for his fleas. Unit 731's Third Division, in "South Block", Harbin, was set to work baking casings in their long kilns. Sub-Lt Segoshi described the work:

> To manufacture these bombs, clay was taken, ground to a powder, mixed with water and then brought to the required consistency. The stuff was then poured into a special plaster mould. The mould was shaped like a shell. In view of the fact that plaster absorbs moisture, the upper surface of this stuff dried. Later, the plaster mould was removed, the liquid stuff that had remained was poured away and ceramic vessels were obtained in the shape of shells. The finished bodies of the bombs were then dried in special kilns. These bombs were 70 to 80 cms in diameter. At the bottom there was a screw thread aperture. The interiors of the bombs were hollow. A time fuse tube was inserted into the screw-threaded aperture. Zig-zag grooves were cut in the outer surface of these bodies. On the upper part of the bombs there were attachments for stabilizers. Explosives were fastened into the grooves for the purpose of exploding the bombs. Dropped from aircraft, these bombs were supposed to explode above the ground.[24]

A 25 kg bomb was completed, designed by Maj Jun'ichi Kaneko and civilian technician Yamaguchi. Called the *Uji*, it was filled with fleas, oxygen to sustain them, and sand, through an opening in the nose stopped by a metal screw cap. Its capacity was 10 litres with apertures for nose and tail fuses as well as stabilising fins. The nose contained an impact, delay fuse and a bursting tube of 500 grams of TNT. The tail fuse exploded the bomb at a height of 200 to 300 metres by means of 4 metres of primacord. Should the tail fuse fail and the primacord not function, the detonation was guaranteed by the explosive train in the nose. Like an eggshell the bomb would shatter into a million fragments leaving no trace. Even its fins were made of combustible material so as to leave no tell-tale signs. Except for the sound of the explosion the bomb would leave no evidence.[25] Packed with oxygen the fleas could withstand high altitudes and could be dropped from beyond the reach of anti-aircraft fire. Full testing on the bomb was probably not completed before July 1944, when Umezu left the Kwantung Army to become Chief of the General Staff. But his successor Otozō Yamada declared that the bomb was an effective technique.[26]

Later in 1944 a "mother and daughter" bomb was developed by Lt-Gen Gondō at the secret weapons 9th Army Technical Research Institute which was located at a place called Noborito, just outside Kawasaki City, Kanagawa Prefecture, Japan. This device accurately controlled the optimum altitude of detonation. Tested by Unit 731 this "smart" bomb was in two parts – mother and daughters – connected by a radio link. When the mother hit the ground the link was broken. Its still airborne cluster of daughters would, at this point, be detonated, releasing their payloads at the most effective altitude.[27]

Next came field trials. Anta test site, a large area of the Manchurian plain 146 kilometres from Pingfan, was where Unit 731 carried out many weapons delivery experiments. Special sentries were on guard to prevent unauthorised entry to the area. Ishii's *Uji* bomb was tested there, and elsewhere, by means of static and drop tests.

Unit 731 had its own air squadron of seven aircraft called the Heibo 8372 Field Aviation Unit. In tests at Anta, flags were erected and smoke signals lit to guide the squadron's aircraft to the drop site. All round the test zone were laid thousands of boxes containing sticky paper. Set roughly 2 metres apart they covered an area of 2 square kilometres. After the bombs, each containing approximately 30,000 fleas, were dropped, workers would laboriously count the number of live fleas in each box to assess dispersion. The survival rate was 80 per cent.[28] With one bite fatal, Ishii knew he had an effective weapon.

Porcelain bombs carrying tetanus and anthrax bacilli were considered suitable for use at the battlefront. Those carrying typhoid and dysentery were thought best for attacking troops concentrated in the rear.

Unit 731 experimented with many other agents and delivery systems. Two types of artillery shell, the "H", an ordinary gas shell, and the "S", a 75–80 mm shell with bacterial suspensions replacing the powder charge, were investigated, but had already been found impractical by 1937.[29]

The *Ha* bomb was designed for anthrax spores. Anthrax is a deadly disease, both to humans and animals. The bacterium *B anthracis* is strong and easy to cultivate and disseminate. In its natural form the disease primarily affects herbivorous animals. But it can also affect human beings, through the skin, digestive system and lungs. It was particularly suited to aerial spraying, forming spores which have an outer protective layer that shields the genetic material against hostile environments. In direct sunlight the spores may survive for a number of days; in soil for decades. After inhaling an infective dose, man is likely to develop pulmonary anthrax symptoms within four days. Untreated, the mortality rate approaches 100 per cent. The onset of the disease is mild and may resemble a cough, but thereafter the disease progresses very rapidly, the victim developing high fever, vomiting, laboured breathing and aching in the head and joints. He soon collapses and may die within two days or less.

The *Ha* had a thin steel wall and contained 1,500 cylindrical shot immersed in half a litre anthrax (or tetanus) emulsion. Their anti-personnel shrapnel effect on impact would create anthrax-infected wounds over a diameter of around 40 metres. The *Ha* was designed for battlefield use against troops whereas the *Uji* was for use against civilians and feeding herds. There were hundreds of bomb experiments. Nine different types of bombs were made: the *I*, *Ro*, *Ha*, *Ni* and *U* were made of iron, the old type *Uji*, *Uji*-type 50, *Uji*-type 100 of porcelain, and the *Ga* of glass.[30] For this last type Unit 731 employed a leading glass blower.

Unit 731 researchers searched through many infectious diseases to find other possible agents. Botulism, brucellosis, cholera, dysentery, gas gangrene, glanders, influenza, meningococcus, salmonella, smallpox, tetanus, tick encephalitis, tuberculosis, tularemia, typhoid, typhus as well as more exotic agents such as *fūgū* (blowfish) toxin, epidemic haemorrhagic fever, and tsutsugamushi fever were studied.

In the field of low level or clandestine warfare Ishii found severe intestinal pathogens, such as the causative agents of typhoid fever, dysentery and cholera, to be highly effective. They involved much lower technology and achieved far more extensive and positive results. But to release them at an effective location involved great personal risk to the saboteur.

This method of warfare could involve contaminating water supplies or releasing plague-injected rats soaked with fleas into areas of dense population. Kajitsuka recalled some of the techniques:

Speaking about the infection of foodstuffs, Ishii told me that in the researches in this field, the germs of cholera, dysentery, typhoid and paratyphoid were being used, and that vegetables, fruit, fish and meat were so infected. Vegetables were found to be the most suitable for warfare: especially such as had numerous leaves, cabbage, for example; root crops, having smooth surfaces, proved to be less suitable. The injection of bacteria into food products, for example, was found to be more effective than infecting their surfaces. The most suitable medium for spreading infectious diseases, according to what Ishii said, were vegetables; next in order came fruit, fish and last meat.[31]

Ishii left practically no stone unturned. He tested dropping feathers infected with bacteria. For assassination squads he invented, decades before the poison umbrella killing of the Bulgarian dissident Markov in London, plague flea sprayers in the shape of fountain pens or walking sticks. These assassination weapon researches were so successful that as early as 1944 a draft roster of weapons for the use of a sabotage group, drawn up by the 2nd Land Forces Division of Japanese Imperial Headquarters, showed fountain pen pistol sprayers issued at the rate of four per platoon and three per company headquarters.[32]

Anthrax-infected chocolates were made, and, in conjunction with the 9th Army Technical Research Institute, plans were considered to use giant balloons to transport germs to their target.

Special self-destroying paper containers were also devised. They were described in one account:

The container is a strong paper cylinder which can split open along the middle. The cavity of the cylinder is divided into two or three compartments. It has a paper or rayon parachute attached to its head, and a heavy weight and detonator below; and there is a fine fuse connection between the detonator and the parachute.

Twelve domestic rats and six wild rats, all infected with plague bacilli, are put in the paper cylinder. At the same time fleas carrying bacteria after feeding on these animals are wrapped in thin paper packages and put in the cylinder.

After being dropped from the air behind the enemy's lines, or over his military stations and bases or important cities, the paper cylinder splits into two pieces on touching the ground or before. The small animals and fleas in the cylinder immediately disperse. The detonator under the cylinder then sets fire to the container and the fuse so that both the cylinder and parachute are burnt without leaving any trace.[33]

Floating bottles were also invented.

The floating bottle is a long necked flask of about 5 litres capacity. The bacterial suspension is put into the flask, the mouth of which is provided with explosive as well as a clock-like timer. The bottle is so managed that when put in water only the mouth of the bottle is exposed above the water surface. This bacterial apparatus is used to attack streams, swimming grounds at the sea sides, and dock-yards in which vessels are gathering. It is also used in special conditions of battle. For instance when the combating forces of both sides are located on the banks of a river, and one side is on the upper stream while the other is on the lower stream, the former having ascertained that the enemy is using the river for drinking and bathing purposes, the floating bottle can be used. The velocity of the stream is determined, the clock-like timer is properly set so that when the bottle reaches the enemy front by floating, it explodes. The contents of the bottle are set free and the stream water is contaminated. In the case of sea water the speed and the direction of the tide should be determined before this method of attack is applied.

Dysentery bacilli, typhoid bacilli and cholera vibrios are used in bacterial attacks for river water, while the cholera vibrios are most suitable for sea water.[34]

Ishii's work was not confined to spreading animal diseases. He had a squad of eleven workers under Dr Yukimasa Yagisawa researching crop destruction. For their target areas, Siberia and the Pacific North-West, this squad selected stinking smut of wheat and nematosis as agents. Yagisawa proposed collecting these agents as by-products of flour-milling operations in Manchuria. For nematosis he discovered that as little as 5 kilogrammes per acre would ensure complete destruction of susceptible varieties. Experiments showed that most Japanese and Australian varieties were 80 per cent suscep-tible; Russian varieties 25 per cent and American ones somewhere in between.[35]

From small beginnings Ishii had built, in little more than a decade, a mighty research empire. Hundreds of talented scientists and thousands of ordinary workers laboured day and night for him. Ishii's "troops" were now attached to every division of the Japanese Army. He had given Japan a weapon which in theory had the power to rival the Manhattan Project, America's programme to build the atomic bomb.

But he had one more sinister reason to feel confident.

Chapter 4

THE SECRET OF SECRETS

Hidden from the outside world at the centre of Unit 731's *Ro* block was Ishii's "secret of secrets". So carefully was its existence kept secret that many junior members of Unit 731 had no knowledge that it was there at all. For prisoners to pass through the tunnel entrance was to start a journey of no return. Only two things were certain – agony and death.

Three of the Ishii brothers, including Takeo, Mitsuo and of course the youngest, Shirō, worked at Pingfan. Takeo was the prison's commander. The prison's guards were second or third sons from the Ishii brothers' village, Kamo. They were called the Special Squad. Tied by bonds of peasant loyalty to their lord and master, they worshipped him. They called him "the Honourable Ishii" or sometimes in reverence "War God Ishii". Most were uneducated, but all were unswervingly loyal. To ensure that allegiance Ishii paid them extra allowances for their terrible and dangerous duties, the sort of money sent home which would support whole families through the difficult times to come, even pay for their brothers' and sisters' education. No Kamo villager has ever publicly spoken, even today, about their former life in Manchuria. The village is silent. The Ishii family name is still revered for its kindness. Asked about Unit 731 older residents will apprehensively reply: "I have nothing to say because it concerns the secrets of the Honourable Shirō Ishii."

Ishii based his Unit in remote northern Manchuria so he could experiment on human beings. There, in what was a police state, he could be given an uninterrupted supply of human guinea pigs. With the unique data gained from human experiments Ishii believed Japan could outstrip the rest of the world in developing this new weapon of war. No other country would have such accurate details about how epidemics spread, and how to protect against them. Only Japan would fully master the twin fields of biological warfare – offence and defence.

From the earliest days after the Manchurian Incident Ishii appears to have employed human guinea pigs.

"It was performed on prisoners who were sentenced to death at

31

Harbin prison," recalled Lt-Gen Saburō Endō. "At first Ishiwara*
brought the prisoners, but later that became the work of the [Kwan-
tung Army] strategy staff."[1]

After Ishiwara returned to Japan in August 1932, Endō himself
took over his predecessor's duties directing the overall activities of
the Tōgō Unit and handing over in cash Ishii's secret funds.[2] Japanese
forces had not entered Harbin until February of that year, dating the
start of Ishii's human experimental activities to the spring or summer
of 1932. At that time, according to Endō, each prisoner was placed in
a closely guarded cell while the experiments took place. After death,
the bodies were burned in an electric furnace to leave no trace. He
described Ishii's work as too important at that time to delegate to the
Kenpeitai.[3] Other evidence also suggests that Ishii built a laboratory
outside Harbin on the route to Ch'ia-lin at Beiinho (Haiinga) that
summer.[4] Bacteria production chief Karasawa was unsure exactly
when the experiments began.

"I am not certain, but I think these experiments were begun
immediately after the Mukden [Manchurian] Incident," he said.[5] "In
the winter of 1939," he added, "Lt-Gen Ishii told me that he
had experimented on cholera and plague on the mounted bandits
of Manchuria during 1933–4 . . ."[6]

By 1935, motion pictures of human experiments were customarily
being shown to senior staff officers of the Kwantung Army. According to a close associate of Tōjō, Japan's wartime premier, but then
chief of the Police Affairs Section of the Kwantung Army Kenpeitai,
Tōjō was personally shown the films by Ishii. After two years in that
position Tōjō served as Kwantung Army Chief of Staff in 1937 for one
year. Although not at first, this associate recalls that towards the
end of Tōjō's term in the Cabinet, the premier was said to have
developed an aversion to viewing such films.[7]

When Ishii's Unit was established at its two-storey red brick
headquarters in Harbin near Pinchiang (Sunkashu) station, the basement floor was the site of human experimentation. This room,
however, became too small to accommodate an adequate number of
personnel for human experiments to be carried out in a systematic
manner.[8] By the time the Pingfan Special Military Zone was established in 1938, human experimentation was a routine procedure.

Occupied Manchuria, and Harbin in particular, was an ideal
location for supply of human fodder. Harbin, a multi-racial city of
shifting minority groups, was a nest of spies. In addition, Japan's
occupation had brought forth strong resistance from both Chinese

---

* An intimate of Ishii's, and a principal architect of the Manchurian Incident.

Nationalists and Chinese Communists, as well as indigenous Manchurians and Mongolians. There was also the large White Russian population caught in the middle between Communist Russia and expansionist Japan. To maintain control in these difficult circumstances was the job of the Japanese Secret Service Agency (*Tokumu Kikan*) and the *Kenpeitai*. They did so through the brutal tactics of fear. Anyone who voiced opposition to the self-declared "paradise" of Manchukuo was liable to detention. Many never returned. The Japanese Secret Service's guide to the "fundamental rules for interrogating war prisoners" reveals that world:

62. Sometimes, depending on circumstances, it is advantageous to resort to torture, but often this may lead to harmful consequences, and therefore, before resorting to it, it is necessary carefully to consider whether this should be done or not. Furthermore, torture must be applied in such a way as not to lead to bad consequences for us.

63. Torture, the infliction of physical suffering, must be sustained and continued in such a way that there shall be no other way of relief from suffering except by giving truthful information.

Torture is advantageous because of the speed with which it is possible with relative ease to compel persons of weak will to give truthful testimony, but there is the danger that, in order to relieve himself from suffering, or in order to please the interrogator, the person interrogated will, on the contrary, distort the truth.

In the case of persons of strong will, torture may strengthen their will to resist and leave ill-feeling against the empire after the interrogation.

64. In relation to persons of weak will, torture is usually applied in those cases when the person interrogated does not speak the truth even in the face of evidence, but there is full reason to suppose that this person will speak frankly if torture is applied.

65. It is necessary to bear in mind that the methods of torture must be such as can be easily applied, as will sustain suffering without rousing feelings of pity, and as will not leave either wounds or scars. However, in those cases when it is necessary to create apprehension of death, the harm caused the person interrogated can be ignored, but this must be done in such a way as not to make it impossible to continue the interrogation . . .

68. After the application of torture, it is necessary to convince the person who has undergone torture that the torture applied to him was quite a natural measure, or to take such measures as will induce him out of his sense of pride, sense of honour, etc, not to

33

speak about it afterwards. In the case of persons from whom this cannot be expected, measures must be taken as in the case of those upon whom accidental wounds have been inflicted.

69. Nobody must know about this application of torture except the persons concerned with this. Under no circumstances must other prisoners know about it. It is very important to take measures to prevent shrieks from being heard.[9]

To be a spy or dissident in Manchuria was to risk death by firing squad or decapitation. But there was an alternative far worse – death at the hands of Unit 731. One of the jobs of the Japanese Secret Service was to serve up human fodder for the biologists at Unit 731.

About twenty kilometres from Pingfan the Gendarmerie ran a detention camp called Hogoin. The name is ironical: *Hogo* means 'protection' or 'patronage' and *in* means 'house'. It was alternatively known by the Japanese Secret Service as the "Scientific Research Division". It had accommodation for 150 men and latterly came under the command of Ishii's acquaintance, spy master Maj-Gen Akikusa, chief of the Harbin Secret Service. Here, Russian citizens, servicemen and spies were held. For those who tried to escape, or those who violated the camp's cruel regime or even those who just stirred up anti-Japanese feeling inside its confines, Unit 731 would become their final destination. Akikusa on receiving reports about such troublesome prisoners would agree to their dispatch to Pingfan. Under later interrogation by the Russians, Hogoin's deputy chief Lt Kenji Yamagishi recalled the dispatch of prisoners to Unit 731:

I do not remember the names of all the people sent to Detachment 731 for extermination. I recall Demchenko, a soldier of the Soviet Army, who categorically refused to give any information about the Soviet Union. Physical means of pressure were used on him with my permission. The questioners tortured him by tying him to a beam by the hands or feet. Nevertheless, Demchenko gave no information. I then decided to have him physically exterminated, and sent him to Unit 731 for this purpose . . .

The actual dispatch of the doomed Soviet citizens was carried out by . . . telephone with the gendarmerie in Detachment 731 . . . Detachment 731 always sent their own motor vehicle for the people – a covered car holding about 20 people without belongings . . .

A list of the names of all the people we sent to Detachment 731 was taken by the man from Detachment 731 and the other was kept at the Hogoin camp . . .

During the whole period that I served at the Hogoin camp there was not a single case of any of these people despatched returning to the Hogoin camp.[10]

Russians from Hogoin were only one source of human guinea pigs. Most, around 70 per cent, were Chinese soldiers, intellectuals and local worker agitators apprehended by the *Kenpeitai* and Secret Service throughout Manchuria. They were shipped to Pingfan as "special consignments" (*Tokui-Atsukai*), a category of prisoner defined by the Police Service Section of the *Kenpeitai* Headquarters as being a suspected spy, saboteur, or ideological criminal, perhaps an opium smoker, pro-Soviet and anti-Japanese, "disloyal", of no value for "enlistment", unwilling for "re-education", of no fixed abode or simply whose release was "undesirable".[11] None received formal trial. Dressed in Japanese Army uniform to hide their identity, "special consignments" were put aboard military trains. At Harbin station, handcuffs hidden, they were hurried across the platform to the nearby *Kenpeitai* holding post, to await Unit 731's four-ton Dodge trucks.

The "special consignments" procedure appears to have been instigated during General Ueda's period as Kwantung Army Commander-in-Chief, that is, in 1939 or before.[12] Forms executing such procedures were issued in triplicate. The discovery of a batch of these forms was later to lead to the uncovering of the secret of Unit 731.

Unsuspecting and innocent people were also tricked into the clutches of Unit 731. Some were lured by the prospect of employment. Young boys, mothers and children, even pregnant women, were trapped. The basement of the two-storey Japanese Consulate in Harbin, a cream-coloured Western style building near the city's Cenotaph, was used as their holding post.[13] When researchers required "new material" Ishii would authorise the Unit's General Affairs Section to contact the Harbin *Kenpeitai* to arrange night-time collection in Pingfan's dark-painted windowless trucks.

During Pingfan's existence 3,000 people were sacrificed.[14] Why were human guinea pigs needed and why in such large numbers?

Epidemics can arise quite easily under natural conditions. Attempts to induce them artificially are much more difficult. One of the critical questions is how to find the optimal route of infection, then to find the lethal and infectious doses required to spread the agent. Another is how to find the most efficient way to immunise. Only human experiments could provide quick answers to these questions, short-circuiting laborious, and less conclusive animal experiments, as well as clinical trials. Ishii knew this sort of information would be unique, putting his programme ahead of any similar one in the West. He had already observed that moral scruples against such drastic human experimentation would prevent Allied countries gaining such information so easily. Ishii needed healthy subjects for testing. Medical orderly Naokata Ishibashi carried out check-ups on new "marutas":

I started work for Unit 731 at the age of eighteen in the special section which did the check-ups on new prisoners. We took details of their type of blood, its pulse and pressure and other things. Prisoners were all referred to as "maruta" which is the Japanese word for a log of wood. Although, when they arrived, they had cards each with their name, birthplace, reason for arrest and age, we simply gave them a number. A maruta was just a number, a piece of experimental material. They were not even regarded as human beings. Most were between twenty and forty years old. None were over fifty. They seemed to know their fate.

After arrival marutas were X-rayed to check for chest infections, then photographed.

I particularly remember two girls: one was Chinese and the other Russian. The Chinese girl was twenty-one. I remember that she was married and that it was written on her card she was not a virgin. She had helped anti-Japanese elements by giving them overnight stays and things. The Russian girl was nineteen – the same age as me then – and she came from Kiev. Our section tried to keep them alive after they recovered from each test. One [girl] hadn't seen her face for years so I smuggled her a mirror and some cotton wool. I think the Chinese girl survived for about two years. A friend of mine told me the Russian girl was poisoned in the end. I was very sad. We did terrible things.[15]

The prison was a vision of hell. Through the spyhole cut in the steel doors of each cell, the plight of the chained marutas could be seen. Some had rotting limbs, bits of bone protruding through skin blackened by necrosis. Others were sweating in high fever, writhing in agony or moaning in pain. Those who suffered from respiratory infections coughed incessantly. Some were bloated, some emaciated, and others were blistered or had open wounds. Many of the cells were communal. An infected person would be put with healthy marutas to see how easily diseases spread. In desperation marutas would try to practise primitive preventive medicine to escape contagion.

Through these little spyholes the most acute symptoms of the worst diseases in the world were coldly observed by 731's white-coated doctors. Special squad guards bearing hexagonal clubs patrolled the corridors of the concrete two-storey building. Day and night they could be seen with doctors, choosing new marutas for experiments and helping collect blood samples and specimens from old infected ones. Guards would often tower over the doctors; their special duties required height and strength. Smaller Kamo recruits were sent to work in the animal house with Ishii's next eldest brother Mitsuo. But larger ones worked in the prison under another elder Ishii brother, Takeo, to prevent trouble breaking out. Inside their guard room a board displayed the schedule of experiments and the research group to which each maruta belonged. They were given instructions by a planning department which charted each maruta's progress.

Unit 731's prison housed around 200 inmates, with capacity for 400, and was divided in half – block seven solely for men and block eight mixed. Marutas were "used up" at the rate of two or three per day. Every now and then the number would be topped up from the holding posts in Harbin. Researchers would submit a requisition to the Unit's commander to gain charge over a new maruta. For the maruta there was no possibility of escape, either from infection or from the prison itself. Diseases could be forcibly injected, or administered through specially developed stick-shaped bacteria assassination guns. They could be sprayed or invisibly concealed in food and drink. Researchers could poison water or fill chocolates, jam buns, melons and crackers with bacteria. Self-protection was impossible. Neither was it possible to break out of the prison, for it was sealed inside *Ro* block by multiple steel doors. Even its small green open air exercise yard was totally enclosed by the square building's inner walls. When some marutas saw the hopelessness of their situation, they gave up hope and took their own lives.

The dichotomy between the doctor's true vocation and the need to build a medically-based weapon was well, and expediently, expressed by an individual (probably Ishii) at the initial assembly of the Unit in 1936:

Our God-given mission as doctors is to challenge all varieties of disease-causing micro-organisms; to block all roads of intrusion into the human body; to annihilate all foreign matter resident in our bodies; and to devise the most expeditious treatment possible. However, the research upon which we are now about to embark is the complete opposite of these principles, and may cause us some anguish as doctors. Nevertheless, I beseech you to pursue this research based on the double medical thrill; one, a scientist to exert effort to probing for the truth in natural science and research into, and discovery of, the unknown world, and two, as a military person, to successfully build a powerful military weapon against the enemy.[16]

One young serologist, Dr Sueo Akimoto, sent from the Tokyo Imperial University to Manchuria by his professor, recalled the horror of discovering the true purpose of an Epidemic Prevention and Water Supply Unit:

> I was very shocked when I arrived and found out about the human experiments. Very few of those scientists had a sense of conscience. They treated the prisoners like animals. The prisoners were the enemy, they would eventually be sentenced to death. They thought the prisoners would die an honourable death if, in the process, they contributed to the progress of medical science . . .
>
> I was very frightened although my work involved no human experiments. I wrote my resignation to Maj-Gen Kikuchi, the research chief, three or four times. But there was no way to get out. I was told that if I left I might secretly be executed.[17]

Civilian researcher Dr Shirō Kasahara was drafted in May 1939 from the world-renowned Kitasato Research Institute in Tokyo. A talented virologist, he researched a new and unknown disease recently broken out at the town of Songo, near the Soviet border.

> I was told to go to Manchuria and work in the Ishii Unit. I was very, very reluctant, but at that time all the population, 100 million Japanese, were mobilised for war so I had no chance to refuse the proposal. Ishii was recruiting all those talented medical scientists who had the rank of assistant professor or professor, or even hospital medical director. And for the people who refused to come to Manchuria he arranged that they were sent a draft note. I was just a civilian member of the Unit. I was called laboratory technician or something like that. In there, those officers who had military rank had great power to control everything.
>
> During the first twelve months . . . I studied the mysterious disease called Songo fever which had broken out in northern Manchuria near the Soviet border. I went there with other officers and medical doctors to investigate the disease . . . I thought that it was caused by a kind of virus, and we named it Songo fever. And then I came back to Tokyo.[18]

Songo, or epidemic haemorrhagic fever (EHF), was a hitherto unknown disease which had broken out at various places in Heilongjiang Province, north Manchuria, during the mid and late 1930s.[19] Pathologist Yasuo Tokoro was flown from Japan to investigate cases of Japanese soldiers being treated at the Harbin Military Hospital, and was first to recognise the new disease.[20] Soon after, in 1940, Ishii, Kasahara, Major Hikotsugu Nishigori of the Clinical and Diagnostic Section, pathologist Tachiomaru Ishikawa, 1st Lt Kiyoshi Ando, civilian technician Hideo Futaki and Lt-Col Takashi Murakami, jointly published a paper on "Songo" fever, so named after one place where the disease had broken out.[21]

Later, Kasahara, who had been unwell but kept on Ishii's payroll, received orders to return to Pingfan from Maj-Gen Masaji Kitano, who, for two and a half years after August 1942, succeeded Ishii as Unit 731 commander. Kasahara continued: "When I arrived . . . Kitano had already started experimenting on Chinese spies."[22]

Kitano was intensely interested in the new disease. A new cycle of epidemics reappeared at Songo in November 1943. He later wrote about his investigation:

When the epidemic broke out in Songo, I went to the epidemic site and conducted tests. Diagnosing the infection process, I believed it most necessary to examine ticks being carried by rats. I had Asahina collect a kind of *toge-dani* [thorny tick, *Lealaps jettmar, Vitzithum*] attached to *Sesuji-nezumi* [rat *Apodemus egrarius*]; on November 6, Dr Kanazawa performed tests on these ticks; subsequently Dr Kasahara took over the tests; on December 14 of the same year I received the pathological opinion of Dr Ishikawa and knew the success of our experiment. After that Dr Kasahara et al. made much effort to determine that the agent was a virus. When Dr Ishikawa was transferred to Kanazawa University, Dr Tokoro took over pathological study and was successful in that work.[23]

In order to perform human infection experiments, Kasahara stated that Kitano made a solution from the ticks, or mites, for injection into marutas.

My work involved supervising the extraction of blood samples from cases previously injected; they would normally show a slight temperature rise to about 37 deg C. These samples were reinjected into a second spy by members of another section, which had nothing to do with mine, and, after the injection, the second generation of patient became infected with haemorrhagic fever

. . . From the symptoms we were able to discern the transmission of the strain . . .

Only on rare occasions did patients die of EHF; normally, they would recover. I have heard rumour that in extremely rare cases, military surgeons, anxious to perform an autopsy, had injected critical and terminal cases with morphine . . . Military surgeons were very active, unlike [civilian] technicians who would not involve themselves in such despicable actions. [Kasahara was here referring to the practice of vivisection.]

. . . when I went to the Unit for the second time in 1942 I had to participate in the experiments of Kitano and the military doctors that were already in progress, namely, injecting people, spies; this was the result of orders and simply had to be obeyed.

I feel very guilty about what I have done and I think I did wrong. There were very few instances but, when a spy did die as a result of human experiment . . . I felt terribly sad and I always arranged for a memorial service to be held in the main hall of the Ishii Unit, which was given by a Buddhist priest from among the soldiers . . . but that's how deeply I was disturbed, and I think I was the only person in the Ishii Unit to arrange such a memorial service.[24]

The onset of EHF is abrupt, with shaking chills, fever, headache, backache, dizziness, eye pain and blurred vision. In the first few days, fatigue, nausea and vomiting are added to the symptoms, producing severe prostration. Patients' faces flush and there is evidence of collapse of some blood vessels, smaller capillaries, rupturing. There is damage to the kidneys. The disease is at its worst between the third and seventh days of illness. Recovery takes three to four weeks.[25] Kitano observed mortality to run at around 15 per cent.

Unit 731's EHF team was large, judging by the number of authors publishing in various military science journals. Added to those already mentioned were research chief Maj-Gen Hitoshi Kikuchi, Lt-Col Motoharu Sakuyama, Masuo Yoshimura and Naeo Ikeda.[26]

Although Unit 731 was vertically organised, researchers assigned to the First, Second and Fourth Division often attended monthly research seminars held in the headquarters' main auditorium and presented lectures. Motion pictures they had personally taken were sometimes shown, including those of human experiments.

Each of Ishii's bacteria research squads were given marutas: Ejima squad for dysentery research, Minato's for cholera, Ōta's for anthrax, Futaki's for TB, Tabei's for typhoid, Utsumi's for blood serum research, Kusami's for drug research, Noguchi for rickettsia, Sekitori's for assassination weapons and Takahashi's for plague.

Takahashi, like Kasahara, used procedures which involved transferring human infected material from maruta to maruta. This was done in the hope of increasing the power of plague bacteria. Those bacteria which survived the onslaught of the first maruta's bodily defences would be strongest. Blood serum from the first could then be taken and injected into a second maruta and so on, each time supposedly increasing the bacteria's resistance. The technique, a dangerous one, had poor scientific foundation, as human antibodies increase in strength at the same time.

Medical orderly Yoshio Furuichi described typhoid experiments:

To test the effectiveness of vaccines fifty Chinese and Manchurians were used as experimental material. First these fifty men were given preventive inoculations, but these were different inoculations – some prisoners were given one, others were given two. Furthermore, different men were inoculated with different quantities of vaccine, and some of these fifty men were not inoculated at all.

Thus, these fifty men were divided into five different groups. All these men were forced to drink water contaminated with typhoid germs and then observation was kept to see what effect these pathogenic germs had in different cases, depending on whether preventive inoculations had been performed on the man or not, how many times, and in what quantities . . .

Most of the men contracted typhoid. Exactly what per cent I do not remember, at all events twelve or thirteen of the men died.[27]

Marutas were also fed typhoid-infected melons to discover if this technique would make a sabotage weapon.

Syphilis was studied. Many female marutas died as Unit 731 endeavoured to solve venereal disease epidemics raging through the ranks of the Imperial Japanese Army as its military hordes marauded across the Asian continent. On one occasion a pregnant woman was deliberately infected with the disease, and when her child was born, both were dissected.[28]

Cruel experiments were not confined to *Ro* block. Five hours from Pingfan by truck lay Anta Proving Ground. Unit 731's Education Division chief Lt-Col Toshihide Nishi took part in one experiment:

. . . an experiment in which I participated was performed in infecting ten Chinese war prisoners with gas gangrene. [Gas gangrene is a wound infection caused by the anaerobic bacteria *clostridia*.] The object of the experiment was to ascertain whether it was possible to infect people with gas gangrene at a temperature of 20 deg C below zero.

This experiment was performed in the following way: ten Chinese war prisoners were tied to stakes at a distance of 10 to 20 metres from a shrapnel bomb that was charged with gas gangrene.

To prevent the men from being killed outright, their heads and backs were protected with special metal shields and thick quilted blankets but their legs and buttocks were left unprotected. The bomb was exploded by means of an electric switch and the shrapnel, bearing gas gangrene germs, scattered all over the spot where the experimentees were bound. All the experimentees were wounded in the legs or buttocks, and seven days later they died in great torment.[29]

Fearing infection, the researchers stood well away, watching through binoculars.

The same technique was used to test the anthrax-charged *Ha* bomb. After the shrapnel blast marutas were given on-the-spot treatment before transportation back to Pingfan, where their death throes were observed and recorded. In some experiments at Anta live plague cultures were sprayed from the air, and plague flea bombs were dropped. An attempt was made to infect marutas with pneumonic plague discharged from a cylinder placed at 10 metres' distance. Field experiments were accurately recorded. Details of temperatures, wind strengths and direction, topography, and results were written into restricted edition scientific papers by Unit 731's printer Naoji Uezono. Many field tests were carried out. Unit 731 experimented on marutas with flamethrowers and in ballistics tests. It was cruelly named "wood-cutting" by some hardened Unit members.

Marutas were generally well fed and looked after before and after experiments. Unit 731 needed healthy test material from which to gain the best scientific results, and to observe different methods of infection and cure. Miraculously, some marutas survived all infection experiments, developing remarkable immunities. But their fate was always the same. Unit 731 had many other uses for human fodder.

The bitter cold of Manchurian winters, where water will freeze in seconds, was a particular problem for Japanese soldiers more used to the temperate climate of their homeland. Some suffered terribly from frostbite – a condition where limbs "go dead" as arteries contract. (In the First World War soldiers called it "trench foot".) Concerned that many would suffer if Japan again went to war with Russia, the Kwantung Army established the *Tōshō* Research Detachment under Colonel Tsuneji Ogata to investigate frostbite. Research was also carried out by Dr Korehiro Ogata into the physiology of human temperature regulation at the Manchurian Medical College and at the South Manchurian Railway's hospital at Suifenho between Mutanchiang and the Soviet border, under Dr Yasuo Inoue. *Tōshō* Detachment was based at Hsinking and Hailar, and its members appear to have used only the acceptable medical practice of researching on themselves or on healthy military volunteers. From this they developed an instrument which gauged wind temperature cooling effect and a drug, *Lebanarin*, successfully used on thousands of Kwantung Army soldiers to increase their resistance to cold. The drug was manufactured at the Tokyo and Mukden plants of the Yamanouchi Pharmaceutical Company.[30]

Unit 731 under Hisato Yoshimura, a civilian researcher from Kyoto Imperial University, used more extreme methods: freezing agony for marutas. Medical orderly Furuichi described Yoshimura's methods:

Experiments in freezing human beings were performed every year in the detachment, in the coldest months of the year: November, December, January and February. The technique of these experiments was as follows: the experimentees were taken out into the frost at night, at about 11 o'clock, and compelled to dip their hands into a barrel of cold water. Then they were compelled to take their hands out and stand with wet hands in the frost for a long time. Or else the following was done: the people were taken out dressed, but with bare feet and compelled to stand at night in the frost in the coldest period of the year.

When these people had got frostbite, they were taken to a room and forced to put their feet in water of 5 deg C temperature, and then the temperature was gradually increased. In this way means for healing frostbite were investigated.[31]

Education Division chief Nishi had more horrific recollections:

I was told by researcher Yoshimura that at times of great frost, with temperatures below −20 deg C, people were brought out from the detachment's prison into the open. Their arms were bared and made to freeze with the help of an artificial current of air. This was done until their frozen arms, when struck with a short stick, emitted a sound resembling that which a board gives out when it is struck. I also read his account of the experiment. A film was made on this subject too.

43

... Yoshimura told me that these researches were being conducted with a view to future war against the USSR.[32]

Sgt-Maj Satoru Kurakazu of the Harbin *Kenpeitai* described what he saw when he worked as a gendarme at Pingfan in December 1940:

When I walked into the prison laboratory, five Chinese experimentees were sitting on a long form; two of these Chinese had no fingers at all, their hands were black; in those of the three others the bones were visible. They had fingers, but they were only bones. Yoshimura told me that this was the result of freezing experiments.[33]

Printer Uezono remembered the terrible sight he witnessed:

Two naked men were put in an area 40–50 degrees below zero and researchers filmed the whole process until they died. They suffered such agony they were digging their nails into each other's flesh. These were the exigencies of military life. You couldn't say I want to do this or that in war, however good or bad. The Japanese way is to obey a superior. It was the same as if the order came from the Emperor. Sometimes there were no anaesthetics. They screamed and screamed. But we didn't regard the logs as human beings. They were lumps of meat on a chopping block.[34]

The danger of frostbite comes when circulation is restored to the affected area too quickly. Yoshimura tried various methods and rates of warming to find the right treatment to avoid the death of affected areas. In October 1941, his published findings overturned the traditional remedy for incipient frostbite, rubbing the suggested part, by suggesting that warmth be applied with lukewarm water at around 40 deg C, never as much as 50 deg C.[35]

Yoshimura found his therapy, but not before many marutas had suffered desperate pain. They could be seen with rotting limbs and skin blackened by necrosis, languishing in the prison. Whole limbs were amputated to preserve their lives for yet more experiments.

Detachment 731 had a sister unit. It was called the 516 Chemical Warfare Unit. Since November 1922, when chemical warfare work was withdrawn from Ishii's patron, Chikahiko Koizumi, the Japanese Army had kept chemical and biological research separate. Chemical weapons were given to one department of the Army Science Research Institute, enlarged in 1941 to become the 6th Army Technical

Research Institute. Based in Yodobashi-ku, Tokyo, this large institute in 1945 employed 715 personnel and had an annual budget of nearly 3 million yen, excluding salaries. (At this time the budget of a large university like Tokyo Imperial University was only 12 million yen including salaries.) In May 1929, the Army Committee for Technology authorised production of mustard gas at Okuno Island in the Seto inland sea, near Hiroshima. It was called the Tadami Weapons Factory and came under the control of the Tokyo Army Arsenal. Its main plant and equipment had been imported from France. By the end of the Pacific War it was to be capable of producing several poison gases.

To train chemical warfare soldiers the Army established the Narashino Chemical Warfare School, in Ishii's home prefecture, Chiba, near Tokyo. Field testing and experimentation with new gases and poisons developed by the 6th Army Technical Research Institute was carried out from 1937 by the 300-strong Manchurian 516 Unit at Tsitsihar.[36] Lt-Gen Masao Oyaizu, director of the 6th Army Technical Research Institute from 1941 to 1944, had general command over the unit. Human experimentation required secrecy, and 516 Unit carried out joint experimental work with Unit 731 at Pingfan and in the small proving ground at Hailar sub-unit. Oyaizu recalled, ". . . prior to our full scale research of CW, the [Geneva] International Congress came to an agreement to prohibit CW. So we were obliged to study CW secretly."[37]

One series of such experiments was held to test mustard gas – responsible for the majority of gas casualties in the First World War. Five marutas were forced to drink liquid mustard gas. Their symptoms included vomiting and diarrhoea. Before the Second World War all the main combatants stockpiled vast quantities of the gas. Mustard gas evaporates from a brown oily liquid. It has a pronounced smell like that of garlic or horseradish, hence its name. It freezes at 14 deg C and is designed to be dispersed as a spray. Its military attractions lie in its effect on the eyes and skin. Exposure to a low concentration of vapour, so low as to be practically odourless, for an hour will cause severe eye discomfort up to twelve hours later. Higher doses cause more severe and longer lasting eye damage, even blindness. Skin damage takes six to twelve hours to appear. Huge fluid-filled blisters form which burst and are followed by ulcers. The body becomes heavily pigmented as if over-exposed to the sun. This is accompanied by throbbing pains. Symptoms may take as long as four weeks to subside. The vapour attacks moist areas of the body. Neck, armpits and genitals are most susceptible.[38]

The mysterious bundle of documents found in the Tokyo bookstore gave details of one such series of experiments with mustard gas, held in September 1940. The symbol dotted across sketch maps stood for a maruta. In one test twenty were involved, placed strategically in the topography of the test site. Some were tied to stakes at the top of hillocks, others in valleys or bunkers; some with gas masks, some not. Vast gas clouds were created as thousands of chemical munitions were exploded over a four-day period around (not nearer than 100 metres from) the marutas. Symptoms were recorded such as skin, eye, stomach and lung conditions.[39]

Units 731 and 516 jointly researched other special toxic chemicals produced by the "secret weapons" 9th Army Technical Research Institute. The human experimental facility at Pingfan was used to test hydrogen cyanide, acetone cyanide and potassium cyanide. Hydrogen cyanide, in particular, received extensive study. A blood gas, often used as the lethal agent in human execution chambers, it was studied by Unit 731 as a weapon for bombs and sabotaging water supplies. Hydrogen cyanide has the faint smell of bitter almonds. Its principal effect is to interfere with the enzyme in red blood cells that controls the transport of exhaust carbon dioxide away from respiring tissue. Marutas who were given large doses became confused and dizzy within a few seconds. They were unable to hold their breath because of the agent's stimulating effect on respiration. Great weakness and muscular inco-ordination occurred simultaneously and within half a minute they fell unconscious, seized with violent convulsions. Except for an occasional gasp they would stop breathing in less than a minute, although their hearts could continue to beat for several minutes. At this point their chances of survival were small, whatever medical aid was given. Tests were carried out in a large cloud chamber, the size of a telephone box. Made of thick steel, it had an agitator in the ceiling connected by large pipes to a gas-producing machine. Marutas were put in a truck, tied to a pole and pushed inside, some naked, some in full Army uniform and some in gas masks. 731 and 516 researchers watched them gasp and convulse to their deaths through the chamber's reinforced glass windows. A young mother and her baby were even put to death in this chamber. She desperately tried to protect her child from the fumes by covering it with her body. She died lying on top of her child.[40]

An anonymous businessman, then a junior researcher at Unit 731's vaccine-producing sub-unit in Dairen, saw experiments with cyanide bombs:

They used a newly developed gas bomb by Unit 516 for human experiments conducted at Hailar. Nearly 100 marutas were used and except one, all of them were killed. Their bodies were carried by truck, ten or twenty at a time, and transported to Haruarushan where tents had been erected for a pathologist to carry out a pathological autopsy. I wasn't involved in the dissection. The person who actually did the dissection was Dr Okamoto. I had to wait outside the tent to obtain the blood that had been recovered from various organs of the autopsies and placed in tubes, and took these to the military hospital in Hailar. There I checked the contents of cyanide in the blood. That was my job.[41]

The Sekitori squad in Unit 731 researched special pharmaceuticals for making assassination weapons. Its particular interest was in potassium and acetone cyanide.

Unit 731's work encompassed more than just chemical and biological warfare. Malnutrition had appeared in units of the Kwantung Army fighting on the Xuzhou front in mid 1938. More than 1,000 troops of the Mixed Second Brigade and the 13th Brigade suffered from persistent diarrhoea, and about half died. Their illness was initially thought to be an unknown disorder. A number hospitalised at Tsitsihar Military Hospital, however, were recognised by the hospital's commander Major Tokuyuki Okazaka to be suffering from malnutrition, something of an embarrassment to the "glorious" Japanese Army.

On November 11th and 12th, 1938, the Kwantung Army Medical Administration held a two-day conference on the subject. Present were Ishii and Kitano. Soon after, Koizumi, then chief of the War Ministry's Medical Bureau, ordered corrective administrative measures, but the problem was massive. For the next two years a research project was carried out aimed at increasing nutrient absorption from food. Kitano, then at the Manchurian Medical College, carried out other studies using normal scientific procedures.[42]

At Unit 731 a more drastic course was taken, as medical orderly Ishibashi witnessed:

I saw the malnutrition experiments. They were conducted by the project team under the technician Yoshimura. He was a civilian member of Unit 731. The purpose of the experiments, I believe, was to find out how long a human being could survive just with water and biscuits. Two marutas were used for this experiment. They continuously circled a prescribed course within the grounds of the Unit carrying, approximately, a 20-kilogramme sandbag on their backs. One succumbed before the other, but they both ultimately died. The duration of the experiment was about two months. They only received Army biscuits to eat, and water to drink, so they would not have been able to survive for very long. They weren't allowed a lot of sleep either.[43]

Maj-Gen Kawashima summarised the marutas' fate at Ishii's death factory:

From 500 to 600 prisoners were consigned to Detachment 731 annually. If a prisoner survived the inoculation of lethal bacteria this did not save him from a repetition of the experiments which continued until death from infection supervened. The infected people were given medical treatment in order to test various methods of cure, they were fed normally, and after they had fully recovered were used for the next experiment, but infected with another kind of germ. At any rate, no one ever left this factory alive. Following anatomical study the bodies of the dead were burned in the detachment's incinerator.[44]

His summary, however, glossed over perhaps the greatest horror of Unit 731 – vivisection.

Unit 731 had two teams of pathologists; one headed by Dr Kōzō Okamoto, the other by Dr Tachiomaru Ishikawa. Anatomical study performed by these squads was not always confined to the dead. Pathology squad assistant Kurumizawa saw vivisections. "Unit 731 did work on living human bodies," he said. "To do this work our sentiments were suppressed."[45]

Epidemic Haemorrhagic Fever (EHF) researcher Kasahara confirmed that sacrificial experiments had been carried out. Military doctors were, he said, more curious to see how the disease progressed inside the body, at progressive stages. A scientific paper of that time guardedly observed that haemorrhaging in the kidneys in experimental monkeys could be seen with the naked eye.[46] It is a medical fact, subsequently pointed out by the same author many years later, that such a symptom only appears in humans.[47]

Some doctors are said to have come all the way from Japan just to see such a dissection. Laboratory assistants got extra pay, called the Chemical Weapons' Allowance, for wielding the scalpel during this dreadful work. Blood is said often to have spurted all over the ceiling of the dissection room as certain incisions were made. Limbs of the dying marutas would flex and jerk involuntarily as the scalpel entered particular parts of the brain. Organs would twitch vigorously after they were thrown into jars of formalin for preservation. Not only were anaesthetics researched, but also bizarre surgical experiments, connecting different parts of the body, are reported to have been performed.[48]

Each squad was given prior notice of vivisections so they could reserve pathological samples. After dissections special forms were filled in, completing the marutas' files. Bits of bodies would end up as specimens kept in hundreds of jars in a special room. There, dead eyes could be seen staring from severed heads.

The world will probably never learn of all the grisly experiments that took place at Unit 731. Among them were pressure experiments, similar to those carried out by Dr Rascher at Dachau concentration camp. Presumably done on behalf of the Japanese Air Force, it was an extremely painful method of killing. Individuals placed in the Unit 731 pressure chamber would suffer terrible agony as their eyes first popped out of their sockets as the eye membrane ruptured, and later as blood forced its way out through pores in the skin.[49]

Marutas had their blood syphoned off and replaced with horse blood in plasma experiments. It is said that a number of these poor men, women and children who became marutas were mummified alive in total dehydration experiments. They sweated to death under the heat of hot dry fans. At death their corpses weighed only one-fifth normal body weight. Others were electrocuted, boiled alive, killed in giant centrifuges or died from prolonged exposure to X-rays. In all some 3,000 are said to have been murdered. Some were just killed off when there was an excess of supply.[50] They were killed like animals in an abattoir; every bit of their bodies mercilessly used up in the name of the terrible medicine of military science.

Ishii's work allowed Japan to make solid gains on the rest of the world in the field of microbiology. In a number of areas of medical research it is claimed she had taken the lead. Perhaps ahead of the United States by several years in the mass-production of penicillin, Unit 731, it is also said, led the world in research on vitamins, especially the "B" complex, and nutrition.[51] But one more scientific field interested Ishii – the different genetic susceptibilities to disease of various races. It was vital to the success of his project.

From the history of medicine Ishii knew that most races suffered from the same diseases. But this was not always so. History also showed that some genetic groups had been wiped out after exposure to a new unknown disease and that others showed striking immunities. What if he had selected particular diseases or disease strains for BW that would be ineffective against their target? With Japan at war with so many racial types, now including the Anglo-Saxon races, he could not afford such an oversight. Vast resources had already been spent on his project; he could not afford an error over something possibly quite easy to check. Blood tests would perhaps suffice. Unit 731 was handicapped by the fact that its human guinea pigs were overwhelmingly of "Mongol" extraction. There was a small, but crucial chance that some of his weapons might not work on American or Anglo-Saxon racial groups. Doubts grew in his mind. A project team to study the problem was set up at Pingfan under his old Kyoto contemporary, pathologist Professor Zen Kawakami. In 1943 researcher Utsumi was sent on trips to Inner Mongolia to study the immunities of Mongolians and other races. Another had already been sent to a place called Mukden.[52]

Chapter 5

Prisoners in Mukden

Warren W. Whelchel, known more familiarly as "Pappy", came from Tulsa, Oklahoma, and was a Master Sergeant with the US 200th Coast Artillery Anti-Aircraft Regiment. On April 9th, 1942, Bataan fell. On May 6th, so did Corregidor. Pappy Whelchel and 88,000 other Americans and Filipinos were captured.

Pappy remembers: "It was the beginning of one of the most dehumanising experiences ever perpetrated on humans . . ."

Whelchel and his fellow-prisoners had to endure the familiar ill-treatment the Japanese meted out to prisoners-of-war, a proceeding that is understandable only if viewed from the Japanese standpoint that to die in battle is honourable but to surrender is to be shamed. But it was also dehumanising because, unknown to him, he was to become a "guinea pig" in Japan's experimental programme as they sought to build the weapons of biological warfare.

Whelchel was to spend three years of his life as one of 1,485 American and British, Australian and New Zealand prisoners-of-war who were herded into a special prison camp in Manchuria, at Mukden.

Major Robert Peaty of the Royal Army Ordnance Corps walked through the gates of Mukden prisoner-of-war camp on November 11th, 1942. He was appalled by what he saw. The living accommodation was a series of wooden huts, perhaps "5½ yards [5 metres] wide and as long as a cricket pitch" (22 yards – 20 metres). They were partially sunk into the ground and the roofs were made of single boards, packed tight with earth. "I was reminded of Dante's *Inferno* – 'abandon hope all ye who enter here . . .' Inside the huts, the mud was covered by more boards and rush mats the Japanese called *tatami*. I wouldn't have kept my garden tools in such a shed . . ."

Peaty was to be the senior British officer in the camp for more than three and a half years, responsible for more than 100 British and Commonwealth troops.

Like the Americans who would join them in Mukden, the British and Commonwealth troops had had to endure appalling privation on the way to Manchuria. A thousand troops had been herded aboard

51

the *Fukai Maru* in Singapore and for forty days and nights they had survived overcrowding, lack of food – one bowl of rice and a pickled prune or a piece of seaweed, twice a day – and filth, for there were only four lavatories for the thousand men. They had disembarked at Fusan in Korea and had taken a train to Seoul. For a time they had been billeted in a warehouse. Then 100 of them were marched to Seoul railway sidings, driven on to trains and taken across the Yalu River into Manchuria.

The route the 1,000 American prisoners took to Mukden began with what became known as the Bataan Death March. "We were subjected to beatings, killings, forced marches during the heat of the day. We were deprived of food, water and any medical attention whatsoever," as Pappy Whelchel remembered.

They were penned into two camps on the Philippines – at Capas Tarlac and Cabanatuan. Hundreds more died, both in the camp and from suffocation as more than 100 were crammed into box cars on the journey from one camp to another. Then, in October 1942, about 1,000 US troops had been singled out and marched to Manila, the capital of the Philippines. They went aboard the Japanese vessel the *Totori Maru*.

From the moment we went aboard that hell-ship, they were experimenting on us. They threw us on board to see how much we could stand and many of us died. They took us from the tropics to a bitterly cold climate, and that took its toll on us. They gave us a few crackers and a little rice to eat and I feel that it was a systematic way of beginning to test us, to find out how much the Americans – and the British and Australians – could endure.

This was said by Greg Rodriquez Snr, retired now from his career as a foreman in Henryetta, Oklahoma. Rodriquez was a private in 59 Coast Artillery Corps, US Army. He survived the journey to Mukden and three years in the camp itself. It was an opinion since questioned by experts but echoed time and again, on both sides of the Atlantic, with the advantage of forty years' hindsight. Yet, at the time, life in Mukden apparently had its advantages for prisoners-of-war.

Robert Peaty remembers:

Even when I was there, I formed the opinion that Mukden was in some way out of the ordinary. A propaganda camp. We had so many visits from the Japanese Propaganda Corps who brought cameras and took reels of film of the Americans playing baseball.

They photographed the men marching to work – with the Japanese guards and their kendo sticks well out of sight – and they encouraged the quizzes, spelling bees, camp orchestra, the choir and church services at Christmas.

Peaty, as Senior British officer, organised many of the events. He kept a daily diary of life in Mukden. And, amid the battles over the need for more soap or food or bedpans, there runs a thread of medical inspections and care not apparent in many another Japanese prison camp. Peaty himself thought little of it at the time; the job of survival was all-important and totally consuming. But, culled from the pages of a daily diary recorded on scraps of paper torn from exercise books or saved from the daily ration of a single sheet of toilet paper, lies a story of consistent medical surveillance, in stark contrast with other Japanese POW camps. The extracts, written in a secret code to confuse the Japanese, read:

25 Jan 43 Today there was an inspection by a general of the Japanese Army Medical Corps.

30 Jan 43 Everyone received a 5 cc Typhoid-paratyphoid A inoculation.

13 Feb 43 About ten Japanese medical officers and twenty other ranks arrived today to investigate the cause of the large number of deaths.

14 Feb 43 Vaccination for smallpox.

15 Feb 43 Two Americans died in hospital, autopsies being performed on the corpses by visiting Japanese. Owing to the frozen ground we have been unable to dig graves for some time, and all the bodies have been kept in rough board coffins in "cold storage".

18 Feb 43 The medical investigation is still in progress. Inspection by a Lt-General of the Japanese Army Medical Corps. Many high-ranking officers have inspected us since our arrival. The purpose of their visits seems, as a rule, to be mere curiosity, for we do not observe that anything happens as a result of their inspection.

19 Feb 43 Several officers have been questioned about dysentery and diarrhoea.

20 Feb 43 Factory work was suspended, while everyone was tested to find carriers and sufferers from dysentery and diarrhoea.

21 Feb 43 Graves for eighty-five coffins are being dug today, but ground is still frozen and progress is slow.

23 Feb 43 Funeral service for 142 dead. One hundred and eighty-six have died in 105 days, all Americans.

24 Feb 43 The medical investigation is completed. The findings are "that ordinary diarrhoea, not normally fatal, plus malnutrition and poor sanitation, and insufficient medicine, have proved a fatal combination of circumstances".

19 Apr 43 Another Japanese medical investigation started to-day, as apparently the findings of the first did not meet with approval.

24 May 43 Diarrhoea is increasing.

25 May 43 While waiting for medicine for diarrhoea (which was not forthcoming) men were ordered to exercise by playing baseball. The ball could not be found!

26 May 43 Diagnosis of diarrhoea consists of running the men around the parade ground (I saw some of them with bare feet). Those who do not mess their pants, or drop from exhaustion, are reckoned to be liars, and are told to "go back". A protest has been made and a change is expected in both methods and personnel.

4 June 43 Third Japanese medical investigation started.

5 June 43 Anti-dysentery inoculation ½ cc including Flesher Y.

8 June 43 Diarrhoea still steadily increasing.

13 June 43 Second anti-dysentery shot, 1 cc.

6 Aug 43 There are now 208 dead.

29 Aug 43 1 cc TAB* inoculation, and anti-dysentery.

19 Sep 43 Everyone was subjected to the Mantoux test.† Each man also had about 40 cc of blood drawn off for a sedimentation test.

9 Oct 43 Everyone X-rayed for TB.

10 Oct 43 Anti-cholera 1 cc inoculation.

21 Nov 43 There are now over 230 dead.

5 Feb 44 Vaccination of the whole camp.

7 Mar 44 Everyone is being stool-tested for round-worms.

12 Mar 44 The stool-tests show that 41 per cent of us have worms. The Japanese say no remedy is available at present and we can't expect it to be forthcoming.

14 Apr 44 The stool-tests showed: worms, assorted, 500 men; amoebic dysentery: 3 men; trichinosis: 10 men. We can obtain no information as to when medicine may be expected.

18 Apr 44 Inspection by the Surgeon-General of the Japanese Medical Corps.

---

* TAB – Tetanus – anti-bacillus.

† Mantoux test – a blood test usually associated with tuberculosis. At the time, the rumour among the prisoners was that it was some kind of test more usually associated with pregnancy!

28 Jan 45 Everyone was vaccinated today.
27 Feb 45 Everyone was given 2 cc TAB* injection.
6 May 44 We all had 1 cc TAB inoculation.

Today, Major Peaty comments, wryly: "Much of this work must have been done by the scientists of Unit 731 – though we didn't know as much at the time."

Jack Roberts from Bedford was a sergeant in the Royal Army Medical Corps. He worked in the camp hospital, which was no different from any of the other huts partially buried in the ground. He says: "It was pretty obvious to me that we were being used as guinea pigs for some reason that we were not aware of and that we hadn't been told about." He remembered prisoners being measured with calipers, and series of injections and inoculations he was ordered to give on the grounds that it would do the prisoners good. "This group of strangers appeared in the camp from time to time. I don't know where they came from. We were never given any information. They were dressed differently from the normal camp staff. They carried out these duties and after this series of visits they disappeared and we never saw or heard of them again . . ."

The Americans shared the experience. Again, Pappy Whelchel remembers:

A group of five or six Japanese medical personnel entered our barracks and called out various prisoner-of-war numbers that we'd been assigned. They gave us various shots discriminately; not all the prisoners were given the same shots. Then, some were tested through oral or rectal smears. Later, some were inspected for the welts the injections had caused, and more rectal and oral smears were taken. At that time we were the only ones to be given this particular treatment and the Japs were keeping accurate records of every one of us in this one barracks.

For Greg Rodriquez, one of the oddest incidents took place when he was too sick to leave the barracks.

A Japanese came in and looked me over and then placed a mirror in front of my nostrils. At the time, I thought: "Well, he's just checking to see if I'm still breathing." But, after a little bit, he came back again with a feather. He ran that feather up and down under my nostrils – and, later on, I discovered this was one of the methods used to get prisoners to ingest bacteria.

*   *   *

55

It is also a way of collecting bacteria.

Rodriquez dreaded the winters when the temperature dropped until "even the mercury froze! I never thought I would survive. When the going got really tough I used to cling to the thought: 'This, too, will pass!' But I got to the point where freedom, my life back home in the United States, seemed like a dream."

And, always, there were these white-coated strangers who came back, and back again, to Mukden to inject, to test, to measure. Jim Bird, from Fremont, California comments: "We thought they were doctors. I don't know if they were scientists or not."

Greg Rodriquez has a theory. "It was the Americans who died. I wonder if the British and Australians were the control group for the experiments, and we Americans were always given the doses, the real shots . . ."

Dr B. J. Brennan from Croydon, New South Wales, Australia, was one of those doctors in the camp hospital. He too kept a diary that he protected from discovery by concealing it under the mattresses of those prisoners stricken most severely with tuberculosis – and near whom the Japanese refused to go. Dr Brennan remembers three specific visits by these "strangers" from outside Mukden. The first, under a doctor named Tanaguchi, behaved, he recalls, perfectly properly. They had carried out dissections of those who had died, and they had taken samples, clearly labelled. They had been highly critical, however, both of conditions in the camp and of the inhuman travel conditions that had killed so many – an attitude that was not shown by the white-coated scientists in either the second or third parties to visit the camp. Dr Brennan says:[1] "They 'rubbished' Tanaguchi and the work he had done, but, if the Japanese were experimenting on the men, they will have used the samples he had taken at the end of that first winter and which I believe were removed to the laboratories at the local university."

One other memory has always puzzled and disturbed Brennan. "The camp guards made a great fuss one day, and singled out about 150 American prisoners. They then partly dressed them in British and American uniforms, lined them up and marched them out of the camp. They never came back and I never heard of any of them again . . ."

Arthur Christie, then a private in the Loyals Regiment of the British Army, now living at the Post Office in the village of Bryncir, Garndolbenmaen, in Wales, was so sure that something odd was happening in Mukden that he became part of a chain that carried news of what was going on there to the world outside.

Christie's Mukden number was 1210; when he was captured in

Singapore, he had been attached to Military Intelligence. In Mukden, he eventually became part of a work detail that went every day to a factory outside the camp. After he'd been working there some weeks, he fell into conversation with one of the policemen at the factory. The man spoke English. He was Chinese, by name Kim Hua. He had been working for the Japanese police since 1937, he said. Could Christie steal electric spare parts from the factory machinery, and sell them to Hua? Christie reacted with horror. Steal machinery? To sell to a *policeman*? Kim Hua persuaded him that he was working for Chinese Intelligence. He produced photographs of himself in the British Army Royal Artillery Mess in Shanghai. Christie began to be convinced.

"So I stole an electric motor and smuggled it to him. Nothing happened, except he gave me money I used to buy drugs, heroin from the Chinese for the camp hospital. Once it had happened once, I reckoned we were OK. After all, if we'd been caught, I was a dead man – but so was he."

Hua used the electric motor, and other spare parts Christie was able to supply to him, to build a transmitter to contact other Chinese Intelligence agents. The year was 1944. Till 1945 their lives were in each other's hands. The war's end divided them and they have never met since.

Christie is in no doubt about what was happening inside the camp. "The injections were supposed to be beneficial but we had no idea what was in them. Blood samples were regularly taken – but we never seemed to receive treatment. I understand now. We were guinea pigs . . ."

The testimony of these men who survived the Mukden experience must necessarily be subjective. But, in 1985, there was also detailed first-hand evidence to support the feelings and impressions they have held for the past forty years. This came from Japan, from men who worked for Unit 731 in the headquarters at Pingfan, 350 miles from Mukden.

Most crucially, Naoji Uezono spoke at length for the TVS documentary. He was a member of Unit 731 for four years. He was the Unit's printer and, as such, he had the opportunity to read all the most secret documents as he printed them. A dignified seventy-year-old with a flowing white beard, he said:

As regards the white prisoners at Hōten [Mukden], many of our scientific teams went there and I don't know for what purpose but they certainly did go there . . . Whenever important experiments or assessments were carried out in the Unit, at least fifteen or sixteen copies of a report had to be prepared for circulation to senior officers. There were so many in the four years I was there that I don't remember precisely what was in the reports about the prisoners at Mukden. But, to the best of my recollection, those prepared were almost wholly related to malnutrition and I also seem to remember the phrase: "It is considered unwise to bring these prisoners to Pingfan."

Unit 731 was also working in the military hospital at Mukden. So the fact that it was necessary for our scientists to visit the prisoner-of-war camp as well indicates that some type of work was going on there.

For weeks, by telephone, letter and personal approaches, we tried in Japan to talk to those who had worked in sections which might most obviously have had contact with the Mukden prison camp, might have need of what the European and American inmates had to offer.

The clue lay in something Uezono had said to us. "Most of the work there was on dysentery . . ." Among the list of those men who had worked in the dysentery group of Unit 731 was Tsuneji Shimada. Shimada, then seventy-four and waiting to go into hospital "for observation, because of hypertrophy of the heart", lives in Osaka, in a small house tucked away between river and railway line. We telephoned him, and recorded the conversation. He declined an interview. But he confirmed that he had, for seven years, "been attached to the Minato group, the dysentery group" (a group run by researcher Minato). He had been with them from early 1939 until the end of the war.

Could he not, then, discuss whether or not his investigations into the use of dysentery as a weapon of war had any connection with the prisoner-of-war camp at Mukden?

"Researcher Minato visited there frequently. He frequently went with one of my professors with bacterial strains . . . I went there once to see what it was like."

Yes, he said, blood samples *were* taken from the Americans and British prisoners. And he believed there was a balloon bomb factory at Mukden.

What had Unit 731 put into balloon bombs?

"Epidemic germs. They used cholera and typhus."

But what about the prisoners-of-war, the Americans, Australians and British?

"Well, I was in the dysentery group, remember. We studied

whether this could be used as a weapon. Now the cholera group constantly required serum and other things."

That is, blood samples from the prisoners?

"Yes, they required them for their research."

Research records?

"This becomes a long story. We did not experiment on soldiers, but we carried out dissections. Normally, we gave them infected materials to drink and carried out autopsies to ascertain the symptoms. We had to observe the progress [of the diseases] and we had to ascertain the potency of the various viruses."

So are you saying they made the Americans drink various infected liquids?

"Yes, because we also carried out the same experiments at the headquarters of Unit 731 [at Pingfan]."

So the *American* prisoners were made to drink –

" – Yes, of course . . ."

Eventually, Shimada agreed to meet us, in order to let us have a photograph that he didn't mind us reproducing. He was a little, wizened man, on a bicycle . . .

There is documentary evidence that the Caucasian troops herded into Mukden were specially chosen by the Japanese for study and examination.

The evidence was later to be hinted at in the Tokyo War Crimes trial (see Chapter 12) and in documents the true significance of which would be kept from the court in Tokyo. Parallel studies on prisoners were being carried out at the Army Medical College and at prisoner-of-war camps in Tokyo, at Osaka, and elsewhere. The aim was "the physical examination of the quasi-malnutrition cases . . ." and ". . . to make a study of the differences due to the racial differences from a pathological point of view.[2] What if the impact of the germs was dramatically different on Caucasians from what it had been on the hundreds of Manchurians, Chinese and Russians who had already died as part of Unit 731's research?

Ishii was directly responsible for these studies. He needed the raw material to carry out the exploration of racial differences close at hand in Manchuria. Originally, the Mukden prisoners numbered 1,485, men brought to Ishii, to quote an official Japanese report, "for a certain purpose".[3] By the time a Red Cross inspection took place in November 1943,[4] the number had already been reduced to 1,274, presumably by deaths. Of these eighty-four were British, sixteen were Australian and 1,174 American . . .

*   *   *

A battle Major Robert Peaty never won was that which he waged to gain free access to the camp hospital.

"The Japanese tried to keep me out of the hospital, away from the sick people, as far as they could. They made it pretty obvious that I would be very unwelcome to pry into any sort of sickness or ill-health."

Jack Roberts, of the Royal Army Medical Corps, and Frank James, a sergeant in the US 409 Signal Company, could not have been better placed to record one of the most bizarre incidents in the whole history of the Mukden camp. In that first winter, 430 men died. This posed the problem of what could be done with the bodies. The ground was as hard as granite and they could have been buried only with the greatest difficulty. Major Peaty and the senior American officers conferred, but the Japanese took the decision. All the bodies would be taken to a single shed and stacked – some in makeshift board "coffins", some wrapped in cloth or sacking. Many were piled up "like cords of wood" as Jack Roberts remembers. By this time, Roberts was becoming quite used to visits from this

group of organisers – men who weren't apparently military personnel but, if they carried only civilian status, none; the less wore a paramilitary type of uniform. They appeared mysteriously from somewhere . . . and would instruct Japanese orderlies to give out various medicines. On one visit, I remember they produced each morning a large flask, which they told us was a solution of glucose which could and should be injected into the patients in ordeı to assist their recovery from the symptoms of starvation. It all became quite routine . . .

But in the middle of one of these visits, Jack heard a rumour. The bodies were being moved. And they were being dissected. One morning early in 1943, Frank James was assigned to burial detail.

I was pretty sick myself but I wouldn't go to the hospital because nobody that went in ever came out. I went round to the hut and there must have been, I reckon, 340 bodies stacked there.

Each body had a tag attached to his toe. There were two or three men who I took to be Japanese doctors there. They were all masked, 100 percent. All the time they were there, their faces were covered. Another fellow and I were told to lift the bodies up and put them on autopsy tables.

Then, they began to cut them open. They went deep into the stomach, the bile, the small intestine and they also took what looked like pancreas and lungs. They also operated on the heads and took part of the brain . . .

James carried body after body from the shed, and set them on the floor of the building in which the dissections were taking place. He laid the men out, he remembers, quite neatly, the tallest at one end, the shortest at the other. He saw the Japanese "doctors" putting some of the specimens they had dissected into containers and marking *all* the dissections with the dead prisoner's PoW number.

A meticulous record was being kept of each man. Strictly speaking, the Japanese had a duty under international law to ascertain the cause of death. To fulfil it in this way was unique, as far as we can ascertain. The specimens were trucked away from Mukden and that's the last that Frank James, or anyone else imprisoned in the camp, ever saw of them.

For the prisoners the end of their incarceration in Mukden was quite matter-of-fact. After days of rumour, Major Peaty's diary records for August 16th, 1945. "Six men were brought into camp this evening, and from the fact that they were smoking more than the regulation distance from an ash-tray, we knew they were not prisoners-of-war. After an unusually good supper, all prisoners were released from the guardhouse. Red Cross food supplies are to be 'inspected' tomorrow." The six men were an American mission, sent primarily, of course, to rescue the American prisoners.

The diary continues for August 20th:

At about 7 p.m. a small party of Russian officers arrived and announced that we are now "Svobodo" – (free), and that they would enter into conference with our senior officers at once to discuss details regarding our departure. Later in the evening the Japanese guard were disarmed on the parade ground, and, headed by their colonel, they were marched in single file right around, guarded by us, now wearing their equipment and armed with their weapons, and escorted into their own guardhouse in front of every man in the camp. The Russian officer in charge said "Here they are – do what you like with them, cut their throats or shoot them, it is all the same to me", but this was translated diplomatically as "He says he hands them over to you . . ."

For Major Peaty and the hundreds who had survived the privations of Mukden, the victory was theirs in every sense. They had no need, they decided, to seek reprisals. "It would have been," said Major

61

Peaty, "beneath our dignity. It would have reduced us to their level. After all, they had to live the rest of their lives with what they'd done . . ."

Chapter 6

WAGING GERM WARFARE

It is certain that Ishii's Unit 731 had achieved, by various horrifying means, the capability of waging germ warfare. That they also used this capability is now beyond doubt. This seems to have begun as early as 1935, when five Russian spies carrying ampoules containing bacteria were caught by the *Kenpeitai* inside Manchuria. These men were saboteurs, Ishii's protégé Masuda later claimed, and their ampoules were filled with dysentery organisms (Shiga and Flexner) as well as bacteria-spore mixtures of anthrax and cholera to spread disease against the Japanese.[1]

Other allegations were added. Chinese guerillas, acting under Russian influence, had poisoned wells with cholera in the Shanghai area causing the death of 6,000 Japanese soldiers. Saboteurs spreading anthrax had killed 2,000 Army horses during the building of the Peiangchiang to Heihō railway in 1934 or 1935.[2]

True or false – they were probably elaborate disinformation – Ishii used the allegations subtly to further his cause. The Army General Staff, schooled in less technical aspects of conventional warfare, could be alarmed and at the same time were in no position to challenge the validity of his claims. Ishii used them to legitimise his requests for funding, and to begin justifying the need for "retaliation in kind". To prove his weapon's worth, he needed official approval for battlefield experiments. Opportunities were soon to arise.

Throughout the 1930s the Japanese occupation of Manchuria had brought frequent border conflicts with Russia. There were hundreds of incidents. Most were minor, but some developed into major conflagrations, the most severe at Nomonhan* in the summer of 1939.

Far to the west of Harbin on the ill-defined borders of Mongolia, the Nomonhan area was essentially a desert region of sand dunes, low grass cover and a few salt water lakes. Japanese demands for "rectification" of those ill-defined boundaries after a border transgression by the Soviets, a rectification which incidentally would have greatly improved Japan's military position along the 50–60 km stretch of the

---

* The Russians customarily refer to it as the Khalkhin-Gol River Incident.

Mongolian frontier involved, were the excuse for war. Typically, it was the sort of action brought by the Kwantung Army in defiance of central authority. The conflict lasted five months between May and September. Japanese forces were sucked in by the Soviets and eventually routed. In the process they lost tens of thousands of men; dead, wounded or taken prisoner by Marshal Zhukov's forces.

Water resources during the conflict were critical. During the first part of the incident, until the end of July when the Kwantung Army's 23rd Division was destroyed, Epidemic Prevention and Water Supply Units (WPUs) of 100 men were supplying around 30 million litres of water to the front each day. They were also given the more unpleasant, and secret, task of transporting "cargo" – the dead and wounded – to the rear. However, on August 10th, the Kwantung Army's strategy changed and so did the role of the Ishii units. Hastily organised under Gen Ryūhei Ogisu the 6th Army was thrown into battle.[3] So too was a suicide squad by Ishii under the command of Surgeon Maj Tsuneshige Ikari.

The education chief at Unit 731, Lt-Col Toshihide Nishi, later read about the suicide squad's actions:

In July 1944, I was transferred from the Songo branch of Detachment 731 to Pingfan station, as chief of the training division. I took over from my predecessor, Lt-Col Sonoda, who left for Japan the very same day. In his safe I found documents showing that the bacteriological weapon had been employed at the time of the Nomonhan Incident, that is, the incident at the River Khalkhin-Gol. There were photographic negatives of that period, a list of the suicide men who had taken part in the operation. I remember that the Suicide Squad consisted of two officers and about 20 non-commissioned officers and privates. At the foot of the list were signatures written in blood.[4]

Beneath squad leader Ikari's signature operational instructions were detailed. As Japanese troops retreated, the suicide squad was to contaminate the Khalkhin-Gol River with the germs of severe intestinal diseases: typhus, paratyphus and cholera. Fully exposed during the ignominious Japanese withdrawal Ishii's men faithfully performed their dangerous task.

Fighting at Nomonhan eventually terminated on August 30th, the day before Germany invaded Poland. The Russo-German Non-Aggression Pact, announced only seven days previously, had shattered Japanese faith in an Anti-Comintern Pact, and forced a fundamental re-evaluation of her vulnerability to the USSR.

The Japanese Cabinet fell. On September 15th an armistice was signed.

For the detachment's bravery and courage, General Ogisu granted Unit 731 a testimonial of praiseworthy conduct. The heroic citation was later printed alongside a photograph of Ishii in the May 23rd, 1940 edition of the *Tokyo Asahi Shinbun* newspaper. Under the caption ". . . The awarding of a commendation, in particular to the hygiene unit commanded by the Ishii Unit, was the first such honour ever accorded a hygiene unit in the history of our country . . .", it made grandiose reading.[5]

The following year Ishii prepared further ambitious plans for biological attack, this time against China, with whom Japan had been at more or less full-scale war since the so-called Marco Polo Bridge Incident of July 1937.

Naokata Ishibashi, an eighteen-year-old youth drafted to Unit 731 in 1938, witnessed preparations for this raid. Unit 731 recruited hundreds of young trainee technicians, teenagers of high intelligence from poor families unable to afford high school education. Because of a shortage of laboratory-trained assistants, these teenagers, some as young as fourteen or fifteen, were trained in bacteriology by Pingfan's Education Division. In 1940, Ishibashi, a rather meticulous young man, was batman to Major Hikotsugu Nishigori, a Kyoto Imperial University graduate with whom he worked in Unit 731's Clinical and Diagnostic Section. Ishibashi kept a detailed diary of his wartime experiences. He documented part of Ishii's secret raid on China.

I went by train from Pingfan to Hangchow in China. On this train there was loaded a small plane and there were some cars and bombs. We arrived at night, and visited a hangar which stored damaged aircraft. It had once been part of the air training school of the Chinese Army. The freight was unloaded from the train and transported.[6]

Kwantung Army Commander Umezu, on July 25th, 1940, had authorised this special journey, requiring that his subordinate Lt-Gen Kusaba, chief of the Field Railway Administration, transport the forty-man *Nara* Detachment of the *Kamo* [731] Army Unit to Central China. Kusaba's orders stated that "the freight consists of special material which calls for secrecy, and for this reason is not named in the waybill." Also shipped from Pingfan were 70 kg of typhoid germs, 50 kg of cholera and 5 kg, approximately 15 million, plague fleas.[7] Ishibashi continued the story:

The raid was to scatter fleas which had been cultivated on rats. The fleas were not in bomb form but were to be scattered from the air. They were packed in special drums to be transported separately by air to Hangchow. When colleagues of mine were loading the plane, one of the drums broke open, scattering fleas all over the place. They were very frightened even though I think all of them were wearing masks. A massive amount of insecticide was used to kill all the fleas. Later I saw that all the grass had changed colour and died.

The airplane left early in the morning and I knew by the distance that they were to attack the port town of Ningpo. I believe food was arriving for Chiang Kai-shek's Army . . . they must have been making a film because I saw a 16 mm camera unit.[8]

Great importance was attached to the raid. Ishii himself had headed it. Much hope had been placed on the new plague flea weapon. Poor results had been given with the earlier technique of spraying "bare" bacteria from aircraft. A success was needed. To gather results a special team under Major Nozaki remained behind.[9]

The following year research chief Kawashima found Ishii in his office poring over a Chinese medical journal. Ishii, with evident satisfaction, read some pages aloud to Kawashima. Several outbreaks of plague had been recorded in the Ningpo region, south of Shanghai. A total of ninety-nine people had died, in an epidemic which persisted in the area until November 1940. Perhaps more worrying was the fact that the journal had made special reference to the epidemic's strange character – humans had been infected first, without the customary prior outbreak of the disease in the rodent population.[10] The Chinese undoubtedly suspected the epidemic's artificial nature.

To spread the news of his success at Ningpo, Ishii released a special film of the raid. Training chief Nishi described what he saw:

It first showed a receptacle containing plague-infected fleas being attached to the fuselage of an aircraft. Then the spraying apparatus was shown being fastened to the aircraft's wings . . . The plane took off, and it was explained that it was on its way to the enemy's territory. The plane was next seen over the enemy's positions. Then followed shots of the aircraft, of the Chinese troops in movement and of Chinese villages. A cloud of smoke was seen detaching itself from the aeroplane's wings, and it transpired from the explanation that this smoke consisted of plague fleas, which were being sprayed on the enemy. The plane turned back to the airfield, and a caption appeared on the screen: "Operation Concluded". We then saw the plane landing. A squad of disinfection orderlies drove up to it, and the plane was shown being disinfected. People were seen alighting from the plane: the first to alight was Lt-Gen Ishii . . . This was followed by a caption: "Results", and a Chinese newspaper was shown, with a translation in Japanese. The explanatory text stated that a severe epidemic had broken out in the Ningpo area. The concluding shot was of Chinese orderlies in white overalls disinfecting the plague area.[11]

On March 1st, 1941 Ishii was made a Major-General. The plague flea demonstration had obviously impressed, although it may not have been a complete technical success. Kawashima summarised Unit 731's operational status around this time.

In the summer of 1941 the chief of the detachment, Ishii, called a conference of all the chiefs of divisions and informed us that an instruction had been received from the Chief of Staff of the Japanese Army, the substance of which was as follows . . . that all attention must be focused on the mass production of fleas . . .[12]

Ishii noted that the detachment had managed in the most successful cases to bring the breeding of fleas up to 60 kg in 3–4 months, but now the amount had to be increased to 200 kg for the same period.[13]

This call for increased production, Kawashima said, was with a view to going to war with the Soviet Union (the Kwantung Army's so-called Kan-Toku-En plan).*

The reality of international events, however, was somewhat different. Despite their Tripartite Pact of September 27th, the previous year, Germany, Italy and Japan never worked out any comprehensive joint strategy. In fact, Japan was not even given any advance warning of Germany's invasion of Russia. She had on April 13th signed a Neutrality Pact with the USSR. When the news arrived of Germany's invasion of Russia on June 2nd, 1941, Japan was mortified. Earlier in this year, moreover, because the Japanese Army had become so bogged down in China, the home government and its political and military authorities had already agreed to take the southward option. In her last major confrontation with Russia in Manchuria, at Nomonhan, the Kwantung Army had been completely

---

* The status of this plan for military manoeuvres has subsequently been disputed by historians. Most non-Soviet historians merely regard it as a normal Army contingency plan. It was by no means a clearly agreed part of Japanese government policy at the highest level.

routed. Since then, not only had morale suffered, but the Kwantung Army had been stripped of troops dispatched south to the Chinese zone. Considering the disastrous effect on the Tokyo governments caused by the international outcry over the Manchurian and Marco Polo Bridge Incidents, the Army did not wish to bring about another political upheaval which would surely follow another clash with Russia.

Japan's southward advance would inevitably lead her into conflict with Britain and America. Although she wished, if possible, to avoid hostilities with those major powers, Japan rated low the ability of the Allied countries. So while Germany was knocking on the doors of Moscow, Japan, on December 7th, 1941, sank most of America's Pacific Fleet at Pearl Harbor. The war had taken a different course, Ishii, too, for the time being, was forced to change direction.

In the autumn of 1941 Unit 731's 2nd Division chief Kiyoshi Ōta led a second raid on China. The Japanese High Command wanted Ōta's squad to demonstrate the plague fleas' effectiveness in dislocating Chinese lines of communication. Changteh City, an important communications point near Lake Tung Ting, was designated as the operation's target. Ōta selected a 100-strong team, including thirty bacteriological specialists. On November 4th, one of Unit 731's aircraft launched an attack spraying plague fleas over sections of the city. The raid caused a minor epidemic, claiming twenty-four lives.[14]

Unknown to Ishii, this attack was to have an unforeseen effect. For the first time, the slumbering web of the Allied Intelligence network was awakened to rumours of Japanese attempts at biological warfare. Albeit at first with much disbelief, Japan's actions were soon to be debated at the highest level in Washington and London.

Ishii's star continued to rise that year. In October, the month that War Minister Hideki Tōjō became Prime Minister, Tōjō himself publicly and personally presented Ishii with an award, the highest accolade for technical achievement. They were photographed together in the newspapers.[15] It can be presumed that the award was for Ishii's highly innovative plague flea weapon. The following year yet another raid was planned.

General Shunroku Hata, Commander-in-Chief of the Japanese Expeditionary Forces in China, had that year ordered an offensive with the aim of driving Nationalist forces from their new capital, Chungking. It was a campaign both of punishment and pre-emption. In April 1942 America had mounted the surprise "Doolittle" air raid on Tokyo from carriers in the Pacific. Bombers dropped their payloads over military targets and then flew on with the intention of landing in free China. In response the Chekiang campaign was aimed as a reprisal against Allied airfields in China. In the Japanese terror campaign that ensued, fuelled by this Allied air raid, a quarter of a million Chinese were killed, an appalling retribution for the ninety killed including several dozen children when an American bomber mistakenly strafed a school.

Hata implemented orders from Imperial General Headquarters (*Dai hon'ei*) to clear the region of the Central Chinese province of Chekiang, along the main railway line connecting the towns of Kinhwa, Lungyu, Chü Hsien and Yüshan. The whole of the Japanese 13th Army was involved. Ishii arrived at 13th Army Headquarters on August 24th for a secret conference with senior officers. The same day, after dinner, he left for Nanking, leaving behind a handful of aides. His plan this time was to contaminate on the ground as well as from the air. When the 11th and 13th Armies staged a strategic retreat from the town of Chü Hsien his units were to stay behind to contaminate abandoned ground. These units, of approximately 300 men, were left to spray germs and infect water supplies in and around the cities of Yüshan, Kinhwa and Futsing. Then, it was hoped, Chinese forces would invade the territory and be engulfed in epidemics.

Pingfan struggled to supply part of the massive quantity of germs required for the operation, producing 130 kg of anthrax and para-typhoid which were placed in special glass bottles, sealed with paraffin wax and cellophane, put fifteen or sixteen to a box marked "Water Supply" and ferried by truck to the Unit's aerodrome. Together with Unit 731's expeditionary party, the germs were flown to China by order of Kwantung Army Commander Umezu. The rest of the Chekiang Campaign germ payload was supplied by another large Ishii BW unit at Nanking, and its satellite sub-units.

During the operation that followed, the germs of cholera, dysentery, typhoid, plague, anthrax and paratyphoid were all used. Flasks containing pure germs were poured by BW cadres into reservoirs, wells and rivers. Containers were also tossed into houses.[16] Three planes from Nanking Unit under fighter escort dropped germs from the air.

So great were Chinese losses resulting from Unit 731's activities during the Chekiang Campaign that one authority later described them as "inestimable".[17] But Ishii's BW strategy was also a disaster for the Japanese. Thousands of her own troops were infected as the BW weapon accidentally boomeranged.

Despite the fact that Ishii had provided fifty-man decontamination and immunisation squads for each battalion, casualties upward of 10,000 resulted within a very brief period of time after Japanese soldiers inadvertently overran a contaminated area. Regular soldiers were not told about the use of bacteria, such knowledge not generally requiring dissemination below division commander level. Victims, most suffering from cholera, were rushed to hospitals in the rear, mainly the Hangchow Army Hospital. Statistics kept at the Nanking headquarters showed that 1,700 had died, most from cholera and some from plague and dysentery. A captured Japanese soldier, Med Lt-Cpl Isamu Chinba, formerly a member of Ishii's Nanking Unit, later revealed that actual deaths were almost certainly much higher, "it being a common practice to pare down unpleasant figures".[18] Another account reveals that as late as the following summer thousands of those soldiers were still being kept in a special isolation enclosure in the exercise yard of Hangchow Army Hospital. On average each day three to five victims died.[19]

Further sabotage tactics employed by Ishii during the Chekiang Campaign involved various acts of Japanese "philanthropy". In two of the province's prison camps, 3,000 Chinese PWs were given special "presents", rolls syringed with typhoid and paratyphoid. After the gesture was photographed to illustrate Japan's benevolence to her enemies, prisoners were released to take their infections back behind enemy lines. At bivouac sites, cakes contaminated with typhoid were scattered, as if forgotten; a deadly fodder for the unsuspecting Chinese peasant.[20]

If disaster struck for the Japanese during the Chekiang Campaign, Ishii appears never to have publicly admitted it. Later, in the presence of Kawashima, he declared the operation a complete success.[21]

Around the time of the Chekiang Campaign Ishii left his position as commander of Unit 731. His place was taken by Maj-Gen Masaji Kitano. Ishii and Kitano were well acquainted. Both had joined the Army in 1922; Ishii serving in the 3rd Regiment of the Imperial Guards, Kitano in the 4th. Both had been instructors at the Army Medical College. When Ishii left the main flow of a military career to take his world "observation" trip, Kitano joined the Sanitation (or Hygiene) Section of the War Ministry's Medical Bureau. Their careers met again in 1936. Both left their positions as instructors at the Army Medical College; Ishii to head Tōgō Unit at Harbin, Kitano to become professor of the Manchurian Medical College at Mukden. Kitano, a graduate of Tokyo Imperial University, a competent bacteriologist and researcher, retained his military status and was thus the absolute authority in the Manchurian medical community. He regularly attended Kwantung Army medical conferences and carried out joint studies on malnutrition with Pingfan's researchers, long before taking over Unit 731.

Although Kitano later stated that Ishii never lost overall control over Unit 731, the new commander launched pioneering studies of EHF and tick encephalitis and reportedly improved the all-round scientific aspects of the detachment's work.[22] Human experimentation continued, as did limited BW attacks. During the winter of 1942, plague appears to have been deliberately spread in the troublesome No-an suburb of Hsinking, making evacuation necessary and thus denying subversives a safe haven.[23] In August 1944, when Ishii's friend Kajitsuka visited Pingfan, Kitano reported that large quantities of plague fleas had been dropped from high altitude over densely populated Chinese territory south of Shanghai.[24]

Ishii's movements after the summer of 1942 are quite difficult to trace. His military biography states that he left his position as Unit 731's commander, and from August 1st, 1942, took over as chief of the 1st Army's Medical Administration, followed by a period as an instructor at the Tokyo Army Medical College until March 1945.[25]

Ishii later stated that he required a posting to a field Army to attain the rank of Lt-General.[26] It appears to have been a source of bitterness to Ishii that officers in the Surgeons' Corps were precluded from rising to the rank of full general. Others have said that Ishii once again became involved in corruption, colluding with a military supplier to embezzle funds earmarked for construction at Pingfan.[27] Perhaps Ishii was in disgrace after BW backfired in Chekiang.

It now appears that Ishii was in Tokyo during this time, building and consolidating his BW empire. His Epidemic Prevention Research Laboratory, the *Bōeki kenkyū-shitsu*, had by then become a high-security establishment surrounded by two separate guard fences.[28] In April 1942, its funding was made secret from National Diet scrutiny, a distinct departure from the open financing of the Faculty of Health and other departments at the Army Medical College.[29] It is said that a large underground BW factory was built in the cellars of the *Bōeki kenkyū-shitsu*.[30] Later, a sophisticated mass bacteria production conveyor line was transported from Japan to Pingfan. Was it devised here? Here also, at his BW Defence Intelligence Institute, Ishii planned the special training or personnel in technical intelligence gathering. Lectures were also given to the *Kenpeitai* on how to assist Army medical officers in their BW duties.[31]

From the *Bōeki kenkyū-shitsu* Ishii visited Japanese universities to recruit the cream of their young medical scientists. At Kyoto Imperial University he lectured each year on how students could help the military, even screening a film containing scenes of human experimentation.[32] Each year, Ishii also hosted a research seminar and lavish banquet at the *Bōeki kenkyū-shitsu* for researchers receiving grants from him. In return for presenting their research report, researchers were paid a stipend of 300 yen a month, a sum far greater then than their university salary.

The *Bōeki kenkyū-shitsu* was also the centre for vaccine research and it was through such work that Ishii encountered the new process of lyophilisation or freeze-dry preservation. He recognised the dramatic effect it could have on BW, vastly increasing its potential. In 1942, Ishii gained the co-operation of Makoto Yanagisawa, an assistant professor at Tokyo Imperial University, in developing dried BCG vaccine.[33] Also that year, Surgeon Major Motoharu Sakuyama, one of Ishii's Nomonhan veterans and a Pingfan researcher, delivered a lecture on the freeze-dry process before the 11th Japan Academy of Medicine conference. His conclusions reveal that the importance of the process was clearly understood:

. . . dry preservation makes possible the shipment of disease toxins and the conservation of serial inoculation of animals.

Infection via the nostrils by means of a drug powder was successful.

The success of the dry preservation of disease toxins made possible the contamination by a pulverized spray applied to the nose, eyes and wound.[34]

The lyophilisation process – where biological substances are rendered stable by rapid freezing and subsequent dehydration under high vacuum – held much promise for Ishii. Germs accumulated for BW attacks would no longer need to be kept alive in "blood juices" during storage and transportation, a cumbersome and dangerous process. There was also the possibility of a significant increase in the weapon's potency, gained in the ability of direct infection through the respiratory tract. In 1943, Ishii recommended the study of large-scale drying for BW. An experimental facility was established at Pingfan, and twenty desiccation units built.[35] It is unclear whether this work was successful. Lt-Col Ryōichi Naitō and Tomosada Masuda, two of Ishii's close aides, later claimed it was never brought to fruition, though their reasons for such an assertion remain contradictory.

Naitō stated that the lyophilisation units were too busy working on plasma and vaccines.[36] His colleague claimed, on the one hand, that no work was done on offensive BW because of excessive cost, and on the other, because of danger to workers.[37,38] He was, however, in no doubt that dried organisms would have vastly improved aerial dispersion.

Throughout this time Ishii, the orator, administrator and propagandist, was undoubtedly championing his cause in the upper hierarchies of Japan's military machine. A measure of his ability to hold an audience spellbound is to be found in the report of a lecture he gave the War Ministry's Grand Conference Hall in 1939. The *Military Surgeon Group Magazine* recorded that Ishii packed this vast hall with practically the entire officer staff of the War Ministry and Headquarters Staff for a full two-and-a-half-hour address on the subject of the "real situation with frontline health and sanitation during the latest Sino-Japanese incident". "His Imperial Highness, Prince Chichibu, broke away from his busy military responsibilities and honoured the meeting with his royal presence and listened most intently to the proceedings," the magazine added.[39]

During this period of the war, Ishii carefully dovetailed his organisation into the Japanese Army across all the war zones. He was already well organised in Manchuria through the Operations Division of the Kwantung Army. As the war shifted south, so too did the tentacles of Unit 731. Main permanent Epidemic Prevention and Water Supply Units like those at Pingfan and Nanking were established at Canton, Peking and Singapore, each with their own satellite sub-units. Water Purification Units (WPUs) of up to 500 men commanded by a full colonel were also attached to armies in the field. At divisional level smaller WPUs roughly half the size carried out similar functions, excluding research and education.[40] An 8 mm home movie taken by Ishii's protégé Masuda shows he visited such WPUs in Rangoon, Mandalay, Bangkok, Saigon and Bandung[41]. In total, there were thirteen Army WPUs and more than forty divisional units. As many as 5,000 men are estimated to have been employed at the eighteen larger WPUs in China. These units were separate from each army's Medical Administration, and generally came under the direct control of military commanders in the field.

Ishii, it is said, extended his personal empire from Harbin to the Dutch East Indies and from the island of Hokkaidō to the Celibes.[42] From Manchuria, bacterial aggression against Russia was supplemented by another unit of the Kwantung Army.

The Kwantung Army had created another unit for waging BW besides Unit 731. It was known as Unit 100, otherwise as the Hippo-Epizootic Unit of the Kwantung Army or more simply the Kwantung Army Stables. It was commanded by a veterinarian, Lt-Gen Yujirō Wakamatsu, not Ishii. As with Unit 731 Maj-Gen

Tetsuzan Nagata once again appears to have been the driving force behind the Unit's formation.

The Unit was fully formed in 1936, at the same time as Unit 731, and based 10 kilometres south of Hsinking at the village of Menchiangtung (Mogatong). Staffed by veterinarians the 700-strong force researched animal diseases and other related subjects. For example, the second division worked on vaccine and sera manufacture for horse herds, and its various sections were responsible for bacteriological research, horse poison studies on potassium cyanide and strychnine, and early BW studies of anthrax, glanders and sheep and cattle plagues; pathology; experimental animals; organic chemistry, and botanical and plant pathology, and studies into the spreading of red rust and mosaic plant diseases.[43]

In September 1941, however, the Unit was ordered to begin mass-production of glanders, anthrax and red rust germs for fully-fledged BW research. Tests on the effectiveness of spreading animal diseases in the climate and topography of the Soviet-Manchurian border region commenced in mid 1942.

In the summer heat, a specially trained squad pushed rubber dinghies out into the flow of the River Derbul. Not far downstream Russian troops were garrisoned near the river's confluence with the Argun, whose flow marked the Soviet border. As the boats drifted downstream, squad chief Major Muramoto ordered his team to tip containers full of glanders germs overboard. This was done every 100 metres. Stretches about one kilometre long were contaminated. Other Unit 100 members on land cultivated anthrax in a special field laboratory. They then contaminated land and lakes in the nearby Tryokhrechye area of North Khingan province with these germs. To test durability, horses, sheep and guinea pigs were put out to graze on the affected areas.[44] Unit 100 researcher Lt Zensaku Hirazakura described more preparations for BW the following year:

In December 1943 at a joint conference of senior personnel of Detachment 100 and Kwantung Army headquarters attended by Maj-Gen Yujirō Wakamatsu, the chief of Unit 100, his deputies Lt-Col Koremichi Hosaka and Maj Bunji Yamaguchi, engineer Kiyoshi Ida, and Lt-Gen Takaatsu Takahashi, chief of the Veterinary Service of the Kwantung Army, a plan was elaborated for forming under the 2nd Division a sixth section, called the "bacteriological". This section was designated for the mass preparation of germs and their storage in special basement storehouses . . . And indeed, a large quantity of germs and chemical agents was prepared in the 6th section . . . Research on forms and methods of carrying out sabotage was also conducted in Detachment 100; for instance, the question of employing aircraft for this purpose was carried out . . .[45]

Although smaller than Unit 731, Unit 100 was substantial in size. Its annual bacteria production capacity was projected to reach 1,000 kg of anthrax, 500 kg of glanders and 100 kg of red rust. Equipment shortages, however, prevented this target being attained. The Unit also experimented on humans, though again on a smaller scale than its sister unit. Senior Sgt Kazuo Mitomo described some experiments:

I put as much as a gramme of heroin into some porridge and gave this porridge to an arrested Chinese citizen who ate it; about 30 minutes later he lost consciousness and remained in that state until he died 15–16 hours later. We knew that such a dose of heroin is fatal, but it did not make any difference to us whether he died or lived. On some of the prisoners I experimented 5–6 times, testing the action of Korean bindweed, bactal and castor oil seeds. One of the prisoners of Russian nationality became so exhausted from the experiments that no more could be performed on him, and Matsui ordered me to kill that Russian by giving him an injection of potassium cyanide. After the injection the man died at once.[46]

Bodies were buried in the unit's cattle cemetery.

In April 1944, Kwantung Army Commander Umezu ordered Unit 100 to carry out reconnaissance of North Khingan province with a view to spreading disease in the event of war. Hirazakura, who led the party, was asked to calculate livestock figures in adjacent regions of Mongolia and Russia. The squad inspected rivers, reservoirs, pastures, cattle numbers and the seasonal transfer of livestock and reported back to Umezu and, later, his successor Yamada. Later, Unit chief Wakamatsu ordered Hirazakura to purchase hundreds of head of livestock and put them to pasture along the Soviet border north-west of Hailar ready to be infected by airborne dispersion. It was hoped that in the event of a Soviet invasion these infected livestock would mingle with local herds to cause epidemics destroying food supplies.[47]

Ishii had given Japan the ability to wage BW on a mass scale by 1945. His single-minded determination and flair had undoubtedly played a major part. But who else had taken a role? Who had sanctioned Ishii's work? Who had allowed him to execute his plans? It is clear that BW was integrated into Japanese military planning at the highest level. Therefore, some of the country's foremost military personalities had certainly been involved. Who were they? And did the Emperor know? Later, people were to go to extraordinary lengths to obscure the answers to these questions.

Viewed today, the chain of command inside Japan's military hierarchy appears complex. It is difficult to discern with complete accuracy exactly who was involved. But much of the picture can now be recreated.

One clue to understanding it is to look at the funding of the Unit. It was responsible to three separate authorities. Firstly, it came under the overall command of the Kwantung Army. Secondly, in matters concerning offensive BW research, the line of authority went directly to the Army General Staff's 2nd Operation Section. Finally, the War Ministry exercised some control. General "political" supervision came from its Military Affairs Bureau, and the Sanitation Section of the Ministry's Medical Affairs Bureau held direction over the detail of research work.[48]

Unit 100, it is known, was funded by the War Ministry via the Kwantung Army: 600,000 yen from the War Ministry for personnel costs, and 1 million yen for offensive BW work via the Kwantung Army's 2nd Division, the Intelligence Division.[49] Unit 731 had a budget of 10 million yen which was channelled, it is believed, entirely through the Kwantung Army's 1st Division, the Operations Division. Three million yen was given for personnel, 200,000–300,000 yen for each of the Unit's divisions, and a staggering 6 million yen for germ production, experimentation and research.[50] The budget of Tokyo Imperial University, with its 369 professors and assistant professors and 7,800 students, was only 12 million yen at that time. None of Unit 731's budget was scrutinised by the National Diet, and Kwantung Army Chief Veterinarian stated that he considered BW funding a bottomless pit.[51]

From the earliest days Lt-Gen Chikahiko Koizumi promoted Ishii's work. Koizumi later became Army Surgeon General. Between July 1941 and July 1944, Koizumi was Health Minister, linking Ishii's work directly with the Tōjō Cabinet.

Also from the early days, Ishii received support from Maj-Gen Tetsuzan Nagata, chief of the War Ministry's Military Affairs Bureau, one of the most powerful military men in Japan, and the guiding spirit of the Army's Control Faction.

Remarkably, Ishii again managed to straddle the gulf separating the opposing Imperial Way and Control Factions, gaining help from the former's leader, War Minister Gen Sadao Araki. Araki later went on to hold the important position of Education Minister.

From the earliest days, therefore, the highest echelons knew of Ishii's work. To these must be added many in the Kwantung Army. Shortly after the occupation of Manchuria, one of the principal architects of the Manchurian Incident, Lt-Col Kanji Ishiwara, personally delivered both funding and human experimentees to Ishii. Records clearly implicate three commanders-in-chief of the Kwantung Army in Ishii's work. General Kenkichi Ueda (March 1936 to September 1939) originated the order for "special consignments" of human experimentees. This practice was continued by his successors General Yoshijirō Umezu (September 1939 to July 1944) and Otozō Yamada (July 1944 to August 1945). Umezu personally authorised Ishii's BW raids on China, and Ueda presumably did likewise at Nomonhan.

After his tour of duty with the Kwantung Army, Umezu became Chief of the Army General Staff. As such he was a signatory to the Instrument of Surrender that ended the Pacific War. Yamada had known of Ishii's work before commanding the Kwantung Army. As Inspector-General of Military Education, one of the Three Chiefs Council (the Army's "big three"), a position he had held since October 1939, Yamada had been responsible for military publications which had included a sabotage manual referring to BW.[52]

Tōjō, who at one point jointly held the three positions of Prime Minister, War Minister and Chief of the Army General Staff, had seen films of Ishii's human experiments in his period of service at the Kwantung Army. Between 1935 and 1937 he had been the Kwantung Army's *Kenpeitai* commander, and later the Kwantung Army's Chief of Staff. The month he had become premier Tōjō personally awarded Ishii a commendation for outstanding technical achievement.

Other leading Kwantung Army figures with knowledge of Unit 731's work would certainly have included Heitarō Kimura, Chief of Staff from October 1940 to April 1941. He later became Vice-Minister of War from April 1941 to March 1943, then commander of the Burma Area Army. Kwantung Army Commander-in-Chief from 1934 to 1936, General Jirō Minami, would certainly have known of the human experimental work if such films were being shown at Kwantung Army headquarters at that time. Knowledge might also have extended to General Kuniaki Koiso, Chief of Staff of the Kwantung Army from 1932 to 1934. Koiso, a former War Minister, became Japan's premier after the downfall of Tōjō in 1944.

Outside the Kwantung Army, General Shunroku Hata, Commander of the China Expeditionary Army from March 1942 to November 1942, would certainly have known that biological weapons had been deployed during the Chekiang Campaign in the summer of 1942.

Hata, Tōjō, Kimura, Umezu, Koiso, Minami and Araki all subsequently became defendants at the Tokyo War Crimes trial. They were joined in the dock by General Kenji Doihara, chief of the Mukden Special Services Agency (*Tokumu Kikan*), and Colonel, later General, Seishirō Itagaki, Manchurian Incident conspirator, Kwantung Army Chief of Staff between 1936 and 1937 and War Minister from 1938 to 1939. Doihara and Itagaki would have joined their colleagues in their knowledge of Ishii's work.

It is clear that most leading Army figures, many of whom rose to positions of supreme power, knew of or had sanctioned Ishii's work. Outside military circles, it is probable that the Foreign Ministry was aware of the secret work at Pingfan. The basement of its Harbin consulate had been used as a holding post for marutas. This sort of information would have been relayed to Tokyo without interference by the Commander-in-Chief of the Kwantung Army who, although Ambassador to Manchukuo, did not control the country's diplomatic service.

Did knowledge go even higher? Did members of the Imperial family know? The Emperor's brother Prince Mikasa honoured Unit 731 with a visit. Unit photographer Yamashita recalled his inspection:

> I was the photographer for a memorial photograph-taking session for senior members of Unit 731 and Prince Mikasa. I didn't actually go round on the Pingfan tour with Prince Mikasa so I don't know how much he saw of Unit 731. Unfortunately, the photograph I took happened to have a reflection from Mikasa's glasses, so you couldn't see his eyes too well. Ishii was very annoyed and strongly suggested we correct the photograph. He said that since we were in the mecca of science we should be able to do such a correction. Because of this incident I remember the visit of Prince Mikasa very well.[53]

Prince Mikasa in his recently published memoirs refers, somewhat obliquely, to biological warfare. The extract reads:

> I heard from a young officer – and the shock was much the greater for the fact that he was my contemporary in Army officer training – that he used exclusively live prisoners for bayonet training to enhance soldiers' thrusting power. I was also shown films where large numbers of Chinese prisoners of war brought by cargo trains

and lorries were made to march on the Manchurian plain for poison gas experiments on live subjects. A high ranking military doctor who took part in these experiments was telling me that prior to this, at the time when Lord Lytton with his group was dispatched by the League of Nations in order to investigate the Manchurian Incident, they attempted to give this group some fruit infected with cholera but did not succeed. So, in fact, these were the kind of things that went on in the show of "The Holy War".[54]

Another member of the Imperial family, the Emperor's cousin Prince Takeda, held executive responsibilities over Unit 731. Takeda, known as Lt-Col Miyata to protect his royal identity, joined the Kwantung Army as a staff officer in the Strategic Section of its Operations Division in August 1943, following a period at the Japanese equivalent of the Pentagon, the *Dai Hon-Ei*, or Imperial General Headquarters.

"Miyata was especially detailed from the Operations Division for liaison between the Operations Division and Detachment 731," recalled Operations Division chief Matsumura. "In immediate charge of issuing passes to Detachment 731 was the Deputy Chief of the Strategical Section . . . Prince Takeda," added Matsumura. "The person who visited the detachment returned the passes to Prince Takeda."[55]

The Kwantung Army and Unit 731 were in daily contact, the Operations Division exercising guidance over bacteria production requirements, technical equipment supplies and the training of special cadres for Unit 731. Furthermore, inside the Kwantung Army a special commission had been set up to study methods of employing bacterial weapons. Takeda, the chiefs of Units 731 and 100, and the Kwantung Army's Commander-in-Chief and Chief of Staff were members. Films of germ bombs were shown at these conferences.[56] It is also known that Lt-Gen Yukio Kasahara once ordered Takeda to visit Unit 731 to report on munition production, and that he accompanied Yamada on an official inspection of Pingfan.[57]

"I worked in the headquarters building of Unit 731 next to the front gate," recalled Unit printer Uezono, "so every time we had some important visitors there was a memorial picture-taking session, and they posed in front of that gate. I remember one occasion when Prince Takeda, the Emperor's cousin, visited Unit 731 and had his picture taken."[58]

Did the Emperor know about his country's BW work? Some have said the Emperor actually sanctioned the work. The Emperor's personal seal was affixed to orders forming Unit 731, and reportedly also on various decrees expanding the detachment. Thousands of military and civil documents, however, carried this seal. Frequently it was no more than a rubber stamp. Top Army personnel were not customarily required to provide detailed explanation of the content of each order requiring Imperial approval.

Ishii frequently invoked his Emperor's name to boost his troops' morale. "He often stated that his work came directly under the orders of the Emperor," recalled Unit doctor Akimoto. "Again and again he would repeat that he was just doing what the Emperor wanted him to do."[59] Such exhortations by Japan's fiercely nationalistic Army officers were commonplace. In fact, the history of events in Manchuria quite clearly shows that Kwantung Army officers frequently abused the Emperor's "Supreme Command" over the military forces as a way to justify defying their political masters.

Other spurious accusations have sought to link the Emperor's interest in biology to BW. His interests, however, were in slime mould, micro-organisms far removed from disease-causing bacteria.

In the Emperor's defence, it is said that he intervened to prevent the Imperial Navy from studying germ warfare for use against the United States.[60] It is known that the Navy tested experimental bacteria bombs, one called the Mark VII, in Tokyo Bay during 1943.[61]

On the other hand, BW was considered of the highest importance; it was known at the highest military and political levels; both the Emperor's brother and cousin were aware of it, and his seal did rest on the document forming Unit 731.

Under Japan's Meiji Constitution legal responsibility rested with the Emperor. Emperors were acknowledged to have supreme command of the Army and Navy under the provisions of that constitution, and theirs was the power to declare war and conclude treaties.[62] The Emperor of Japan's signature was on the 1899 Hague Convention.

Chapter 7

THE END OF PINGFAN

The tide of the Pacific War turned with America's attack on Saipan in June 1944, a 1,000-mile leap forwards from the Marshall Islands. American casualties were 14,000 dead and wounded; the Japanese death toll alone was 24,000, and 1,780 prisoners were taken. Many Japanese, seeing their garrison fall, threw themselves from clifftops to their death. The loss of Saipan caused Premier Tōjō's downfall.

Unit 731 had been preparing to supply bacteriological weapons for the Pacific conflict since May 1944. Ishii laid plans to attack American forces at Saipan. From among the best and most capable members of Unit 731 Ishii chose seventeen officers to lead a large assault team. Ishii planned to deny the Americans the use of Saipan's airstrip by sprinkling the runway with plague-infected fleas. The team was put aboard a ship. But before reaching its destination the ship was sunk by an American submarine. There was only one survivor.[1]

American progress in the Pacific was now relentless, although they paid for every inch in blood. Guam fell in October and that month the first B29 raids began on Tokyo. That same month two-thirds of the Japanese fleet was destroyed in the 2nd Battle of the Philippine Sea. After Iwo Jima's fall in February 1945, Ishii again proposed a BW attack. In March he asked General Umezu, now Army Chief of Staff, for permission. Umezu conferred with Surgeon-General Hiroshi Kanbayashi, but Kanbayashi turned the plan down on practical grounds. It would not change the war situation, he said.[2] His chance to participate in the Pacific gone, Ishii was posted back to Manchuria in March for a final and desperate task.

Japan's ally Italy had already surrendered and Germany was on the point of defeat. Even the once crack Kwantung Army was a shell of its former self, progressively stripped of equipment and its best men during the long years of war. Ishii remained undaunted. He had just been promoted to Lt-General, the highest rank he could attain in the Medical Service, and he had been posted back to Manchuria on the orders of Lt-Gen Kaneshirō Shibayama, the Vice-Minister of War. Shibayama had also ordered the Kwantung Army Commander, Yamada, to help Ishii raise output of bacteria weapons.[3] Ishii's family joined him after the intense night air raid over Tokyo on March 10th, which, by turning 16 square miles of residential areas into a raging inferno, had claimed the lives of more than 100,000 civilians.[4]

Even before Ishii's return operations chief Matsumura reported to his Chief of Staff Yukio Kasahara that bacteriological weapons should be employed deep behind the lines in the Soviet Union, around the cities of Voroshilov, Khabarovsk, Blagoveshchensk and Chita.[5] To raise output Unit 731 was resupplied with new equipment including a conveyor bacteria mass-production line. Bacteria factory chief Karasawa inspected sub-units in Manchuria to see whether further installations were possible, and to consider dispersion of production in the event of enemy air strikes. Songo, Hailin and Lin-k'ou branches were given more equipment.

Thus Ishii's Unit was in fair shape. Events, however, worsened. The following month Russia repudiated her five-year neutrality pact signed with Japan on April 13th, 1941 and it was now only a matter of time before Russia entered the war. Daily lectures were given to Ishii's troops, urging greater effort.

Ishii expected the final and decisive battle would take place between June and September 1945 when America attempted to land on Japan proper. Okinawa, Japan's own island bastion, fell in June. The month before, Germany had surrendered. Russia, urged by Britain and America at Yalta, turned her attention to Manchuria. Forces swelled on both sides of the Soviet-Manchurian border as millions of troops remained at standoff point.

Tanaka's flea factory was expanded and given more staff. With 4,500 flea breeding machines in operation, 100 million insects could be produced every few days. Ishii planned to breed 300 kg, approximately one billion plague fleas, in the run-up to war.[6] Special training courses in flea breeding were set up at Pingfan in June, and sub-unit members ordered back afterwards to establish their own production bases.

To propagate plague cultures and to feed the fleas, rats were needed in their thousands. Yamada ordered every land unit of the Kwantung Army to trap rats.[7] And Ishii ordered Pingfan's Chief Quartermaster Major Satō to calculate the feed required for 3 million rodents, and to have it in readiness by September.[8] Storehouses held grain, millet and soybean flour to the height of four-storey buildings. The putrid stench of rat urine was everywhere. Rats, rabbits and other animals were even bred in their hundreds in the back yards of Unit members' homes.

Karasawa's new conveyor system was working round the clock producing plague, typhoid, cholera and anthrax organisms, which were sufficient, if correctly dispersed, to infect half the planet. To distribute the biological weapons eighty trucks were procured. For safety some facilities and equipment were moved from Pingfan to more secure positions in Korea and Manchuria. Unable to believe that Japan would ever yield in the war effort, Ishii had intended to move his facilities to a new site built in Korea since the spring.[9]

Research continued, although somewhat hindered by a riot in the prison. Printer Uezono recalled:

> I think it was two months before the end of the war . . . Normally, the Special Squad looked after those two buildings and no one else but them could go in. But one day when a prison warder tried to give a prisoner lunch . . . the maruta had cut off his wrist manacle. He attacked the warder. The officer was slightly injured and escaped, but he left the master key behind. So this maruta opened all the cells, and all the prisoners came out and started rioting.[10]

Every maruta in Block 8's second floor tried to escape the prison. But the only way out, a thick steel door at the end of the corridor, had been closed by the escaping guard. Uezono continued:

> There was an emergency call to the headquarters building where I was working. We were ordered to mobilise to help at the scene. And I was very curious about that building, so I rushed to the scene. I was one of the first people. I had to wear a poison gas-proof mask, and I was supplied with a gun. I saw the riot. I think it was caused by a Russian. He screamed something I didn't understand. Our interpreter Ogawa translated what this Russian screamed. He said they had been deceived and taken to this prison. Japan had been defeated so they should be released. All of us were very excited and we tried to persuade them for about one hour to be obedient and go back to their own cells. And then our senior came and ordered the use of gas. So we brought gas bombs, and a tank and a rubber hose. A ladder was put up from the inner courtyard to put the hose into the cell block. We used the gas bombs and the rubber hose to poison them. I think it took about one hour to kill them all.[11]

Sixty marutas died of phosgene poisoning.*

The prison was replenished, and the new group of marutas was required to dig a large hole in *Ro* block's inner courtyard.

---

*Accounts of the riot differ. One account states that more than 100 marutas escaped from their cells in June or July 1943, and were suffocated when rod-shaped containers were lit, vaporising chloropicrin gas. It is possible that there was more than one riot.[12]

Between midnight and 1 a.m. on the morning of August 9th, after Hiroshima had been devastated by the atomic bomb, the Soviet Army swept across the border into Manchuria and Korea, with a massive force of 1½ million men, 5,500 tanks and 5,000 aeroplanes. The Kwantung Army was thrown into panic. Confusion broke loose. That day, or the day after, Yamada ordered the destruction of Units 731 and 100. A nearby sapper unit was ordered to blow up Pingfan's main headquarters. The Unit's personnel were to destroy all evidence and be evacuated south to Seoul in Korea. A second bomb was yet to be dropped on Nagasaki.

Shortly before our evacuation from Harbin [recalled Ishii's daughter Harumi] I heard my father whispering with his men something about an "uranium bomb" . . . I remember that my father said, "Shall we use it then?" I didn't have any idea as to the nature of "it", but now I realise he meant the germ weapons his team of researchers had developed.

Later, I heard that the plan was dropped because the Emperor opposed it.[13]

At 6 p.m. on August 10th, after the Kwantung Army song had been sung, Unit 731 members heard a broadcast newsflash on the Soviet invasion. Branch sub-units were contacted, and three days later ordered to put to the torch all buildings, living quarters, equipment, materials and documents. Branch chiefs were asked to issue their entire personnel with potassium cyanide for use if captured by the Soviets. Many took to the hills and prepared to commit collective suicide.

At Pingfan, marutas were the first to be destroyed. Members of the 516 CW Unit gassed the marutas by throwing Erlenmeyer flasks of toxic chemicals into their cells. Six hundred local Manchurian and Chinese labourers who worked at the Yagisawa plant disease farm and elsewhere at Pingfan were machine-gunned.[14] Potassium cyanide poison was also put in the marutas' breakfast food.[15]

"All of us had to begin the evacuation work," said Uezono. "First of all the marutas were killed. Then their bodies were put in the incinerator. The specimens taken from human bodies were also put in, but there were so many that they just wouldn't burn. So we took them down to the Sungari River and dumped them in."[16]

Some bodies were thrown into the Ro block courtyard pit, covered with heavy fuel oil and set alight. Hot bones, all that remained, were collected, put in straw bags and dumped in the river along with hundreds of pairs of manacles.

The local sapper brigade under Maj-Gen Ube took a full three days to demolish the main buildings. So rigid were some of the concrete structures that they resisted dynamite. Finally, the eighty unused Ford trucks were loaded with 50 kg bombs and set to ram the buildings. Ishii's ceramic *Uji* bombs were smashed. Those loaded with fleas were taken to the boiler room and incinerated. With blackened and charred faces Unit 731 members slaved through yet another nightmare of their own making.

On the 11th at 3 p.m. most family members were loaded into open freight cars brought to the Unit's shunting yard for the evacuation.

Because I was the commander's daughter [said Harumi], I was ordered to lead a group of youths and children. There were thousands of women and children riding that train. We witnessed many dramas . . . a baby was born aboard the train, though the mother died after giving birth to the boy. The train was re-directed towards Fusan after we were informed that the war had ended . . . When the train stopped at a station in Korea, people brought fresh water for the passengers. But we were ordered not to drink it out of fear that it might be poisoned.[17]

The rest of Unit 731, excepting a few left behind for final clearing up, assembled on the 13th and 14th at the shunting yard. Ishii made a formal speech, extolling the memory of Unit 731 and its diligent research. As if in mockery of him, it was interrupted by the sound of the prison exploding. Members were issued with phials of poison. Ishii had originally wished every branch member and all families in Tōgō village to commit suicide. But this proposal met the violent disagreement of Maj-Gen Hitoshi Kikuchi, 731's research chief.[18] Nonetheless, some took their lives without orders from Ishii.

In fifteen freight trains the 2,000 or so personnel were shunted off from Pingfan first to Harbin, then south to Hsinking. Trains were given special clearance by Kwantung Army Headquarters, and military police were posted at transit stations to ensure their right of way.

On August 15th the Emperor broadcast Japan's defeat and surrender. It had never occurred to Ishii that Japan might give in. He had to confirm the broadcast before believing it. Such was the shock that according to one account, Ishii was seen in a listless condition, utterly crestfallen, at Kwantung Army Headquarters.[19]

That day in the late afternoon the Unit 731 train arrived at Hsinking. There, on the following night, Ishii made a final address to his erstwhile troops. He swore them to "life in the shadows" for the rest of their lives. In the light of a candle held by an aide-de-camp, Ishii ordered them never to speak of their military past, never to take official positions in the future, and never again to contact each other.[20] It is a promise that some have kept to this day.

Late in August, Ishii's convoy passed south through Korea, reaching Fusan, the port where nearly four years previously the American prisoners-of-war had disembarked bound for Mukden. It was a sorry end for the once proud and arrogant officers of Unit 731. The pathetic end of Japan's once mighty BW effort was to let loose thousands of infected rats in the neighbourhood of Pingfan. It caused a local plague epidemic which claimed many innocent lives into the summer of 1946.[21] At Unit 100 a handful of infected horses were freed after the surrender.[22] The balloon bombs once considered for carrying disease against the United States were never used, prohibited on technical grounds by the upper echelons of military command.[23] At Ishii's *Tama* Detachment in Nanking, rats and mice were incinerated and officers moved ping-pong tables upstairs to the fourth floor where human experimentation had taken place.[24] At the Dairen sub-unit members systematically tore out from all volumes of journals in the university and departmental libraries articles which had any connection with BW.[25]

Kawashima, Karasawa, education chief Nishi, Yamada, Ishii's friend Kajitsuka and Kwantung Army Chief Veterinarian Takahashi were captured by the Russians, as well as various members of Songo and Hailin sub-units.

Ishii, Ōta, Kikuchi, Masuda, Kaneko, Yoshimura, Okamoto and printer Uezono were among the overwhelming majority of Unit 731 members who escaped. Kitano had been posted to China in March.

On August 19th, the night after the war's end, several uniformed men arrived at the ancient Noma Shrine in the western Japanese city, Kanazawa. The shrine's head priest Nobemura was told they had come from an Army unit evacuated to Maizuru Harbour. He was asked for accommodation. Although the twenty or so men refused to identify themselves, Nobemura offered to clear the first floor of his rooms. That night several trucks arrived and unloaded a mountain of food. It was too much for the needs of twenty men in starving Japan. The "officers" wore civilian clothes. Two resembled Ishii's elder brothers Takeo and Mitsuo. Their younger brother, Shirō, had naturally arranged that Special Squad members were among the first to be evacuated. The mysterious party kept close watch on the movements of the American Occupation forces. Their camp was guarded by an armed man at all times. Each day new men, members of Unit 731, arrived at the Detachment's makeshift headquarters, collected money and supplies, changed into civilian clothes re-tailored from military uniforms and then quickly departed. On September 22nd, the shrine was vacated.[26]

During part of this time, Ishii was at the 2nd Army Hospital in Kanazawa clearing up his papers. Finally, Unit 731 left Kanazawa. Its effects were loaded into two trucks at Kanazawa University Hospital, where former Unit 731 pathologist Tachiomaru Ishikawa had taken up a professorial appointment. The truck set off for Tokyo. When it arrived Ishii was there to greet his two subordinates, Kikuchi and Ōta, outside a boarding house opposite the shattered Army Medical College in Wakamatsu-chō. Fearing for their lives, Kikuchi and Ōta soon set off in different directions to go into hiding. Japanese military authorities had already ordered the obliteration of every scrap of evidence about BW.

In preparation for the American Occupation of Japan, those authorities set about the systematic destruction of all military documentation. A "Special Research Conduct Outline" issued on August 15th by the War Ministry's Military Affairs Section reveals that particular attention was paid to Units 731 and 100, as well as *Fu* (the codename for balloon bombs) and other weapons created by the "secret weapons" 9th Army Technical Research Institute.[27]

During the latter part of the war, mass germ production and other records and facilities are believed to have been transferred from the *Bōeki kenkyū-shitsu* to military medical establishments in Akita Prefecture and to Niigata. American B29 bombers had already done much of the destruction work that April when they razed the Army Medical College to the ground.[28] Nonetheless, one account records that hundreds of human pathological samples were dumped between August 10th and September 15th in a pit, 15 metres by 10 metres, dug by members of the college's education section in ground next to Ishii's old epidemic prevention laboratory.[29]

Ishii and his colleagues began their long and nervous wait to see the reaction, if any, of the American Occupation authorities. Ishii's patron, former Health Minister Chikahiko Koizumi, had resigned as Health and Welfare Minister, four days after the fall of the Tōjō Cabinet on July 18th, 1944, devoting the final year of his life to his work as director of the Japan Red Cross. On September 11th, after the war's end, Tōjō himself unsuccessfully attempted suicide with a pistol. Two days later, in the early evening Koizumi was visited by a Japanese police officer who informed him that Allied Headquarters wished to see him the following day. Koizumi took supper that night with his daughter and nephew, bringing out a bottle of sake he had received from the Emperor. After supper he went to his bedroom, put on formal Japanese dress and entered the tea room, which doubled as a Buddhist prayer room. Lighting an incense stick, he picked up some Buddhist prayer beads and sat in front of the altar. He placed a short military sword in front of him, and a pistol at his side.

At 11.25 p.m., he made a cross-shaped incision in his stomach. Then, after fixing his robes, he cut the blood vessel in his right armpit, ending his life. He left no suicide note.[30]

PART 2

DISCLOSURE

Chapter 8

What Allied Intelligence Knew

Glasounoff, a laboratory technician at the Rockefeller Institute for Medical Research in New York, hurried to finish his Sunday morning's work, feeding laboratory animals and recording the temperatures of infected monkeys. Turning his car into 68th Street as he arrived for work that morning, a man had stepped out, flagging him down. The stranger, inconspicuous in appearance and of medium height, glanced at Glasounoff's car number plate and came over. After confirming Glasounoff's name and without identifying himself, the stranger stated he knew something of interest to Glasounoff. Curiosity aroused that it might be more family news, he agreed to meet at 1 p.m. on Exterior Street on the East River between 67th and 68th Streets.

At the appointed hour Glasounoff drove to the rendezvous, parking opposite the high blind wall bounding the Institute's animal house. A car pulled up behind him. Rain was thundering down but through his steamed rear window he could make out the vague outline of a four-door 1939 Buick sedan. A man got out, glanced into Glasounoff's car then got into the front seat. Around forty, with a small moustache, this new stranger wore a brown coat and hat, and blue suit with a red stripe. Making conversation about Glasounoff's work, the stranger, speaking with a slight foreign accent, was obviously refined and well-educated. Like the man that morning he refused to identify himself, but he did, however, state that he was working with a famous person, again anonymous, but a very distinguished scientist. Their research, he said, was handicapped by lack of proper material. Could Glasounoff help? he inquired. He wanted cultures of yellow fever virus, specifically a virulent unmodified *Asibi* strain.

Glasounoff, quite properly, suggested he contact the laboratory's director Dr Wilbur Sawyer. The man, however, replied that he preferred not to use that route, as professional jealousy was involved. Both the Rockefeller and his laboratory, he explained, were planning rival work. Glasounoff declined to help, whereupon to his surprise the stranger offered to pay $1,000. Worried, the laboratory technician demurred. The stranger persisted, raising the sum to $3,000 –

91

$1,000 now, $2,000 on delivery. Glasounoff, countering the man's increasingly insistent advances, explained that cultures were locked in an icebox. Not put off, the stranger suggested bleeding a monkey, then desiccating the virus.

Glasounoff at this point moved to reach into the back of the car. Alarmed, the stranger's hand flashed over and caught his. Glasounoff was ordered not to move a muscle as the stranger pocketed the car's ignition keys. A final offer was given to comply with the request. But on receiving an equally final refusal, the stranger jumped out of the car, slammed the door and screeched off southwards in his car.

Excited and frightened, Glasounoff hurried back through the rain to report the incident to the Institute's authorities. In the confusion of the incident Glasounoff failed to notice the stranger's car registration number, and it was decided therefore not to report the matter to the police, which might only invite unwelcome newspaper publicity.[1]

The incident assumed importance because it coincided with another strange occurrence. Three days previously, on February 3rd, 1939, the laboratory had been visited by a Japanese Army doctor, bearing an introductory letter from his country's military attaché in Washington. The young doctor, an assistant professor at the Tokyo Army Medical College, was one of Ishii's men, Dr Ryōichi Naitō. His letter stated that he had been asked by the Superintendent of Tokyo Imperial University's Institute of Infectious Diseases (*Densenbyō Kenkyū-jō*) to obtain the yellow fever virus strain used for vaccination, and the unmodified and virulent *Asibi* strain.

Naitō gained an interview with laboratory director Dr Sawyer. But the request was refused because of resolutions passed by the Far Eastern Bureau of the League of Nations' Health Section and by the Far Eastern Congress of Tropical Medicine, in which the governments of India, Netherlands and others agreed to prohibit, indefinitely, the introduction of yellow fever virus for any purpose whatsoever into Asiatic countries. Undeterred, Naitō returned to the Institute's laboratories badgering researchers with questions about the virus, particularly where the virus used in Brazil was prepared. In conversation Naitō revealed that he had spent the last one and half years at the Robert Koch Institute in Berlin and that on his imminent return he would probably be sent to Manchuria for field service.

Both incidents were investigated. A private detective followed Glasounoff for several weeks. Nothing suspicious occurred. The matter was reported to the State Department, and a copy found its way to the offices of the Army's Surgeon General – the first, and almost unrecognised, hint to America of Japan's interest in BW.

Six months later, Dr Yonetsugi Miyagawa, a famous bacteriologist and director of the Tokyo *Densenbyō Kenkyū-jō*, again requested the virus. A boyhood friend of Koizumi's and also physician to Prince Fumimaro Konoe, Japan's premier 1937–39 and 1940–41, Miyagawa stated in a letter that a Professor Koybayashi would attend the Third International Congress for Microbiology in September and requested Dr Sawyer to furnish him with the virus. Again Sawyer refused.[2]

It was one and a half years before the significance of these incidents was recognised. Aware of the theoretical possibility of BW, Colonel James Simmons of the Surgeon General's Office signaled his fears to G-2, the War Department's Military Intelligence Service (MIS). Concurring with Simmons, G-2 noted: "The Japanese are endeavouring to obtain virulent strains of yellow fever virus for the purpose of bacteria warfare."[3] Steps were taken to prevent the virus falling into Axis hands from Rockefeller sources in Brazil and Colombia.

Reliable information gained in February 1941 indicated that Japan had a bacteriological detachment attached to each of two CW regiments, and that more than 2,000 parachute troops had been trained.[4] Also in early 1941, it was reported that the Japanese government had suspended fishing near Otaru, Hokkaidō, after bubonic plague cultures were inadvertently dumped into the sea after flood damage to the laboratories of the city's university.[5]

That autumn, two months before Pearl Harbor, America's War Secretary Henry Stimson became sufficiently worried about BW to write to Dr Frank Jewett, President of the National Academy of Sciences:

Because of the dangers that might confront this country from potential enemies employing what may be broadly described as biological warfare, it seems advisable that investigations be initiated to survey the present situation and the future possibilities. I am, therefore, asking if you will undertake the appointment of an appropriate committee by the Division of Medical Sciences of the National Research Council to examine one phase of the matter. I trust that appropriate integration of these efforts can be arranged.[6]

Wisconsin University bacteriologist Dr Edwin Fred was appointed to gather together, in utmost secrecy, a special working group known as the WBC Committee, the War Bureau of Consultants, comprising twelve prominent scientists plus representatives of the Army Chemical Corps, Ordnance Corps, Surgeon General's Office, the Navy Bureau of Medicine and Surgery, and the Department of Agriculture and the Public Health Service. The committee reported in February 1942, that BW *was* distinctly possible.[7] Prompted by accounts of the devastating impact of the first gas attack at Ypres, the WBC Committee urged immediate defensive preparations, concluding that:

> The value of biological warfare will be a debatable question until it has been clearly proven or disproven by experiences. The wide assumption is that any method which appears to offer advantages to a nation at war will be vigorously employed by that nation. There is but one logical course to pursue, namely, to study the possibilities of such warfare from every angle, make every preparation for reducing its effectiveness, and thereby reduce the likelihood of its use.[8]

In response to the renewed interest and volume of inquiries about BW, *Military Surgeon* magazine reprinted, nearly a decade later, a pioneering article entitled "Bacterial Warfare" by Major Leon Fox, which argued that in wars before the twentieth century disease had always caused more casualties than those killed or wounded in combat. Ishii himself had read the original.[9]

In May 1942, as Ishii was preparing his full-scale Chekiang BW offensive, President Roosevelt, hoping to avoid public alarm, authorised the Federal Security Agency, a civilian organisation, to make preparations "to promote social and economic security, advance educational opportunities and promote public health". It, in turn, established the War Research Service (WRS) under Dr George Merck to study BW. Quickly realising that discovery of the necessary protective measures against BW would require massive facilities, the Army's Chemical Warfare Service (CWS) was given responsibility to perform exhaustive investigations that November. Aware of Japan's gas warfare activities – 900 reported incidents in China before 1941 – the CWS had already, in August 1941, formed a "Special Assignments Branch" to pursue BW research.[10] Roosevelt, in June 1942, unequivocally warned Japan against using CW, stating his "desire to make it unmistakably clear that if Japan persists in this inhuman form of warfare against China or against any of the other United Nations, such action will be regarded by this government as though taken against the United States, and retaliation in kind and in full measure will be meted out."[11]

Cloaked in the deepest wartime secrecy, the CWS acquired, on March 9th, 1943, Detrick Field near Frederick, Maryland, and began building America's own BW establishment. Camp Detrick was initially staffed with eighty-five officers and 373 enlisted men. Three months later building costs had already risen to an estimated $4 million.[12] Rivalled only by the Manhattan atomic bomb project in secrecy, Camp Detrick was still only tiny compared to the thousands of men at Ishii's disposal.

Intelligence gathering about BW was stepped up. Overseas commanders were alerted, and the WRS asked Military Intelligence Services, the Office of Strategic Services* and the FBI to try to uncover enemy intentions and capabilities. Information began to trickle in. The difficult job of piecing the puzzle together was given to Lt-Col Howard Cole, chief of the CWS's intelligence branch.

The MIS in Washington reported in March 1942 yet another Japanese attempt to secure yellow fever virus. A Dr Kiyoshi Hayakawa† had approached the Rockefeller laboratory in Brazil.[14] Fortunately, that source had already been blocked. The month before, the FBI were told by a Los Angeles informant that Japanese saboteurs, armed with five or six cans of a jelly-like substance, reportedly a mixture of typhoid and plague germs, planned to poison the city's water supply, but disaster never struck.[15] Late in December 1943, the Office of Naval Intelligence was told that the Japanese Army maintained a BW laboratory in Kyoto and that a 1st Lt Mutsubu Isayama, previously a medical student, had been assigned to the laboratory, located in a three-storey brick building west of the city's old palace grounds. Remarkable was the fact that the source, a friend of Isayama, had left Japan as early as 1928 – the Americans concluded this to be evidence of a remarkably early start to BW activities in Japan.[16]

But the most revealing harbinger came from China, from the town of Changteh, an important and embattled business centre of 50,000 people, situated on the western shore of Tung Ting Lake on the northern bank of the Yuan River in Hunan Province.

One misty morning at 5 a.m. early in November 1941, a lone enemy plane was seen making three low passes over the town's Chi-ya-hsiang and Kwan-miao Streets and East Gate district. Air raid sirens were sounded, people dashed for cover, but no explosions were heard. Surprisingly, the plane seemed only to drop a mixture of wheat

---

* Forerunner of the CIA.

† Hayakawa had been attached to one of Ishii's Water Purification Units at Nomonhan, and had been in charge of media preparation at Pingfan from 1937 to 1940. He studied brucellosis at the University of Michigan for six months in 1939, and from 1942 until the end of the war worked at the Singapore branch of Unit 731 classifying salmonella organisms, particularly paratyphoid, and certain studies differentiating scrub typhus from tsutsugamushi fever.[13]

and rice grains, pieces of paper, cotton wadding and other un-identified particles. There were many eye-witnesses, including Mrs E. J. Bannon, Superintendent of the local Presbyterian hospital. Twelve hours later, after the all-clear sounded, some of these strange "gifts" were collected, and sent by police to Mrs Bannon's hospital for examination. There, the presence of micro-organisms resembling plague was detected.

Town life carried on normally the following week. Then, suddenly, Tsai Tao-erh, an eleven-year-old girl from Kwan-miao Street, fell ill with a high fever. She died two days later in the missionary hospital. Blood smear tests and a post mortem examination of her internal organs revealed the presence of plague-like organisms.

Five more cases were soon to appear. The sixth, Kung Tsao-sheng, a man of twenty-eight, who had been staying in Kwan-miao Street, died just as a specialist investigation team arrived from Kweiyang. Headed by plague specialist Dr Wen-kwei Chen, director of the Department of Laboratory Medicine at the Central Emergency Medical Service Training School at Tuyunkuan and also a consultant to the Chinese Red Cross Medical Relief Corps, the team started work immediately. They proved that the last death had been caused by bubonic plague. Culture and animal tests backed up the post mortem examination findings.

Chen issued a report on December 12th. He asked the following searching questions: was plague present in Changteh? How did it arise? Could any connection be established between the outbreak and the alleged infective material scattered by the enemy plane? Did plague exist prior to the "aerial incident"? Did plague come to Changteh from contiguous districts known to be plague-stricken?[17]

His summary of findings found enemy BW activity probable:

A) That Changteh has never been as far as is known afflicted by plague. During previous pandemics and severe epidemics else-where in China, this part of Hunan, nay this part of Central China in general, has never been known to come under the scourge of the disease.

B) That the present outbreak may have been due to direct contiguous spread from neighbouring plague-infected districts is also untenable on epidemiological grounds. Epidemiologically, plague spreads along transport routes for grain on which the rats feed. The nearest epidemic centre to Chü Hsien is Chekiang, about 2,000 kilometres away by land or river communication. Further-more, Changteh, being a rice producing district, supplies rice to other districts and does not receive rice from other cities. Besides, all the cases occurring in Changteh were native inhabitants who had not been away from the city or its immediate environs at all.

C) That all the cases came from the areas from within the city where the strange objects dropped by the enemy plane were found, and that among the wheat and rice grains and cotton rags there were most probably included infective vectors, probably fleas. The fleas were not noticed on the spot because they were not looked for and because the air raid alarm lasted some twelve hours with the result that the fleas must have in the meantime escaped to other hiding places.

D) That there was no apparent evidence of any excessive rat mortality before and for some time after the "aerial incident". About 200 rats were caught and examined during the months of November and December, but no evidence of plague was found. However, toward the end of January and the first part of February this year [1942], among seventy-eight rats examined there were eighteen with definite plague infections. As plague is primarily a disease of the rodents, the usual sequence of events is that an epizootic precedes an epidemic; but that did not take place in the present case. The infected fleas from the enemy plane must have first attacked men and a little later the rats.

E) That all the first six human cases were infected within fifteen days after the "aerial incident" and that infected fleas are known to be able to survive under suitable conditions for weeks without feeding. The normal incubation period of bubonic plague is three to seven days and may occasionally be prolonged to eight or even fourteen days. The time factor is certainly also a strong circumstantial evidence.[18]

American intelligence in Chungking moved quickly and by November 27th, the CWS had received a paraphrased report, later relayed by the British Staff Mission in Washington to the War Office in London. By that time, however, MI 10 had already independently relayed the information to the Biological Section at Britain's top secret Chemical Defence Experimental Station at Porton Down, set, as today, in the gently rolling landscape of Salisbury Plain. News about the Changteh incident was passed to the British government by Cambridge biochemist Dr Joseph Needham, then serving as scientific counsellor in His Britannic Majesty's embassy in Chungking.

Britain had become interested in BW several years ahead of America. Late in 1936, Minister for Co-ordination of Defence Sir Thomas Inskip asked the Committee of Imperial Defence to establish

97

a sub-committee on bacteriological warfare. Top academics from the Medical Research Council and London School of Hygiene and Tropical Medicine as well as Army, Navy and Air Force medical chiefs were required "to report on the practicability of the introduction of bacteriological warfare and to make recommendations as to the counter measures which should be taken to deal with such an eventuality". The sub-committee was chaired by Sir Maurice Hankey, Secretary to the Committee of Imperial Defence, Secretary to the Cabinet and Secretary of the Privy Council – the most powerful British civil servant of this, and arguably the most brilliant of any other, century. It met for the first time on November 17th, 1936, and considered various "scrappy" Intelligence reports. With familiar Anglo-Saxon penchant for understatement it was recorded that "there were . . . certain indications that Germany was not neglecting the subject". Japan was not mentioned. Hankey stated that it was "unthinkable" for Britain to contemplate adoption of offensive BW, but argued that certain defensive aspects needed study.[19] By late January the following year, remarkable progress had been made. Discussions about the main points of a report they were soon to submit to the Committee of Imperial Defence showed extraordinary foresight into the problems of BW: the difficulty of distributing the germs without destroying them in the process, and the danger of infecting friendly troops or, indeed, populations.[20]

Nonetheless, it was felt that BW was sufficiently possible and dangerous as to demand careful watching. Becoming a permanent feature of the Cabinet committee system, the sub-committee reported annually and liaised with the Intelligence services. Even before America, Britain not only received but assimilated a piece of evidence that Japan was using BW. Intelligence, questionable as it formed part of "so-called evidence" at recent trials in Moscow, was laid before the Committee of Imperial Defence that the Japanese had instigated Russian collaborators to spread bacteria on troop trains.[21] The sub-committee's first annual report concluded "that the likelihood of an attempt by an enemy to introduce bacteria into this country directed against human life, animals or crops, is, for the time being, small, but that information is at present so scanty as to demand a frequent review of the situation and a close watch being kept upon activities in foreign countries".[22]

It was not until December 1939, that Porton's CW experts were informed or involved.[23] In 1940, Hankey, by then a peer and Minister without Portfolio in the War Cabinet and in charge of unorthodox counter-invasion and scientific warfare, decided that early BW appraisals had not been based on sound experimental work. It was, incidentally, about this time that Hankey sparked the first estimate concerning the practicality of producing an atomic bomb. Hankey felt that evaluation of BW by, albeit gifted, "amateurs" was insufficient.[24] As a result a handful of biologists, mainly bacteriologists, under Dr (later Sir Paul) Fildes were housed in the new experimental animal laboratories of Porton's Medical Division. Fieldwork was supervised by a small committee presided over by Air Vice-Marshal Peck. More generally the work came under the Ministry of Supply's auspices, with policy direction laid down by a joint committee under the Chiefs of Staff.[25]

Throughout the war years this small but brilliant team carried out pioneering research, providing most of the original ideas and research later taken up and put into production by the larger American (and Canadian) BW teams. In January 1942, while Fildes was considering the Changteh intelligence, Winston Churchill's War Cabinet Defence Committee agreed with a recommendation from Hankey that measures should be taken to enable Britain to retaliate in kind if the enemy resorted to BW. The measure mentioned was to manufacture, largely in America, two million cakes infected with anthrax, to be dropped from aircraft if retaliation proved necessary.[26] There is even evidence at Britain's Public Record Office that Churchill, at one point, considered first use of BW.[27]

A. Landsborough Thomson at the Medical Research Council commented on the Changteh incident:

> It is an unlikely story. The circumstantial evidence seems weak, and plague bacilli in rice or other material would almost certainly be harmless – only the dissemination of infected fleas or rats would lead to cases of the disease, and even then only under very favourable conditions.[28]

Fildes, at least initially, was not so dismissive. He reported to the War Cabinet Office:

> I have had reports that work is being carried out in Germany under Japanese tuition on the production of plague rats for use in England, and that the Institut Pasteur at Garches has been turned over entirely to the preparation of anti-plague serum. I have also had reports about Changteh. It seems to me that they should not be dismissed too lightly. I see no reason to suppose that plague could not be started by dropping infected food for the local rats. In any case, it is essential to follow the matter up and obtain a definite statement as to whether the continuing investigations have

revealed the plague bacilli. If they have, the conclusion is certain that an attempt has been made, even though a futile one. Will you please inform me whether you are in a position to obtain this definite information, and if so will you please do so.[29]

On March 21st, a copy of Dr Chen's report was forwarded from the All India Institute of Hygiene and Public Health in Calcutta. Fildes added:

From a survey of this evidence there is no reason to doubt that something was dropped from the aircraft and that cases of plague occurred, but since no plague bacilli were found on the materials alleged, but not proved, to have been dropped, nor in local rats, and since no fleas were found, there is clearly no proved connection between the aircraft and cases of plague. Furthermore, the evidence does not seem convincing that natural plague in the neighbourhood could be excluded. Thus, while admitting the possibility of the account and its value for propaganda . . . an impartial reader can hardly admit that it constitutes a case on which action can be based.[30]

Fildes later altered his conclusion as doubt hardened still further:

From a survey of this evidence there is every reason to doubt whether anything was seen to drop from the aircraft. Certainly no plague bacilli were found in materials alleged to have been dropped. There is thus no proved, or even reasonably suspected, connection between the aircraft and the cases of plague, nor is the evidence convincing that the district was normally free from plague. For these reasons, this incident cannot be accepted as a proved instance of BW.[31]

Given the quality of her BW team, Porton's dismissive response to the Changteh allegations was surprising. Perhaps seeing themselves and Britain as the vanguard of world bacteriology, they found it difficult to conceive that Japan, so new to the modern industrial world, could have had such foresight and skills.

By the time Chinese Nationalist leader Gen Chiang Kai-shek formally approached the British government on the issue in July, via his Ambassador in London, Dr Wellington Koo, Porton experts had more or less dismissed the issue and closed the file. Cabinet memoranda described as "tiresome", Koo's repeated requests to have allegations of Japanese BW and CW brought before the Pacific War Council. Grudgingly, Foreign Minister Anthony Eden conceded in the end that it would be impossible to prevent the issue being placed on the agenda. Winston Churchill saw the relevant papers and agreed to the circulation of documents for the next meeting.[32]

Although the Chinese persisted in producing reports of BW incidents, their cries, for the time being anyway, increasingly fell on deaf ears. In India, British experts scribbled on the reports comments such as "please return when you have finished smiling at the attached", and "glance at this muck".

Such arrogance was misplaced. Koo's report was startlingly accurate. Four incidents, other than Changteh, were described:

On at least five occasions during the first two years the Japanese armed forces have tried to employ bacteriological warfare in China. They have tried to produce epidemics of plague in Free China by scattering plague-infected materials with aeroplanes. The facts thus far collected by Chinese and foreign medical experts are as follows:

1 On October 4th, 1940 a Japanese plane visited Chü Hsien in Chekiang. After circling over the city for a short while it scattered rice and wheat grains mixed with fleas over the western section of the city. There were many eye-witnesses, among whom was one named Hau, who collected some grains and dead fleas from the street outside his house and sent them to the local Air-raid Precautionary Corps for transmission to the Provincial Hygienic Laboratory for examination. Although the laboratory examination result was that "there were no pathogenic organisms found by bacteriological culture methods". Yet on November 18th, thirty-eight days after the Japanese plane's visit, bubonic plague appeared in the same area where the grains and fleas were found in abundance. The epidemic in Chü Hsien lasted twenty-four days, resulting in twenty-one deaths. As far as available records show, plague never occurred in Chü Hsien before.

2 On October 29th, 1940 bubonic plague for the first time occurred in Ningpo in Chekiang Province. The epidemic lasted a period of thirty-four days and claimed a total of ninety-nine victims. It was reported that on October 27th, 1940 Japanese planes raided Ningpo and scattered a considerable quantity of wheat grains over the port city. No one at the time seemed to know the enemy's intention and no thorough examination of the grains was made. All the plague victims were local residents. The diagnosis of plague was definitely confirmed by laboratory test. There

was no excessive mortality among rats noticed before the epidemic outbreak and despite careful investigation no exogenous sources of infection could be discovered.

3 On November 28th, 1940 when the plague epidemic in Ningpo and Chü Hsien was still in progress, three Japanese planes came to Kinhwa, an important commercial centre situated between Ningpo and Chü Hsien, and there they dropped a large quantity of small granules, about the size of shrimp eggs. These strange objects were collected and examined in a local hospital. The granules were more or less round, about 1 mm in diameter, of whitish-yellow tinge, somewhat translucent with a certain amount of glistening reflection from the surface. When brought into contact with a drop of water on a glass slide, the granule began to swell to about twice its original size. In a small amount of water in a test-tube, with some agitation it would break up into whitish flakes and later form a milky suspension. Microscopic examination of these granules revealed the presence of numerous gram-negative bacilli, with distinct bi-polar staining in some of them and an abundance of involution forms, thus possessing the morphological characteristics of *P. pestis*, the causative organism of plague. However no plague occurred in Kinghwa and it indicated that this particular Japanese experiment in bacteriological warfare ended in failure . . .

5 A serious epidemic of plague occurring in Suiyuan, Ninghsia, and Shensi Provinces has been recently reported. From the last week of January this year to date there have been some 600 cases. According to a recent communiqué from the local military in the north-western frontier, "a large number of sick rodents had been set free by the enemy in the epidemic area." However, considering the fact that plague is known to be enzootic among the native rodents in the Ord region in Suiyuan, one must wait for confirmation of this report. Technical experts, including Dr Y. N. Yung, Director of the Weishengahu North-west Epidemic Prevention Bureau, have been sent there to investigate and help to control the epidemic.

The enumeration of facts thus far collected leads to the conclusion that the Japanese army has attempted bacteriological warfare in China. In Chekiang and Hunan they scattered from the air infective materials and succeeded in causing epidemic outbreaks of plague. Aside from temporary terrorization of the general population in the afflicted areas, this inhuman act of our enemy is most condemnable when one realizes that once the disease has taken root in the local rat population it will continue to infect men for many years to come.[33]

It was as late as early 1944 before Allied Intelligence agencies were put on full alert to the Japanese BW threat. In America, CWS Intelligence chief Howard Cole began passing a regular digest of information to Porton. Porton reciprocated. That January, America's Intelligence chiefs began briefing field officers on how to spot signs of BW. They were asked to look for:

a) Any mention of "biological", "bacteriological", "germ", "microbe", "microbiological", "microorganism", "living agent", "virus" warfare.

b) Any mention of the use of toxins, venoms, or biological poisons in weapons.

c) Troops trained for these types of warfare.

d) Means of protection or immunisation against infectious diseases, toxins, venoms, viruses or other biological agents.

e) Special gas masks or filters for masks, hoods, or other protective devices.

f) New munitions developed for dissemination of special agents . . .

g) Research institutes devoted to special studies of secret nature.

h) Islands or isolated places where experiments involving animals are performed.

i) Farms or research institutes where large numbers of rats, mice, rabbits, sheep, goats or eggs are used.

j) Breweries, sugar refineries, distilleries, or other plants which are heavily guarded and which employ large numbers of scientists, particularly bacteriologists or chemists.

k) Any type of bomb or munition which contains a powder or liquid of unknown composition.

l) Report of the appearance of infectious disease in locality where such disease is not prevalent.

m) Report of abnormal numbers of rats, or death of large numbers of rats, in any locality.

n) Development of unorthodox weapons such as darts.[34]

For security reasons only senior military staff, the CWS and medical and Intelligence services were put in the picture. The War Department in Washington on February 14th issued an urgent warning to all commanding generals:

. . . Neither Germany or Japan will be influenced by humanitarian motives in making their decisions to employ biological warfare.

From information now available, it appears that two principal types of biological warfare are to be guarded against. One of these is what might be called a mass tactical or external attack, such as the Japanese used in China. The other is sabotage, or attack from within, such as the attempts of the Germans in World War I to spread glanders and anthrax among the horses in France and Rumania. Intelligence officers and others concerned must be alerted for indications of either type of attack.[35]

Washington ordered prompt dispatch of all information and exhibits to G-2.

Cole, in his first report to Fildes at Porton, claimed Japan's BW capability was large, that she had been interested in the subject for several years and that many of her bacteriologists were highly trained. "She will not hesitate from humane motives to use this weapon and can do so on the many islands of the Pacific with little risk to her own troops," he added.[36]

A breakthrough for the Allies came in May. Captured notebooks belonging to an enlisted flying trainee and an engineer contained references to a "bacillus bomb". Described as "military most secret" for "special circumstances", the experimental 1 kg weapon was colour-coded with green-purple, grey-purple markings and called the Special Bomb Mark 7. Its designated targets were reservoirs, animals and personnel.*[37]

G-2 gave the information high credibility. Commanders in the Pacific and China, Burma, India theatres were alerted to the munition's existence, and asked to search thoroughly captured enemy airfields and ammunition dumps for any evidence of it.[38]

Confirmation of the weapon's existence followed earlier and worrying intelligence about a vast shipment of bacteria bombs. In March 1944, the *Nanking Evening News* had reported that Japanese Imperial Headquarters had since just before the beginning of the year sent around 30,000 bombs containing typhus, diphtheria and bubonic plague germs to China. Further information suggested that the bombs had been made at the Osaka Chemical Research Institute, then shipped to Shanghai where, at the city's Tungyen Club, Central China Branch, germs were cultivated. Later, the weapons had been sent to Hangchow bound for war zones in Yunnan, Kweichow, Szechwan, Kwangsi and Hunan provinces. The Chinese special agent originating the report said the bombs, containing powders and

* The Mark 7 Bomb was an experimental weapon created by the Japanese Navy, not Ishii's Unit.

solutions, were to be dropped over urban industrial areas. Trials, he said, were to be made "in accordance with the suitable breeding quality of the germs".[39]

ATIS, the Allied Translator and Interpreter Section, reported on June 16th the publication in the January edition of *Fuji Magazine* an article entitled "The Fighting Scientist", which stated that a young Japanese scientist, Seiji Arakawa, working under Dr Yaoi at the Tokyo University Institute of Infectious Diseases (*Densenbyō Kenkyū-jō*) had succeeded in making a serum for the treatment and prevention of dengue fever. The discovery, the magazine added, could become "a weapon with which to threaten the enemy".[40]

Another unconfirmed report received by the US Army's 14th Air Force Intelligence suggested that the Japanese in Canton and Kwang-chauwwan areas were training women and children to spread germs in unoccupied China. And from the local press in Kweilin, China, it was learned that the county's once best-equipped hospital, the Peking Union Medical College, had been transformed into a "virus culti-vation centre". Cole added:

The enemy have also assembled a large crowd of beggars and street sleepers in the hospital for the purpose of lice breeding. They also distribute cloth bags to all households, requiring each to deliver to them twenty flies [fleas?] and one live rat (or mouse) per day. Failure to do so is met with severe punishment. It is said that the Japanese are cultivating large quantities of virus for spreading bubonic plague, pneumonia, relapsing fever, cholera and other epidemics among Chinese or Allied troops.[41]

Cole noted the similarity of this request for "one live rat (or mouse)" to an earlier Japanese document captured in Burma, and asked to learn the source and authenticity of the newspaper's source.

Cole's fourth "Special Projects Periodic Intelligence Report", July 1st to August 15th, 1944, however, claimed there was no sinister motive behind Japanese rat-catching activities.

"This information was first looked upon with suspicion as an attempt by the Japanese to use rats in the spreading of BW . . . most recent reports . . . confirm that the Japanese are attempting rat control for the purpose of avoiding a plague epidemic in territory under their control," he wrote.

A vital clue had been mislaid.[42]

ATIS translated various captured documents linking BW with Manchuria, even though these all concerned possible Russian bacterial sabotage there: there were allegations of intention to spread typhus, plague and anthrax.[43]

Elsewhere in Cole's fourth report a captured Japanese civilian bacteriologist named Ishii as the leading figure behind bacterial bomb experiments. G-2 checked the PoW's information and found Ishii's name on several previous reports, notably an ATIS bulletin, dated November 14th, 1943, which stated that on "November 14th, 1941 – Technical Meritorious Medal (A), citation, medal and highest degree of supplementary decoration were conferred upon Medical Maj-Gen Ishii by Ministry of War, Medical Bureau, Sanitation Branch Commander." Although the PoW considered the medal had been awarded for Ishii's water filter work, intelligence chiefs concluded it might have been given for BW bomb development.[44]

Intelligence about these Japanese BW bombs was, however, again thrown into doubt in Cole's fifth digest of intelligence (August 15th to October 16th, 1944). A military attaché report from New Delhi claimed an earlier report on the dispatch of 30,000 bacteria bombs from Japan to China was largely fictional.[45] Nevertheless, other tell-tale details kept emerging.

Glass bottles mentioned in connection with BW tallied with another report of a glass bacillus bomb.

Feathers unloaded from the air over Futsing, China. G-2 took technical advice, and were told that the infectious psittacosis virus could be spread in this fashion.[46]

A water filter technical manual found referred to precautions against BW, as well as poisoning by mercuric chloride, hydrocyanic acid and arsenic. G-2 commented: ". . . previous captured documents refer to poisoning wells, water supplies and food by Chinese and Russians. These facts indicate one of two things (a) either the Japanese are contemplating poisoning water supplies, beverages and food, or (b) that they suspect us of planning to do so. Their accusation . . . may be for the purpose of building up a cause to justify their own use of such agents."[47]

The frequent discovery of highly complex, technical, and expensive medical and water purification equipment in all war zones, including a complete "anti-disease" suit found near a battlefront.

A captured commando manual containing details about "Raiding Diversionary Units", which stated that "great results" could be gained by contaminating enemy food and drink by "bacterial strategy". Porton consulted their Japanese language experts, Archdeacon Moule and his brother Mr Moule. The Moule brothers confirmed G-2's translation of key words in the document –

"bacteria – if necessary". It was possible, said the Moules, that the spoken meanings of the Japanese characters which appeared to read *saikin*, could have been "a small defect", "reappointment", or "latest or nearest"; but agreed that the two characters: *sai*, which meant "minute", and *kin*, which meant "mould" or "fungus", were more likely to represent the word "bacteria".[48] It was decided, as a result, that strict precautions must be taken in moving into areas voluntarily occupied by the enemy.

Cole's next report, to December 15th, 1944, highlighted:

Rumours of a BW unit based in Manchuria. A PoW gave information about experiments by a water purification unit at Hsinking in which a bacterial gas or fog was sprayed from the air. The agents, glanders and another organism, were then collected in gelatin trays laid out over the test site, it was stated. Cole commented that mention of a water purification unit tied the work in with "the activities of Maj-Gen Shirō Ishii".[49]

An article in the *Tokyo Mainichi*, dated August 1943, referring to civilian defences against a BW attack aimed at contaminating Tokyo's water supply.

A captured document entitled "How to defeat an enemy possessing superior equipment" which revealed a full range of tactics and dirty tricks including the use of plague-infected rats, malaria-infected mosquitoes, and the dropping of attractive and infected objects and garments over enemy areas.

A near exact blueprint of Unit 731's *Tama* Unit at Nanking, drawn and compiled by captured X-ray specialist Lt-Cpl Isamu Chinba. Chinba also revealed the presence of similar Ishii units at Peking and Kiukiang. G-2 considered Chinba's information reliable, and described him as "very intelligent and sincere".[50]

After a year of intensive effort, a picture had begun to emerge by the end of 1944. It was cause for concern. In response, G-2 decided to interrogate and re-interrogate all Japanese PoWs with experience in the medical service, particularly those who had been in water purification units. Additionally, all advance intelligence centres in the south-west Pacific area were ordered by Washington to take blood samples from captured Japanese in an endeavour to uncover the diseases they had been inoculated against. From samples returned by air to Washington it was found that a certain portion of troops had been immunised against anthrax.[51]

By early 1945 it had become clear to the Allies that the idea of bacterial warfare was firmly established in the minds of the Japanese military. In reports and at conferences, Cole warned that the only deterrent was perhaps the possibility of Allied retaliation. But, he added, taking into account Japanese psychology, the willingness to commit hara-kiri and suicide missions with bombs strapped to the body, this threat might not carry a high rating.[52]

Then on May 24th, the Japanese broadcast from Singapore in English a chilling message:

At the present moment there are Anglo-American forces in India and Burma. They are learning what it is to fall victim to tropical diseases.

As the *Daily Herald* pointed out some time ago, the British 14th Army is a dead army . . . disease and the Japanese forces were responsible for bringing this about.

There is much talk of GIs in Europe being transferred for active service in the East, a tropical death trap. How can they come armed with the medicine to fight against these virulent tropical diseases, and malaria especially, when that most essential drug culture of quinine, is something they do not possess? Natural quinine is absolutely indispensable for the manufacture of anti-malarial medicine, and the Japanese forces in the southern regions have a monopoly on that so very important commodity . . .

The European war was tough and bloody, but there were no such terrors like cholera and malaria to make it unbearable. The war in the East is tough and bloody, but the thing that makes it hell for Americans fighting in that theatre is the presence of diseases. Virulent scourges, waiting to strike them down when they least expect it, deadly as the lashing attack of Japanese fighting men, will be waiting for the showdown. Americans at home, perhaps, envy the lot of doughboys and marines. They're lucky, you think, to get a free trip to this glamorous East. But, no, it is you people at home who are the lucky ones. Your chance of living to a good old age is so much better than theirs. Their life in the East is scheduled to be short and it certainly won't be a merry one.

Goodbye, Americans.[53]

In the closing months of the war, Washington's Military Intelligence Service summarised information to date:

Bacteriological Experimental Center (Saikin Kenkyū shō), Harbin: Four Ps/W verified the existence of this agency, which is Army-controlled, but could not locate it on a map. Experiments are being carried on by Army biologists. There were no civilian officials connected with this center, which is commanded by Maj-Gen Ishii,

Shirō. Nature of the types of experiments being carried on here is extremely secret and their findings were never published for general assimilation.

Bōekikyūsui Bu (Hygiene and Water Purification Dept.), Harbin, 1943: This is one of the main Hygiene and Water Purification Departments of the Kwantung Army and maintains close liaison with the Bacteriological Experimental Center. Ps/W could not give details except that the work of the departments is to collect and evaluate results of all biological experiments carried on by its subordinate units in the field. One P/W thought that this unit and the Bacteriological Experiment Center were one and the same.

Bōekikyūsui Bu, Hsinking, 1943: All experimental results are co-ordinated in Hygiene and Water Purification Department at Hsinking under Maj-Gen Ishii, Shirō. No details.

General: These field units of the various Hygiene and Water Purification Departments check all epidemic and endemic types of diseases at places where they occur. Data on incidence, mortality, treatment, and prophylactic measures are collected with the co-operation of medical officers in these infected areas. Reports are cleared, only through the units immediately concerned, to the Main Hygiene and Water Purification Department, Kwantung Army HQ, Hsinking.

Distributions: The 48 Ind Inf Brigade on Guam did not have this type of unit attached, but the 29 Div did. These units are not attached below divisions. A portion of a divisional detachment is attached to a subordinate unit when necessary.

Gijutsu Shō (I.N. [interpreter's note] – Technical Center(?)), Tokyo: Believed that this center is, also, engaged in biological experiments under Army supervision. Exact location unknown. In 1941 or 1942, Maj-Gen Ishii, Shirō, received a medal for the development of a water purification machine. This was announced in the newspapers.

Personalities:

Lt-Gen Kanbayashi	– CG, Japanese Army Medical Corps, 1943.
Lt-Gen Karizuka [Kajitsuka]	– CG, Japanese Army Medical Corps, Kwantung Army, 1943.
Maj-Gen Ishii, Shirō	– CG, Bacteriological Experimental Center and Hygiene and Water Purification Dept, Kwantung Army, 1943. The date is not known but he was the organizer of the Hygiene and Water Purification Departments.[54]

Manchuria, so remote from the West, was a difficult place to gain intelligence. In south-west Pacific areas, such as New Guinea and the Dutch East Indian Empire, and throughout the Malay peninsula to Burma, the Allies continually suspected more than first met the eye. It was wise to be so suspicious. With the loss of Rabaul, which many Japanese considered the turning point in the war, the pressure to use and the benefits gained for Japan from BW could have been great, especially since many troops had already been vaccinated against suitable agents. Islands in the tropics presented many ideal conditions for BW.

Although there was still some scepticism, the Allied armies had now been alerted. As they cleared the newly liberated areas in the west Pacific – New Guinea, the Dutch East Indian Empire, the Malay peninsula – they were constantly on the alert for clues and reported what they found.

For instance, the unpublished (British) war diary of Maj-Gen W. E. Tyndall of the Medical Directorate of Allied Land Forces SE Asia records surprise at the impressive and valuable research discovered at the Japanese Southern Army's No 1 Central Pathological Research Laboratory at Singapore. Huge quantities of medical equipment were found. "I saw about 300 hand centrifuges on one table!" Tyndall recorded, indicating the possibility that hundreds of technicians may have been at work. (A British toxicologist told of these figures observed that a well-equipped university pathology laboratory in a British university today would only have six or eight such centrifuges.) Tyndall added:

The Japanese took over this research laboratory and maintained a very high standard of valuable research work. It was in [the] charge of a Jap who was very "international" in his scientific outlook. [Almost certainly Kiyoshi Hayakawa, who had studied at the University of Michigan, and who was then classifying salmonella organisms, particularly paratyphoid, and studying scrub typhus at Singapore.]

When in Singapore, I talked over the future of this laboratory with many civilians and in particular with Dr Greene (an internee), who had in pre-war days been intimately associated with the work of the laboratory. Greene was taking over the laboratory from the Japanese and impressed upon me the urgency of ensuring that there was no interruption in the research work which the Japanese had been conducting.[55]

110

In view of the importance of the Japanese work to civilians and troops, Tyndall ordered British Army serologist Colonel Stuart-Harris, then engaged in an important scrub typhus vaccine programme, to drop everything and take charge of the Singapore laboratory.

Dr Leonard Short, an American family physician from New England, volunteered for military service and was posted in 1942 to the China, Burma, India theatre as a hospital doctor. After eighteen months, Short was transferred to the Joint Intelligence Collective Agency and attached to the British 14th Army during its reconquest of Burma. His job was to gather and exchange the latest information on the enemy's medical and technical advances. What he discovered shocked him and came to obsess him in later life. His report is presumably in the British archives, which are not publicly available, but in a letter written decades later, Dr Short recorded the events:

In early 1944 the American Chemical Warfare division called a hasty and highly secret meeting of all intelligence agencies to alert them to the fact that the Japanese were distributing "Christmas ball" [These may have been Unit 731's *Ga* glass ball bacteria bombs] containers, by air, in a regular pattern on the border of Burma–China. They suspected Bacterial Warfare.

Detailed recovery was difficult but it was determined that they were using bacteriological agents.

British authorities thought the Pasteur Institute in Rangoon, now held by the Japanese, might be the Burma centre for such activity since high secrecy levels had been exercised there.

As an Army doctor I was designated as the one to follow up on the minimal and scattered intelligence available. All activities were of course secret.

In time I was able to definitely identify activities as truly bacteriological and the Pasteur Laboratory was indeed the Burma centre for such efforts although the ramifications seemed to extend beyond Burma proper.

Names I was able to obtain from the dark walls of the cells in the basement of the Custom House in Rangoon suggest direct exploitation of live human prisoners in grisly medical experiments. However, due to secrecy and the time element, it was impossible for me to follow through with active investigation.

The many facts were buried and intelligence agents were not allowed to talk.[56]

In an unpublished autobiography, Short added that he and his colleagues had confirmed the Japanese were waging BW and that the epidemic swells they had observed and been subjected to "were most often brought on by direct implantation of a special bacterium, by the enemy, of the offending disease, by germ bombs or native saboteurs who had been enlisted to infect food or water supplies servicing the troops or supporters." During the rollback of Japanese forces, Short was present at the interrogations of Japanese medical PoWs and followed up, camp by camp, on their leads.

Now the facts concerning the use of term warfare have surfaced, [he was able to conclude], my own results of investigation have become supported and verified. We now know that disease was intentionally used throughout Burma, by the Japanese, against British and Allied forces and that the revered name of Louis Pasteur was blemished by germs from the laboratory in Rangoon bearing his name.

In his later life, Dr Short spent much time using the Freedom of Information Act attempting to rediscover those secret reports he had once written. It was to no avail. He died without uncovering them.

Chapter 9

MacArthur: Freedom, Tolerance and Justice . . .

The slate-grey decks of the USS *Missouri*, the most powerful warship in the Allied fleet, were crowded with servicemen and diplomats. The day was overcast and the occasion momentous.

The date: September 2nd, 1945. The place: Tokyo Bay. The event: the unconditional surrender of the Japanese armed forces at the end of six years of world war. For Japan the Foreign Minister, Mamoru Shigemitsu, limped up the gangway and on to the quarterdeck. He was accompanied by the Chief of the Imperial General Staff, General Yoshijirō Umezu, who, as Commander of the Kwantung Army, had helped make the work of Unit 731 possible. For the Allies, the Supreme Commander Allied Powers, General Douglas MacArthur, stood prepared to receive their surrender. The men went in turn to the old mess table set out for the purpose – Shigemitsu experienced difficulty because of his artificial leg. He was also uncertain where to place his signature. MacArthur snapped: "Show him where to sign . . ."[1]

For MacArthur it was a particularly poignant moment.

Defeated in the Philippines in 1942, he had sworn: "I will return." Now his triumph was complete. But the words he spoke were considered rather than triumphant. He said:

We are gathered here, representatives of the major warring powers, to conclude a solemn agreement whereby peace may be restored. The issues, involving divergent ideals and ideologies, hence are not for our discussion or debate. Nor is it for us here to meet, representing as we do a majority of the people of the earth, in a spirit of distrust, malice or hatred. But rather it is for us, both victors and vanquished, to rise to that higher dignity which alone benefits the sacred purposes we are about to serve, committing all our people unreservedly to faithful compliance with the understanding they are here formally to assume.

It is my earnest hope, and indeed the hope of all mankind, that from this solemn occasion a better world shall emerge out of the blood and carnage of the past – a world dedicated to the dignity of man and the fulfilment of his most cherished wish for freedom, tolerance and justice.

MacArthur would devote the next six years of his life to this objective. They would be years during which his admiration for the people of Japan, allied to his obsession that the nation should survive as a democracy when he believed it could so easily become a Communist satellite of Soviet Russia, would put a severe strain on the search for justice about which he now spoke with such fervour.

Douglas MacArthur was intended from his birth for the Army, his father being a hero of the Civil War. He headed the examination lists at West Point and received rapid promotion. In the First World War, he led with extravagant personal courage and won the American Silver Star and the Croix de Guerre. With further promotion he became Superintendent of West Point, saw service in the Philippines, returned to Washington as Chief of Staff. Here, however, he treated the unemployed veterans camped on the Anacostia Flats with such ruthlessness, using tear-gas to clear the demonstrators, that his next move was out of the Army mainstream: he became military adviser to the President of the Philippines.

In July 1941, General Douglas MacArthur was recalled to active service by the US Army. He was appointed Commanding General US Army Forces in the Far East. But, in many senses, for the Philippines it was already "too late". Even though there were plans for an umbrella of B17 bombers to protect the islands and the sea lanes, the defences in the islands themselves were run down despite attempts to reinforce them throughout the autumn. Strategically, the initiative lay with the Axis powers – Germany in Europe, Japan in the Far East. On December 7th, 1941, Japan attacked Pearl Harbor and tore the heart out of the US Pacific fleet. Hours later, they caught the bulk of the US Army Air Force in the Philippines on the ground at Clark Field, Manila.

MacArthur's appointment thrust him immediately into the front line. The Philippines were vulnerable, an obvious first target for Japanese land forces. And so it proved. He commanded both United States and Filipino troops, but he could not repel the invasion by the Japanese 14th Army under Lt-Gen Masaharu Honma on December 22nd. He evacuated to Bataan. On January 19th, 1942, Honma invited MacArthur to surrender. He refused. Washington instructed him to flee with his wife Jean and their son Arthur, now four years old. He refused. The MacArthurs would, he said, remain on the island fortress of Corregidor at the entrance to Manila Bay, there to "share the fate of the garrison".[2]

He anticipated that Washington would send help. He expected his stand to embarrass the government into supporting him. Help never came. By February 22nd, the military situation was hopeless. MacArthur with apparent reluctance accepted he would have to evacuate to Australia to carry on his command from there. He and his personal entourage left the Philippines on March 12th, boarding torpedo boats for Mindanao en route to Australia. It was to be a month before his troops surrendered on the redoubt he had prepared on Bataan; two months before the fall of Corregidor.

MacArthur left behind 88,000 troops, American and Filipino who were to be captured by the Japanese. His decision to go – no less than his orders to his subordinates to "fight to the death" in his absence – left him open to criticism still bitterly felt by those who survived the harsh years of captivity.

Publicly, he explained the situation at the time to thousands of cheering Australians who, in defeat, greeted him in Melbourne in a manner more befitting a hero:

> The President of the United States ordered me to break through the Japanese lines and proceed from Corregidor to Australia for the purpose, as I understand it, of organising the American offensive against Japan, a primary object of which is the relief of the Philippines.
>   I came through and I shall return.

Much of MacArthur's drive over the next two years sprang from his efforts to expunge the bitter memories of the Philippines from his consciousness. Defeat was bad enough. To have left his men was, for him – as it was for them – intolerable.

Gradually, adopting an island-hopping policy, the Allied forces began to roll the Japanese forces back from the threshold of Australia. Tulagi . . . Guadalcanal . . . New Guinea . . . and, in October 1944, MacArthur strode through the surf and on to Leyte, making a speech to the Filipino people that he *had* returned.

By now, he was a hero. His senior officers helped to promote the image of the invincible, soft-capped, pipe-smoking leader of men, who grimly but stylishly dominated the centre of the Pacific theatre of war. The people of the Philippines, accustomed to colonial idolatry, adored him. His stock among the folks back home in the United States could hardly have been higher. It came as no surprise when on the day the Japanese forces surrendered unconditionally, President Truman appointed MacArthur Supreme Commander for the Allied Powers in the Pacific. Mountbatten held a similarly titled command in South-East Asia. But, whatever the title, from that moment MacArthur became effectively the ruler of Japan.[3]

He spelled out as much to the opening session of the Allied Council for Japan in April 1946.[4] He told the delegates – with an eye on the Soviet representative: "As the functions of the Council will be advisory and consultative, it will not divide the heavy administrative responsibility of the Supreme Commander as the sole executive authority for the Allied Powers in Japan . . ."

His seven-point plan for the nation was to disarm all Japanese troops, demobilise them and send them home, divert the heavy industry that had survived the bombing into a more constructive, peacetime role, open all schools (with the provisions there would be no military instruction and that civics and the workings of democracy would be added to the curriculum), give the vote to women, hold free elections and permit the labour force to organise and bargain for its rights.

He supported a policy conceived in the White House and endorsed in Whitehall, that he would resist all efforts to prosecute the Emperor as a war criminal. He would implement the new measures through Hirohito and the machinery of the Imperial government. The agreement reached between Britain, the Soviet Union and the United States at Potsdam in July 1945 had called upon Japan to renounce war. It had now done so, although there were many who believed the promise to be hollow. MacArthur was not among them. He said:

Japan thereby proclaims her faith in a society of nations governed by just, tolerant and effective rules of universal social and political morality and entrusts its national integrity thereto. The cynic may view such action as demonstrating but a childlike faith in a visionary ideal, but the realist will see in it far deeper significance . . .

There can be no doubt that both the progress and survival of civilisation is . . . dependent upon the development of a world order which will permit a nation such as Japan safely to entrust its national integrity to just such a higher law to which all peoples on earth shall have rendered themselves subservient. Therein lies the road to lasting peace.[5]

By September 1946, when he had been Supreme Commander for just a year, MacArthur was reporting optimistically on the growth of democracy as a bulwark against what he saw as a Communist threat. He warned of the influence of "the extreme radical left" and added:

If we would . . . guide the Japanese people the more firmly to reshape their lives and institutions in conformity with those social precepts and political standards best calculated to raise the well-being of the individual and to foster and preserve a peaceful society, we must adhere unerringly to the course now charted – destroying here what yet should be destroyed, preserving here what should be preserved and erecting here what should be erected. This will require all of the patience, all of the determination, and all of the statesmanship of democratic peoples. The goal is great – for the strategic position of these Japanese Islands renders them either a powerful bulwark for peace or a dangerous springboard for war.[6]

The Japanese responded to MacArthur's words and complied eagerly with his wishes. He praised them for their dignity in defeat. In fact, to this race steeped in the traditions of war, "surrender" was a new experience. Japanese society was, and is, rooted in an everlasting desire for harmony and consensus. That consensus had to take some account of power, both temporal and spiritual. In "surrender", the Japanese reasoned, one apparently obeyed the conqueror's commands. Besides, the Emperor had instructed them to do so.[7] Some of the demands of the Occupying Powers were obtuse or demeaning. Nonetheless, the majority of the Japanese accepted the orders – because, it appeared, that was the way defeated nations behaved.

MacArthur's aims and methods in Japan were supported totally by his Western Allies. The British attitude, reflected in a top secret briefing by the Foreign Office, prepared for Viscount Montgomery when, as chief of the Imperial General Staff, he visited the Far East in 1947, took the pragmatic stance: that an independent Japan had to be encouraged if only "to pay her way". She should take part again in international trade – a concession announced on August 15th, 1947 – because "Japan alone is in a position to supply many of the consumer goods which are urgently needed in British territories in South-East Asia . . ."

The briefing also pointed out that the relatively small British and Commonwealth force in the Occupying Army was "manifestly subordinate to the US forces". Further it emphasised to Montgomery, himself a positive, fiery figure, the authority that MacArthur held in Japan. "Responsibility for the implementation of policy in Japan," Montgomery was told, "rests upon the Supreme Commander for the Allied Powers who is the sole executive authority. General MacArthur receives his directives from the United States government . . ."

To the Japanese man in the street, as he gradually became accustomed to the rhythm of the new way of life, the overall character of the Occupation seemed beneficial. Kazuo Kawai, then a newspaper editor in Tokyo, summed it up by saying that "the Japanese couldn't help but be impressed by it."[8] More than that, MacArthur so dominated those post-war months that "the Japanese saw the Occupation personified in his image . . ." Kawai wrote.

One reason for his influence on the Japanese was his dedicated sense of mission. The egoism fringed with mysticism, with which he regarded himself as the chosen instrument for the reformation and redemption of the Japanese people might sometimes be ludicrous and sometimes irritating. But there was no mistaking the sincerity and intensity of his idealism . . . he lifted the tone of the Occupation from a military operation, to a moral crusade.

MacArthur, as he promulgated democracy, ran a personalised dictatorship. Dr John Pritchard, who contributed the Introduction to this book, states:

There is a *leitmotif* that runs through MacArthur's career, from his youth until his final exit from the stage of history. It can be summed up as the sanctimonious usurpation of power, an arrogation of responsibilities by a man who brooked no interference from his superiors unless it suited him, and who tolerated no dissent from his subordinates. He probably half-believed the purple prose of his public declarations: he certainly had faith in its effect. He made a habit of surrounding himself with a suite of sycophants, some of whom were men of ability, but his personal vanity was limitless and tiresome to men of independent spirit. For all of these reasons, he was probably the ideal person to select as Supreme Commander for the Allied Powers in Japan.[9]

Confidently, then, MacArthur pursued his vision of trying to impose democracy on Japan. He did so with style. He took up residence in the American Embassy in Tokyo, with his office in the Dai Ichi Insurance building, close to the Imperial Palace. He was aloof though informal, seldom seen. His daily routine rarely changed. He left the Embassy between nine and ten in the morning, he would work in the Dai Ichi till 1.30 or 2 p.m. and then go home to lunch. Sometimes he would entertain at lunch; normally it was simply a family affair. Afterwards he would take a rest and then return to the Dai Ichi around 4 p.m. and work a further four hours or so. Sunday was a working day, like any other.[10] Occasionally, he would relax by watching a film at his home in the evening. It was usually a Western.

Many felt that by his style and aloofness he was assuming the mantle of the Emperor in the nation he had helped to defeat. That was not part of MacArthur's plan. He needed to use the Emperor in order to achieve his objectives. "The docility of the Japanese was assured once the continuity of Hirohito's reign was established."[11] The *New York Times* had summed up the manner in which the god/Emperor could be employed in an editorial a few days before the surrender. It noted that a "discredited god" would be more useful to the Allies than "a martyred god". These were sentiments shared by most of the world's authorities on Japan. MacArthur wasted little time before assessing the calibre and strength of Hirohito. Frazier Hunt described the meeting[12] between the two men, at the US Embassy building.

The Supreme Commander had his military secretary waiting to meet the Emperor when he stepped out of his old-fashioned black limousine at the entrance to the Embassy. The Emperor was so emotionally disturbed that he was actually shaking. Brigadier General Fellers saluted, and the Emperor almost timidly reached for his hand. The officer greeted him most cordially, and they walked side by side to the study. The friendly reception had a marked effect. The Emperor realized immediately that he faced no trying ordeal.

MacArthur had sent word that the Emperor was to bring his own interpreter, and when the two entered the study the door closed behind them. Only the three were there, and the whole atmosphere was one of complete friendliness and good will. They talked over certain phases and incidents in the long war and other matters of immediate concern. The total result was of immense significance.

Back in America the announcement of the meeting brought violent reactions. The leftist hang-the-Emperor advocates insisted that instead of receiving him so courteously, MacArthur should have him tried and condemned.

It is possible that no single move by MacArthur during his five years in Japan had a more profound effect on the Japanese people than this. As the story of Hirohito's visit spread throughout the Japanese islands, it seemed to put a final stamp of complete acceptance of the realities of the Occupation and of the series of great reforms that were being initiated. MacArthur had proved that he had no intention of publicly humiliating their Emperor. The people everywhere began to understand that the American

Commander who had had such a part in their defeat was now a true friend who was trying his best to help them into a new way of life.

Accepting Hunt's privileged view of events, in that they recorded only MacArthur's remembrance of the meeting and of its impact, it is undoubtedly true that the Japanese took comfort from the relationship between the two men. As Kazuo Kawai put it, MacArthur "emerged with a warm commendation of the Emperor's integrity, sincerity and good intentions". But in doing so, MacArthur took the political risk of treating with a man ultimately responsible for Japan's atrocities in the war against China and, later, in the Second World War.

MacArthur was continuing to follow Washington's instructions. He protected the Emperor's position in the nation's new constitution that came into effect on May 3rd, 1947. There is much of the General in both the sentiment and the language of this fresh blueprint for a nation – so much so that it is still known as "the MacArthur Constitution". No longer was the Emperor the sovereign and fountainhead of all authority. Now, he was "symbol of the State . . . deriving his position from the will of the people in whom resides sovereign power". It provided for a two-house democratic system. It instituted a "Bill of Rights" on civil liberties and gave women certain equal rights. It insisted on a permanent demilitarisation and it called for a strengthening of local government to nurture democracy at the grass-roots of the nation. That, after all, was the over-riding concern. For socialism and Communism – and amid this new-found freedom, trade unions were beginning to flourish – had to be resisted at all costs.

The Allies' wielding of the atomic bomb and fire-bombing of Tokyo had smashed Japan's will and morale. Now MacArthur saw it as his task to reconstruct it. Much that was to happen in the first crucial months of the Occupation was already in his thoughts and his instructions – the need to establish and confirm a Western-style democracy, the casting of Hirohito as a linchpin of the process and, of course, the expectation that those who had perpetrated the most heinous of war crimes would be brought to justice.

Chapter 10

MURRAY SANDERS

The job of finding out what Japan had done in the field of biological warfare fell to a young soldier-scientist, Colonel Murray Sanders. A highly qualified bacteriologist, Sanders had served at Camp Detrick, the secret Maryland headquarters of the US Chemical Warfare Service which had been set up as a consequence of Intelligence reports on biological warfare activity elsewhere in the world.

Its function was to "develop BW defensive measures and to devise means for offensive retaliation in case of biological attack against the United States or its combat forces".[1] It was an enormous task. The mounting threat of the German VI "buzz bombs" that were raining on England from launching sites on the Continent during 1943 spurred the need for BW defences. The US government feared that these self-propelled flying bombs might easily be converted into efficient weapons for a massive BW attack.

How could germs be harnessed as weapons of war? How could they be produced in quantities large enough for wartime needs? What type of bomb or shell could deliver the germs? And, once those questions had been answered, how could Sanders and his team build defences against them, if they were ever used against the Army in the field, or the civilian population in their homes?

A crude rule of thumb to assess the effectiveness of each individual germ emerged early on at Camp Detrick – how many of the investigating team succumbed to it. There were "casualties in the workshop", Sanders admits. Some died. When they began exploring brucellosis, all the people working on an entire floor went down with it. The same thing happened with tularemia. Sanders instituted a system by which scientists were restricted to the laboratory in which they worked. On one occasion he went to Washington for ten days and when he returned he found one entire building, housing the brucellosis experiments, closed and sealed. There had been a leak in a pipe. All ten people in the building had caught brucellosis. "We had some deaths at around that time . . ."[2]

He almost lost a friend who had been one of his students at Columbia, Gifford Pinchot III, son of the Governor of Pennsylvania. "We fought for him, day and night, as we did for all of them.

Sometimes, we lost. This time, we won with a mixture of strepto-
mycin and penicillin. It just worked, we didn't really know why."

Sanders was angry, though not because of the deaths.

Our hands were tied because the authorities didn't seem to realise
what we needed in order to give them the answers they wanted. We
were often playing around with simulants rather than the real
thing. Coloured organisms that were quite harmless, when we
knew the Japanese and probably the Russians were using real
germs all the time every day. My group came to me and said that we
had to have more power to do what we needed to do. After all, they
said, there's a war on . . . even though we had almost lost Gifford
Pinchot III.

I was due that day, by coincidence, to go to dinner in Washington
with Gifford's father, the Governor. Judge Black of the Supreme
Court was going to be there. So was Theodore White, who was
back from China. I decided to break Article 380–5.[3] I told them
what had happened. I laid it all out.

Next day, Maj-Gen Porter, head of the Chemical Warfare Corps
called. "Murray, for Christ's sake, why don't you shut up. You're
under house arrest."[4]

But in Washington Governor Pinchot went to see Secretary of War
Stimson. The result: Murray Sanders was released from house arrest
within forty-eight hours, and promoted to Lt-Colonel.

From 1943 to 1946 he was responsible for research into bacteriology, virology, medicine, pharmacology, physiology and chemistry in
one of the most secret of the top secret laboratories in the United
States.

He and the other members of the team burrowed into their subject.
They confronted the most basic problems – for instance, how the
diseases were passed from person to person. Influenza, pneumonia or
tuberculosis were known to be acquired through the respiratory tract.
But what about the great many other diseases, especially those which
historically had been transmitted to man by fleas, ticks, lice or
mosquitoes? Could infection with their causative organisms also be
induced through the respiratory system? What was the infectious
dose for each disease? Of what size should the particles be to cause
infection?

Different jobs needed different agents. One day in 1943 Sanders
was called to a meeting at one of the National Science Foundation
buildings in Washington. Around the highly polished table were
Secretary of War Stimson; General Porter, head of Chemical

Warfare, George Merck, director of the War Research Service, and his chief of Intelligence John P. Marquand.[5] They came straight to the point.

"We are about to invade North Africa. We need you to put out of commission Germany's secret agent in Casablanca."

Sanders inquired, "Why not kill him? That would be easier."

"We like him. Our agent likes him. They have dinner together every week. Besides, if we killed him, the Nazis would replace him with someone else and our man would have to work at a relationship all over again. No, we simply want him out of action for about four hours."

The plan was to neutralise the German for the crucial four hours around the time of the beach landings. His absence would add to the confusion that always attends these affairs.

Sanders asked, "What does he like to eat at these dinner parties?"

"Apparently, he's fond of oysters."

"Can we depend on that?"

He was assured that he could. He went back to Camp Detrick. A week later he returned to the same room. He carried a phial of staphylococcus. Add this to the oysters, he said. It was carefully borne away.

The invasion of North Africa was successfully accomplished. Soon after, General Porter thanked him: "The staphylococcus worked like a charm." The German spy had been neutralised.

"We were always looking for a way to camouflage a strain so that it would be so difficult to detect and identify that, by the time the enemy had done so, the disease would have done the damage." That is how Lt-Col Oliver N. Fellowes[6] summarised his particular work on virus research and production at Detrick. "We know the enemy were doing the same thing . . . the tension and the security were very much the same as surrounded the building of the atomic bomb. The germs had code letters so that the scientists didn't even refer to them by name among themselves. Botulinus was 'X'. Tularemia was 'UL'."

The Americans worked beside Canadians and Britons. The co-operation, the sharing of discovery and conjecture, was total, says Sanders. "We were more cautious with the French, and we told the Soviets nothing – but Lord Prime, from Porton Down, was always there at Detrick. So was a guy called Henderson.[7] I remember, in fact, he married one of our WAVE officers named Kelly. He was an anthrax man . . ."

Sanders also tried to keep abreast through regular Intelligence briefings of what the Axis nations, Germany, Italy and Japan, were likely to use if they launched an attack on the United States mainland.

One day in 1944 he was summoned to talk with his immediate superior, and by now Scientific Director, Dr Oram C. Woolpert. Intelligence had news of Japanese germ warfare attacks on the Chinese in Manchuria, said Woolpert.

"We think they've killed a lot of people, Murray. We think that they've been poisoning wells and reservoirs."

The germs they had been using were anthrax and plague.

The Germans were active, too. Intelligence reports indicated that, when the Allies returned to the mainland of Europe on D Day, the German forces were poised to use botulinus toxin to throw them back into the sea. Botulinus is a germ that attacks the central nervous system. Sickness is followed by paralysis and rapid death. Sanders called a series of hurried meetings. "It became obvious we would have to make a special effort, however busy we were. We had to have enough anti-botulinus vaccine to inoculate a whole invasion force, we decided. We had to go into production."

Sanders' team set aside a fermenter approximately 10 feet high and 5 feet wide. They filled it with a culture in which the botulinus would grow. A spoonful multiplied to fill the vat in seventy-two hours or so. Enough poison to destroy several armies. The next task was to kill the organism, while retaining the strong antigenic properties, without which a vaccine would be ineffective. Hundreds of thousands of shots were prepared. Though they didn't know it, the men and women who went to France on D Day, June 6th, 1944, were all immunised against botulinus, protected by a vaccine produced at Fort Detrick.

In December 1944, Murray Sanders' deliberations were interrupted by an urgent telephone call. A strange balloon had been discovered in Butte, Montana. Thirty feet in diameter, 91 feet round, apparently made of rice paper. "Leave it alone," Sanders instructed. "I'll be right there." But within hours, other balloons were reported, about ten of them in all. Sanders went instead to Washington and the balloon from Montana was brought there. So was another, found in the water at San Diego, California, reportedly made of rubberised silk.

The balloons were brought in, and we all stood around them, in a circle. All the scientific and military experts, all of us with our own thoughts. We examined them, and then we went away to make our own individual reports. Mine scared them stiff. The balloons had obviously come from Japan. I told them that the prevailing winds would carry most of the Japanese balloons, comfortably, to the mainland of the United States. I told them that if we found Japanese B-encephalitis[8] on any of the balloons we were in real trouble. Mosquitoes were the best vectors [carriers] – and we had plenty of those in the States – and our population had no defences against B-encephalitis. We had no experience of the disease in this country. We were totally vulnerable to it. And four out of five people who contracted it would have died, in my view.

Sanders also conjectured that the balloons could have been contaminated with anthrax.

Anthrax is a tough bug. It's sturdy. It's cheap to produce and they'd used it in China. They could have splattered the west and south-west of Canada and the United States. They could have contaminated the pastures and forests and killed all the cows, sheep, horses, pigs, deer – plus a considerable number of human beings. The hysteria would have been terrible; one of the strengths of BW as a weapon is that you can't see it, but it kills. I was worried . . .

The balloons were cleverly designed.[9] They were built so that they would travel across the Pacific in between thirty and sixty hours at the optimum height to be carried by the prevailing winds. If they went too high, a gadget released a little helium from the sac and the balloon resumed its steady course to the United States. If it dropped too low, another gadget jettisoned one of the sandbags so that the balloon rose once more. Several balloons had been found in Alaska and Canada. On January 10th, 1945, Sanders went to Ottawa to talk to the military attaché. He was given a small, transparent box, found in one of the balloons. The mission was interrupted because another balloon was found at White Horse, Alaska. The North-West Mounted Police arranged for dogs, sleds and parkas. As they were about to leave, a further balloon was reported, in Hawaii. Sanders chose Hawaii. With the transparent box (4½ inches by 7 by 5) in his possession he flew out on January 19th to Washington, en route for Hawaii. That same day, a paper balloon landed miles south of Fort Simpson, in Canada, and there were sightings near Oyster River, Vancouver Island. Another balloon fell in the St Lawrence River and still another at Grand Rapids, Michigan. The incidents built up over the months to indicate a planned campaign against the north and west of North America. Planes shot them down. A sheriff in Montana punctured one with his rifle. Over the Aleutian Islands nine were destroyed in a couple of hours. In the month of March there were almost 100 "confirmed incidents". The Western Defense Command produced a battle plan, code-named Lightning Project, preparing the Army for

125

contamination of an area watershed with disease-producing agents; dissemination over an area of bacterial agents causing disease in humans or animals upon contact or inhalation; implantation of infected insects to act as vectors of disease in humans or animals; introduction of agents to cause plant diseases with resulting economic loss; and distribution of contaminated material for infecting disease-carrying vectors.

Rigid censorship was placed on radio and press reports of the finding of any balloons. There were 200 of them in all. But what lay at the root of this campaign?

Sanders personally examined the balloons found intact. Inch by inch he pored over them. He spent hour after hour in the glass belly of a B19, tracking up and down the west coast of the United States, looking for 30 feet of rice paper caught up in trees or spread out in marshlands or on pasture. Surprisingly, he discovered no trace of any threatening bacteria on any of the balloons. He looks back forty years to that revelation, and says:

The only explanation I had, and still have, is that Ishii wasn't ready to deliver what he was making in Pingfan; that he hadn't worked out the technology. They just weren't good enough at their virus research. If they had been, we were at Ishii's mercy. I mean, a litre of Japanese B-encephalitis, freeze-dried, comes down to about that much powder [he cupped his hands] and I always thought that Ishii was pushed into the campaign. It was in retaliation for Doolittle's raid on Tokyo in April 1942, because the Japanese had sworn that no American plane would bomb the homeland. The Japanese press certainly made enough of the "triumphant" balloon attacks; they were told that the west coast of the United States was a blazing inferno.

Each balloon did in fact carry an incendiary device. But most of them failed to detonate. Even the fire bombs were a damp squib.

The balloon that fell in Helena, Montana, carried an incendiary bomb. It exploded and killed a woman. A balloon that landed in Oregon intrigued a party of men out fishing. They handled the black bomb with the white stripe. It exploded and killed six of them. These were the only casualties of the attempt to change the course of the war through onslaught by balloon.

The implications of the balloon attacks had to be digested and disseminated. In March 1945 meetings were hastily convened at

Omaha, Nebraska, at the headquarters of the 7th Service Command, and in San Francisco at the headquarters of the US Western Defense Command. Senior officers of the Army and Navy, responsible for defending the west coast of North America, from Alaska and Canada to California and Mexico, sat for four days and heard what five men from Washington – among them Murray Sanders – had to tell them about biological warfare. They talked about balloons. They heard of the Japanese germ attacks on the Chinese, using plague and anthrax. They listened as the evidence of Chinese doctors was tabulated before them. They were told that the Japanese had "tried to get yellow fever virus from the Rockefeller Foundation in New York and made similar attempts in Rio de Janeiro and Brazil" and that it was quite possible that Japan "now has that virus . . . through Germany".[10]

The head of the project was described, without naming him as Ishii, and the headquarters was pinpointed as being at Nanking. Pathetic-sounding precautions were listed: "Tie trousers at the ankles, wear gloves, put on a gas mask." Intelligence reports were considered: "We have several documents and prisoner-of-war statements that Japan has a bacillus bomb. This is called the Mark VII, Type 13, Bacillus bomb, experimental." Possible targets, possible means of dispersal, possible biological agents and diseases – all these were discussed.

The anxiety over how best to deal with what many military authorities believed to be Japan's last opportunity to tilt the balance of the war was real and pressing. As Sanders said, one balloon could be carrying enough cholera to start an epidemic, "if conditions were favourable . . ."

That same spring, a group of US Naval warships nosed slowly through the early morning mist to group at a point five miles off the shore of southern California. As a breeze sprang up to clear the way for a new day, there was vigorous activity aboard one of the des-troyers. Valves were operated and the contents of a huge pressure tank, at the stern of the vessel, were released into the atmosphere. The tank contained the germs of influenza. In the weeks that fol-lowed, medical records were checked among the local population. In other, similar tests, simulants were used and testing points estab-lished up to 250 miles inland. Even in the last months of the war, the United States was determined to discover just how vulnerable they were to germ warfare . . .

The impact of the balloon raids was felt as far away as Africa. A new vaccine had been discovered to combat rinderpest. But US

Congressional law prevented Camp Detrick testing the effectiveness of the vaccine on US soil. The United States was, and is, the biggest meat-eating nation in the world. North America's animals were vulnerable to rinderpest. And rinderpest, with its classic high fever, kills most of the animals it infects. So the US turned to the British to carry out the field trials – in far-off East Africa. On June 8th, 1945, at 2100 hours, Britain's Secretary of State for the Colonies urged Sir Philip Mitchell[11] in Kenya to arrange tests of the new vaccine as a matter of "great importance". Half an hour later, the Secretary of State sent a second top secret telegram, explaining that the fear was that the Japanese would try to infect North America with rinderpest.

The Japanese must not "ascertain that these experiments are being carried out".[12]

From Kenya, Sir Philip Mitchell responded with enthusiasm.[13] Trials with forty animals would be arranged in a paddock and field tests on 10,000 animals would follow. Sir Philip invented a cover story for the two Americans and the Canadian scientists due to arrive within a few days and he agreed that the whole affair should be hushed up, for "a new rinderpest vaccine would be headline news from here to Cape Town".[14] The trials, carried out over the next five months, were "completely satisfactory".[15,16] Sanders says: "We were 100 per cent vulnerable to rinderpest. It kills and spreads rapidly. It was one of the most likely biological agents to be used by the Japanese. We had to have the answers . . ."

Most often, the virus to be the subject of experiments carried out by the Detrick team was freeze-dried. Colonel Fellowes remembers:

> We dried the virus in bulk. Then we sometimes mixed the powder with feathers and, though I never discovered where the tests were carried out, I know the mixture was to be delivered in the same way as leaflets were dropped over enemy territory, in leaflet bombs. The system worked particularly well with swine fever. The pigs simply ate the feathers and died.

Once, he admits there was an "incident" at what were euphemistically known as "proving grounds" at Skull Valley, Tooele, Utah. Sheep were tethered on the area for a "controlled" experiment with encephalitis. But the weather forecast was insufficiently accurate and the light wind became stronger. Hundreds of sheep died outside the proving ground. Fellowes remembers, laconically, "There was a lot of explaining to do to the local farmers."

Sanders ruminated:

> We spent a lot of time on what might seem obscure diseases
> because we knew we had little experience in coping with them if
> they were ever thrown at us. But I often think back and realise that
> in fact it was the well-known material and obvious methods that
> posed the greater threat. I mean you could have forecast what the
> Japs would have used, depending on the job they wanted to
> do.
> If they'd wanted to knock out our agricultural areas for fifty
> years, they'd have used anthrax. If they'd wanted to knock out New
> York City, they could have introduced plague into the water
> system and reversed the water flow, so that the germs would have
> come out of the faucets [taps] and the water closets.

Sanders knew this to be true because he tried it. One airless day in
the early summer of 1945, he and two other officers checked into an
apartment house in one of the oldest districts of the city. Each carried
in his suitcase a specially designed screw-topped bottle containing a
quantity of a pink substance. They settled in and, at a prearranged
time, they took the bottles to the wash-basins in their rooms. Each
bottle had been manufactured with an attachment that made a
vacuum. The three officers turned on the taps. The vacuum reversed
the flow of the water and the freeze-dried pink substance was sucked
into the city's water supply.

> I was naïve, I guess, in those days. I was told it would work, and it
> did. The apartment house soon had scores of complaints that there
> was pink staining in the water. And we dropped the bell captain ten
> dollars and went into other rooms in the place to check that the
> water was indeed running pink.
> Oh yes, that would have taken out New York in a matter
> of hours. And though we never said it, I believe we all knew
> that . . .

Then, in the summer of 1945, as British, Indian, Australian, New
Zealand and American troops rolled back the Japanese Army in
Burma, documents discovered on the bodies of dead soldiers indi-
cated that *Bōeki-Kyūsuibū* – "water-purification units" – were at
least present in the area. Lt-Col Sanders was ordered to leave the
United States for Burma immediately, to join General "Vinegar Joe"
Stilwell's staff, presumably to put his biological knowledge into
practice. Three hours before he was due to leave, at the height of a

farewell party at Camp Detrick, the orders were withdrawn. Major Adams* would go instead.

Though only a few in high places knew it for certain, the war was drawing to a close. The first atomic bomb would be dropped on Japan in a few weeks' time. The overriding need was for a cohesive plan to put – in an Intelligence sense – the right people in the right places. Sanders would not go to Burma, he would instead join General Douglas MacArthur, General Charles Willoughby and Karl T. Compton in Manila, to await the assault on the Japanese mainland. Sanders, said MacArthur, was America's top man in biological warfare. He would be needed in Japan. Sanders flew to the Philippines to confer. He knew Compton, formerly president of MIT, the Massachusetts Institute of Technology, now chief of Scientific Intelligence. Compton was still technically a civilian but he wore the three stars of a lieutenant-general. He knew Willoughby as head of G-2, US Military Intelligence. He went straight to MacArthur's headquarters for the first of many meetings. Sanders recalled:

I liked MacArthur and respected him. He was often brusque, particularly when anyone challenged him, but I guess you have to be something of an egotist if you get to that position of authority.

You were aware that he felt very heavily the weight of the responsibility he was carrying. He talked to me for hours about BW and what I thought and what I feared. He and K. T. Compton said: "We need you very badly here." In every way, my position was a privileged one, a very strong one. I was the only one who knew anything about BW. They *had* to take notice of what I said. And I believe they felt, even at that late stage of the war that Ishii – whom we knew about – could and would try a BW attack on our forces.

The planned land, sea and air assault on Honshu, in mainland Japan, was codenamed Operation Olympia. It was decided that Sanders would go ashore at H plus 6 – only six hours after the first bombardment. He would go with the first wave of assault troops – "presumably they weren't worried my test tubes would get smashed."

Then, in August 1945, US planes dropped atomic bombs on Hiroshima and Nagasaki. The war was as good as over, though the surrender would be some weeks away. MacArthur decided to act

* Major Adams was briefed just as Sanders had been, to go to Singapore, there to look at what the Japanese had left behind. Instead, Sanders heard later that Adams had travelled to Chungking, where "through a slip-up of paperwork", he had been posted as a surgeon to a newly formed Chinese division. He was killed in action by the Japanese.

quickly. A week before even he set foot on Japanese soil he de-spatched the SS *Sturgis* to Yokohama, loaded with specialists, including Intelligence experts, to assess the best course of action when the Occupation began. Murray Sanders was aboard the *Sturgis*: his mission – to find out as much as he could, as quickly as he could, about the Japanese biological warfare machine – and about Shirō Ishii.

Sanders was heavily briefed. He was told that he knew as much as there was to know, from G-2 and Scientific Intelligence, about this curious Water Purification Unit. He had been given a photograph which he studied and studied again. It was of a Japanese biologist, Dr Naitō, and Dr Naitō could speak English. As the *Sturgis* docked, Sanders had no problem in effecting a meeting with Naitō. He was among the first to hurry up the gangway. "Dr Sanders," he said. He was carrying a photograph of Sanders.*

Naitō simply said that he was Sanders' interpreter. He was in fact a Lt-Colonel in Unit 731. Sanders laboured on in ignorance – "after all, even if he'd told me, at that stage I didn't even know what Unit 731 was . . ." He showed Naitō other photographs he'd been given by Military Intelligence (G-2) – an array of Japanese scientists. Help me find them, he ordered, and they set off to meet their first "target", Professor Yonetsugi Miyagawa at Tokyo Imperial University. Sanders rated him Japan's best virologist. The meeting was little more than a formality. As the days wore on, Sanders set himself up in an office at Supreme Allied Headquarters in the Dai-Ichi building.

During that first week, Naitō suggested Sanders accept his hospi-tality for a traditional Japanese meal. Together, they went to an hotel and up to a simple room on the first floor. There, Sanders was introduced to a tiny, smiling Japanese who bade him sit down. *Tempura* arrived. This man, said Naitō, is senior vice-president of a major Japanese company, the equivalent of General Electric. "Would Colonel Sanders be interested in earning 5,000 dollars a week for the rest of his life?" Sanders laughed – and left. Naitō apologised. "I didn't consider the bribe for a moment," Sanders says. "I didn't sack Naitō because I needed him."

Naitō was quick, helpful, efficient and very humble. He worked a long day, every day and then, apparently, went home dutifully to his wife. In fact, he did nothing of the sort. He left Sanders' office and made immediately for a rendezvous with senior members of Unit 731 and Unit 100, who were in hiding in the city's suburbs. He went to

* Murray Sanders never discovered where Naitō obtained his photograph. It seems likely that G-2 gave it to him. Sanders remembers the photograph being taken at Camp Detrick.

brief them on what Sanders was finding out – which was precious little – and to indicate the direction of the US investigation. In real terms, he totally controlled the first weeks of Sanders' probing. It was his job to ensure that Sanders didn't find out too much. He succeeded.

MacArthur arrived in Japan on August 30th, 1945. Sanders and other senior officers were waiting for him at the US Embassy. MacArthur began as he intended to continue. He assembled a mighty motorcade of men and equipment, and, under an air-cover of fighters and bombers, he thundered in an extravagant show of strength the short distance from the Embassy, past the Imperial Palace, to the Dai-Ichi headquarters building. Murray Sanders was in the third jeep behind the triumphant MacArthur. "I'll never forget the experience till the day I die. Even today, it sets the hairs rising on the back of my neck thinking about it. You see, there wasn't a single person in the streets to see all this – but we knew they were all watching." At headquarters, MacArthur summoned Sanders. How were the investigations going? he inquired. Badly, said Sanders. Together they pondered the problem and decided to try to bluff Naitō.

> Naitō came in one afternoon and I was sitting there, very dejected. "I've lost face," I said. "I am a total failure as an inquirer. I am being sent home and a much tougher man is being sent to take over the investigation. I've been too kind to you." I'd given him rations and helped his family. Now, I told him I was going to call in the Russians, our Allies. It was time the Soviets were involved, I said. He went home early that day.

Next morning Naitō asked for a little of Sanders' time before the day's interviews began. He then produced a handwritten document. Sanders leafed through its twelve pages. He realised the bluff had worked. Here was a document laying out the organisation of the *Bōeki Kyūsuibū* (Water Purification Unit) and admitting that it had been engaged in biological warfare. We reproduce it in full in Appendix A.

It named names, including Ishii. It showed a chain of command topped by the Emperor – though it stressed he was not directly implicated. It talked of motivation and methods of delivery, by bomb, shell and insect. And it outlined experiments with cholera and plague, salmonella and dysentery.

Sanders was elated. But not too elated to forget one crucial question to which the document did not address itself. He asked the question, and then carefully noted the reply, in his own hand at the end of the document.

"I have asked Dr Naitō whether prisoners were ever used as experimental guinea pigs. He vows that this has not been the case." He signed it "M. Sanders, Lt-Col."

Sanders left immediately to see MacArthur. Willoughby from Military Intelligence was there; so was K. T. Compton.

It was one of the most exciting moments of my life. The document tied Ishii with the Unit and with BW and it even seemed to tie in the Emperor, although Naitō was denying it. It was the breakthrough we needed. It was dynamite because it listed so many senior men – all of them implicated plus or minus. But how were we going to get the scientific details we had to have? I asked. We need to find the scientists themselves. Where was Ishii for instance? The Russians were already demanding to interview him as a war criminal.

The three men debated the matter. Then Sanders said: "My recommendation is that we promise Naitō that no one involved in BW will be prosecuted as a war criminal."

MacArthur said, "Well, you're the man in charge of the scientific aspects of this. If you feel you cannot get all the information, we're not given to torture, so offer him [Naitō] that promise as coming from General MacArthur – and get the data."

Sanders went back to his office and summoned Naitō. He told him the Allies would not prosecute BW workers as war criminals and he had General MacArthur's word on it.

"This made a deep impression on Naitō and the data came in waves after that . . . thick and fast . . ."

So the deal was done. The offer was made and accepted and Sanders began to meet scientists who were suddenly much more ready to discuss their experiments with anthrax and glanders and plague and the rest. But what about that question that Sanders had thought to ask when Naitō had handed him the historic document?

Had humans been involved in the experiments? And did Sanders believe Naitō's vow?

Forty years later, we explored the issue, with a bright-eyed but ailing Murray Sanders, in his ocean-side home in Florida. "I believed him for a very short time."

Did it suit you to believe him?

"Well it made it easier for me to be friends with him."

No, but did it also make it easier for you to protect him and go through with the deal?

"Yes. By all means. I needed that document. It opened the gate and it showed me where to go and what to do . . . And I thank God I thought to ask him that question before I went with the document to MacArthur.''

Yet Sanders' belief that no human guinea pigs had been used was to last only two or three weeks.

As the information flowed in, Murray Sanders ended yet another day's investigations by returning wearily to his bedroom in the Dai-Ichi Hotel. Suddenly, there was a scraping noise outside the window. Sanders looked out and saw the face of a Japanese who had slid down a water pipe to reach his room unobserved. He snatched his revolver from under his pillow.

I checked him out as I let him in. He was a slight man, wearing a beret, a sweatshirt and trousers. He had a blueprint he wanted to give me. It was of a bomb, that was loaded with germs, called the *Uji* bomb. He stayed and we talked. He showed me production figures indicating they'd made more than 100 bombs. He told me the bomb hadn't worked very well.

But he also told me that in experiments they had staked out prisoners at varying distances from the bomb when it had exploded, to see the impact on them. Some of the prisoners had died.

The Japanese – ''he was probably an engineer'' – left. Sanders was shaken. Previously, he had had only second – or third – hand allegations of the use of plague against the Chinese. Now, here was a bomb that had been used to kill prisoners, chained to stakes. And he believed the man who had told him about it. It was, he remembers, ''a helluva dilemma''.

He decided to take the situation and the fresh information directly to MacArthur and Willoughby. They must decide whether to scotch the deal that protected the Japanese scientists from prosecution. He hurried to MacArthur. MacArthur heard Sanders out. ''He raised his eyebrows, and lit his pipe. Then he said, 'We need more evidence. We can't simply act on that. Keep going. Ask more questions. And keep quiet about it.'

''So I did . . .''

In the second week of September Murray Sanders took matters into his own hands. It was necessary, he felt, to see Pingfan for himself.* A B29 would take him there, from Tokyo. The plane was made ready and he went to the airport.

---

* Sanders did not, of course, know that Pingfan had been razed to the ground.

I was excited, hot on the trail. Naitō had let slip the previous day that Unit 731 had chosen Pingfan because, he said "the temperature was ideal, with an average wind speed of ten to twelve miles per hour, the optimal conditions for disseminating the bacteria!" I'd asked him how he knew this; what experiments had been carried out that he felt he wanted to tell me about and he'd got a bit flustered. He'd hedged. Again, he said that no human beings had been involved and that he'd only picked up the information on conditions at Pingfan from conversations he'd had since the investigation had begun. But I knew I needed to get to Pingfan to find as many clues as I could on how Ishii had operated.

Sanders was about to board the B29 when he was suddenly recalled. MacArthur had ruled that the relationship with the Soviet Union was so uneasy that he could not risk a B29 falling into their hands. He didn't want the Russians looking over a B29.

Murray Sanders never saw the ruins of Pingfan to explore the questions he desperately wanted answered.

During the hectic months of September, October and November, Sanders had interrogated no lesser men than the chief of the Army General Staff and erstwhile Kwantung Army Commander-in-Chief Yoshijirō Umezu, Vice-Minister of War Lt-Gen Tadakazu Wakamatsu, Vice-Chief of the Army General Staff and longtime China campaigner Lt-Gen Torashirō Kawabe, Ishii's deputy Colonel Tomosada Masuda, BW bomb expert Major Jun'ichi Kaneko and many others. Army technical expert Lt-Col Seiichi Niizuma, of those interviewed by Sanders, is perhaps the only person still alive today. An officer responsible for establishing and equipping specialist research units of the Army, who had worked at the 9th Army Technology Research Institute, Niizuma was an obvious Technical Intelligence target. He provides a unique perspective on how the Japanese responded to Sanders' investigation.

Sanders started asking me questions as early as September [said Niizuma]. He went on for two months . . . the medical doctor [Sanders] wanted to know all the research I had set up. And about the third time he talked to me, he told me that the following day he was going to talk about fuses. I replied that I was not informed about the subject, and asked him to explain what it was all about.

It transpired that what he was really asked to find out from me was about the Ishii troops. He wanted to know what I knew about what these people had been doing.

Well, this was a subject that nobody wanted to tell them anything about. We all felt it wasn't a very pleasant subject to talk about, nobody volunteered, so I took it on.[17]

Niizuma was present at most of Sanders' subsequent interrogations, attending those of Umezu, Shimomura, Wakamatsu, Masuda, and even a formal interview with Naitō. He continues:

. . . we talked about fuses, cannon burster impact that would cause scattering on detonation, the scattering device within the cannon shell; and the whole subject came up because the Ishii troops had requirements for it. He persisted on that subject, and so I asked of him, turned the question back at him, what on earth are you trying to find out?

And what transpired was all about this "red book"* which they got off the Navy down south . . . it would seem it came from an intercepted airplane . . . and all the interrogations were based on that.

Niizuma's memory is entirely correct. Sanders presented the Japanese with details of the Special Bomb Mark 7 which had been captured by the Americans in the South Pacific in May 1944. A "military most secret" document belonging to an enlisted flying trainee, it had described a "bacillus bomb". Sanders only confronted the Japanese with this hard evidence of offensive BW after his earlier "hands off" approach to interrogations had failed. This followed Naitō's revelations about the reluctance of senior Japanese to reveal the whole truth.

Niizuma appears to have been the first Japanese to be confronted by Sanders with such evidence. Sanders, the following day, went on to explain to Army and Navy Surgeon Generals Hiroshi Kanbayashi and Nobuaki Hori that although *he* was perfectly willing to accept the Japanese version on BW, it would be difficult to convince others that the whole story had been told in the complete absence of offensive data.

Although Sanders may have thought he was getting tough, the reaction he produced from the Japanese was entirely different.

"As soon as I knew that was all he had in his hand to base his investigation upon, I was very relieved," Niizuma recalls. "What mattered was that none of the Army's secret documents had been taken off them."

* Niizuma referred to the notebook as the "red book", as it was customary for red to designate "top secret" in the Japanese Navy.

Niizuma knew that technical collaboration between the Japanese Army and Navy was almost non-existent, and that Sanders' avenue of questioning based on Naval documentation would lead nowhere. Sanders was steered to Commander Hiroshi Ishiwata for an explanation as to why the Navy never actually built the Mark 7 bomb. Masuda was produced to speak on behalf of the Army, and to give a sanitised version of the activities of Unit 731, as Ishii's water purification unit was now known to be called. Ishii was not produced, although Niizuma knew he had returned to Japan. Instead, Niizuma cleverly reinforced what was already the Americans' belief, by telling them that he "presumed" Unit 731's commander was still in Manchuria.

In order to control information reaching Sanders, and to speed the American's departure, Niizuma had offered to collate information. In this he was aided by a Dr Kan'ichirō Kamei, an anti-expansionist politician who for his beliefs had been imprisoned for six months during the Tōjō regime. Kamei, who held his doctorate from America's Columbia University, was much later to hold the key to full-scale revelations about Unit 731's true work.

Murray Sanders switched off the desk lamp and pushed aside the typewriter at which his clerk had been hammering all day. It was late and the report on his investigation in Japan was finished. He gathered it up, left his office and walked down the corridor to find General MacArthur's secretary. He gave it to her, said: "Take good care of it; please make thirty copies, the chief will want to see it" and, stretching, he left the building to grab a jeep back to his hotel. He had been there perhaps an hour when there was a knock on his door.

It was a reporter from one of the wire services. He was holding Sanders' report. "This looks quite interesting," he said. "Can you tell me a bit more about it?"

"Give me that," said Sanders, "where did you get it?"

"There's a heap of them on a desk at headquarters. I picked one up. It's only marked RESTRICTED and the press are allowed anything marked RESTRICTED . . ."

The reporter was quite correct. But, correct or not, a major breach of security was about to take place. Sanders said: "Stay here. Don't move. Give me fifteen minutes, please." He raced downstairs, commandeered a jeep from the desk clerk, US Army Sergeant Watanabe, and drove back to the Dai-Ichi headquarters. He ran to MacArthur's outer office, now in darkness – and there was, sure enough, a pile of his reports. He examined them. They were simply marked RESTRICTED. He counted them; there were twenty-nine. The one in his hand was the only one missing. He took them to the duty

137

clerk. "There's been a mistake," he said. "These are TOP SECRET. Please reclassify them and keep them safe."

He returned to his hotel. He explained the situation, as much as he could, to the journalist. The reporter agreed, in the national interest, to keep the secret. He did not break that promise.

We reproduce Murray Sanders' report as Appendix B.

Nowhere in it, neither with regard to the *Uji* bomb nor to the *Ka* bomb, is there a reference to any human experiments. Nowhere is there a note on the evidence provided by the Unit 731 engineer who produced for Sanders the blueprint and the allegation that prisoners-of-war had in fact been killed in experiments.

All the interviews on which the report was based were carried out by Lt-Col Murray Sanders. But MacArthur's orders had been quite specific – keep quiet about human experiments.

Murray Sanders spent only ten weeks or so in Japan. The first part of his investigation was complete and he was then ordered home, told to sort out a bureaucratic dogfight over the high expenditure of the chemical warfare and biological warfare arms of Military Intelligence. After a difficult journey he arrived in Washington, more tired than he had ever been in his life. He went to Camp Detrick and revealed the existence of the Naitō document. He was home a week; then, he collapsed with a severe haemorrhage. He had tuberculosis. He spent the next two years in bed. He had plenty of time to think.

I pondered about the issue so often while I lay in bed month after month [he says today]. In retrospect, the deal was a mistake. But I didn't know that human guinea pigs had been used when I suggested the arrangement and when we learned about the bacillus anthrax bombs there had still been time to prosecute the Japs at the Tokyo trials. The trials went on for almost three years, remember.

At night I would lay there and try to puzzle out Naitō's place in the whole thing because there's no doubt he successfully pulled the wool over my eyes.

You have to try to understand the Japanese and that's quite difficult. I remember reading Ruth Benedict's wonderful book, *The Chrysanthemum and the Sword*, in which she explains about Ons. You see, the Japanese recognise three overriding obligations – first to the Emperor, second, to their parents and, third, to anyone who saves their life.

Well, I guess I fell into the third category. I had saved Naitō's life, by protecting him. So he was obligated to me – and I believe, over the years, he hated me for it.

I remember the first couple of days that I was in Tokyo, I saw an old guy on his bicycle in the middle of the traffic wobble and tumble off. I automatically ran forward and helped him up from under the wheels of the passing cars. I dusted him down and he turned and spat in my face.

Naitō was with Sanders and the bewildered young US Colonel had in his distress questioned his Japanese interpreter. "I asked: 'Why the hostility? Simply because I'm an American?' 'Not so,' said Naitō. 'It was because he now owes you his life, and he'll *never* be able to repay you . . .' Well, I reckon Naitō came to feel that way about me . . ."
Wasn't that just bitterness talking?

I don't think so. He duped me, of course. But it took me years to realise that. I thought he was a man of good will. He was charming and he visited me in the United States and was welcomed by my wife, Peggy, and stayed in our home. He got a fine job and became president of the Green Cross Corporation in Japan . . . He was highly respected and only since he died in 1981 have I realised how clever he was.

Sanders went back to those days in 1946.

I wasn't completely fooled, you know. I should have returned to Japan once I had briefed my BW colleagues in Fort Detrick on what I'd discovered from Naitō. But I couldn't go back because of my TB. Instead, I talked to Arvo Thompson* who was to carry out the next stage of the investigations. And I remember telling "Tommy" Thompson about the anthrax bomb and the experiments on the human beings. I told him specifically to look for the anthrax experiments and the *Uji* bomb.
Funnily enough, no one at Camp Detrick seemed to take the story of the human experiments very seriously . . .

And that in itself is an amazing admission. Why wasn't Sanders' evidence taken "very seriously"? Was it simply that the germ warfare secrets were being pursued so assiduously that its significance was overlooked? Unlikely. More likely, surely, that Camp Detrick realised that, if Sanders was correct, the information they were about to get was unique – the first comprehensive data on the effect biological warfare had on the human body.
But Sanders was a man of principle. The only medical doctor on K. T. Compton's team, the only man among the investigators to have

* Arvo Thompson committed suicide in 1948.

139

taken the Hippocratic Oath on the sanctity of human life. A man of sufficient scruples to ask the Japanese at the first sign of a break-through in the investigation: Did you use human guinea pigs? In these circumstances, to ruthless commanders such a man of scruples could become an embarrassment.

There are a number of other oddities about Murray Sanders' involvement in the Unit 731 investigation. That he should be chosen for the task is no surprise; he was the best man for the job. But how was it that when they met Naitō had Sanders' photograph, the one taken at Camp Detrick? And why, in an area so security sensitive, wasn't Sanders given an American of Japanese extraction to act as his interpreter, someone who had been positively vetted throughout years in the US Services?

Could it be that G-2 and Scientific Intelligence knew that Naitō had links, at the very least, with Unit 731 and that they failed to pass on this knowledge to Lt-Col Sanders? If so, that would explain how Naitō had Sanders' photograph – G-2 had given it to him. It would also explain why, once the hint of human experimentation had been picked up by Sanders, quick decisions had to be made by MacArthur, Compton and Willoughby: could they afford to keep Sanders in the team? Should they keep running with the information now coming through from Naitō and the Unit 731 scientists?

The decision was made: Sanders might be a hindrance. He was shipped out as soon as the ink was dry on his report. The pawn was simply moved off the board. The illness that followed so rapidly may have been viewed in the rarefied atmosphere of the Dai-Ichi head-quarters in Tokyo as providential intervention. Murray Sanders was never again involved in the germ warfare investigation. He was too ill . . . Other men, uncluttered by medical principles, took over the questioning.

In 1946 Lt-Col Murray Sanders was awarded the Legion of Merit by a grateful nation. The citation read:

Lieutenant Colonel Murray Sanders performed meritorious ser-vice in the development, perfection and standardization of labora-tory methods for detection and evaluation of actual potential biological warfare agents. From August 1943 to November 1945 he was Chief of a unit whose mission was to devise protective meas-ures for our troops against biological warfare agents. This mission was outstandingly accomplished, permitting our high command to feel that sufficient materials and information were on hand to pro-tect our troops and the United States from an attack of this type.

Chapter 11

Ishii Investigated

It was not long before the relief of Sanders' departure was dispelled for the members of Unit 731. The *Pacific Stars and Stripes* edition of January 6th, 1946 and other, Japanese-language, newspapers carried a story quoting Japanese Communist leaders as accusing "members of the Japanese Medical Corps" of inoculating American and Chinese prisoners-of-war in Manchuria with bubonic plague virus. It was said that "Dr Shirō Ishii, former lieutenant-general in the Japanese Surgeons' Corps and former head of the Ishii Institute at Harbin, directed 'human guinea pig' tests both at Mukden and Harbin." It was claimed that experiments at Canton had backfired and that plague had broken out in the city. It was further asserted that Ishii, in spite of having had a mock funeral staged, was alive and living in Japan.[1]

The extremely serious allegations appeared at a critical moment.

The Allies had announced their intention to hold a series of war crimes trials ranging from Class "A", or major cases, tried in Tokyo by the International Military Tribunal for the Far East (IMTFE), to Class "B" and "C" cases tried across the war zones, for the most part by commissions appointed by the US Army and Navy. Every day newspapers published stories of executions carried out throughout Greater East Asia as the sentence of these lesser war crimes tribunals, and the American Tokyo trial prosecutors had recently arrived in Japan and were settling down to their duties.

It is impossible to gauge either GHQ's or the Japanese response to the *Stars and Stripes* article since no records have yet surfaced on the subject, but if MacArthur had known about, and had wanted to prevent publication, then his wide powers of censorship would have enabled him to do so. However, the reason for, and the timing of, publication in all probability resulted from decisions made thousands of miles away in Washington and London.

In December 1945, the British and Americans jointly decided to lift the veil of secrecy that surrounded their wartime BW research. Now that the whole world knew of the Manhattan Atomic Bomb project from the terrible devastation of Hiroshima and Nagasaki, it was felt opportune to announce the two Allies' other great wartime research secret.

Two days before the *Pacific Stars and Stripes* article was published, George Merck, formerly director of the former War Research Service, and now special BW adviser to America's Secretary of War Robert P. Paterson, Henry Stimson's successor, released a copy of his personal report on Allied BW activities throughout the war. And in a late announcement to the press the War Department's public affairs bureau added the following statement:

> . . . There is no evidence that the enemy ever resorted to this means of warfare. Whether the Japanese Army could have perfected these weapons in time and would eventually have used them had the war continued is of course not known. However, defenses against biological warfare were the subject of an active research and development programme in this country.[2]

Merck in important concluding remarks of his report stressed that continued efforts in BW research were vital to America's security.

It is possible to surmise that the *Pacific Stars and Stripes* editor took the Washington announcement as his cue to publish, unhelpful as this might have been to MacArthur. Merck's report, it has been claimed, was withdrawn shortly after the release, because it shocked public opinion.[3]

At any event the Americans had already decided that their Japanese BW investigation was incomplete. Their inquiries were, in fact, to run for years.

In the early days of January 1946, Masaji Kitano – known to have commanded Unit 731 from 1942 to 1944 – was flown for interrogation from China to Japan, presumably with the help of Nationalist authorities. (From the time he had relinquished command of Unit 731, Kitano served as chief of Military Medicine with the Shanghai Expeditionary Force.) When he arrived in Tokyo, two American officers, Colonel Whitesides and Chief Surgeon Schwichtenberg, were waiting for him. They interrogated him on January 11th, five days after publication of the *Pacific Stars and Stripes* article.[4]

Whitesides was determined to find out about Japan's offensive BW work.

"We want to get some information on your Harbin medical installations, chiefly on BW," he demanded. "We realise that on your defensive work you had to work somewhat on offensive to determine your defensive action. What was your position at the Harbin medical installation? Give dates and details."

142

"Up to August 1st, 1942, I was professor of Microbiology at the Manchurian Medical College," replied Kitano. "After that I replaced General Ishii as Water Purification Chief of the Kwantung Army."

"Were you prepared at any time to use BW as a weapon?" asked Whitesides. "If not, why not?"

"No," replied Kitano, "we were not prepared to use it."

"Why were you not prepared to use it?" Whitesides asked again.

"In my opinion, it is not good to use BW in warfare and, if used, it is not effective," Kitano responded.

"Were you prepared to use it if you had been directed to do so?"

"If higher authorities had given the order, I and General Kobayashi* would have dissented."

Kitano's reply was strange, considering it was not the Japanese way to "dissent" from carrying out orders. Perhaps underlying it was the fact that he and Kanbayashi were less enthusiastic about BW than Ishii.

Whitesides changed the questioning to the whereabouts of Ishii. Kitano replied he did not know. Next, he was asked about BW agents tested in the field. Kitano told the two Americans that he had worked with paratyphoid (mostly type A), typhoid, cholera, plague, anthrax, dysentery, gas gangrene and tetanus, but stressed the experiments were not "in the line of warfare".

"What prevented you from developing BW as a weapon then?" Whitesides challenged him. Once again, Kitano replied that it was not "good" to use BW and that, in his opinion, it was ineffective.

Whitesides changed the subject again. "Do you think the Harbin installation is intact?" he inquired.

"The Russians have taken it over and I do not know what has happened to it."

"What amount of time was spent on the research and other work on protection?"

"There was nothing devoted to BW, no time at all," lied Kitano.

"How many BW bombs did they drop in tests?"

"I do not know the exact figures. I think it is several tons."

"Did you know what was in the bombs?"

"Anthrax."

"Who conducted these tests?"

"The second section, under Lt-Col Ikari."

"Did these tests have any connection with the Manchurian Medical College?"

---

* Presumably Lt Gen Kanbayashi, Japan's Army Surgeon General. It is common for Japanese *kanji*, especially in proper names, to be "read" in different ways.

"No connection," replied Kitano, offering no information either on the links with the college in fundamental science, or about his somewhat unusual transfer from "academia" to the most senior military position at Pingfan.

"Where were the bombs made and, chiefly, where were the bacteria made?" continued Whitesides.

"The * section made the bacteria. The bombs were already there when I arrived."

"Did you see the bombs?"

"Yes," replied Kitano. "There were four types." (Kitano may genuinely have been unaware that Unit 731 developed nine bomb types. Some unsuitable ones were abandoned before he arrived.)

"Did they have 'mother and daughter' type?" asked Whitesides.

"I do not know," said Kitano, trying to evade the question. Such a bomb, as Sanders discovered, was tested in 1944, which was during Kitano's period as commander. He did admit, however, having seen porcelain bombs, and being aware of special artillery projectiles. The latter, he added, were effective only at short range and had received attention only during Ishii's time. He told Schwichtenberg that he was unable to estimate the weight of active ingredients, but that porcelain bombs were of two sizes, 50 kg and 100 kg.

Kitano must have been dreading the moment when Whitesides pressed him for information about who the bombs were used against. But he answered calmly: "Monkeys, rats, squirrels and other small animals."

Whitesides followed up quickly: "Did you ever hear of any Chinese prisoners being used in these tests?"

"No," replied Kitano. "No humans at all were used in these tests."

No disbelief was recorded by either Whitesides or Schwichtenberg and they passed on to question him about the effectiveness of testing on small animals. Kitano merely added that he had seen animals die in bomb blasts.

"What type of bomb was most effective?"

"Anthrax."

"What type of bomb was most effective? Fifty kg or 100 kg?"

"One hundred kg."

"What job did General Ishii have when you were in charge of water purification of the Kwantung Army?"

"He was Surgeon General of the 1st Army which was located west of Peking."

---

* Omitted from barely legible transcript that survives.

"How long had General Ishii been with the Kwantung Army when you relieved him?"

"He had been there since the founding of the Unit."

Whitesides and Schwichtenberg concluded the interview. Kitano had avoided revealing Unit 731's war crimes.

Not long after Sanders returned to the United States, the Americans decided to send another officer to complete the BW investigation. His name was Arvo T. Thompson, a Lt-Col in the Veterinary Corps, who, like his predecessor, had been drafted by the Surgeon General's Office to work at Camp Detrick. Sanders and Thompson had worked together since the earliest days of Camp Detrick, and both had investigated the Japanese balloon bombs.

Thompson received his orders the day after Christmas Day, 1945. He arrived in Japan the same day Kitano was interrogated, but was not present. Nearly a week later he was to confront Lt-Gen Shirō Ishii.

Ishii had given the slip to America's Counter Intelligence Corps (CIC) since the cessation of hostilities. But, aided by an informant, CIC finally located him, living in seclusion at his country home at Kamo.[5] CIC then requested the Japanese government to return him to his house in Wakamatsu-chō, Tokyo. Suffering then from chronic cholecystitis and dysentery, it was there that Ishii became available for interrogation on January 17th. He was interviewed through interpreters and by means of questionnaires until February 25th.[6]

Because of her father's sickness, Ishii's daughter Harumi stayed through the interview sessions, taking and typing out transcriptions. It became a daily routine in which she delivered the transcriptions to a GHQ building at the Ichigaya Garrison in Tokyo.*

According to Ishii's daughter, the interrogations became relaxed and the Americans were served meals, sometimes Western and at other times Japanese dishes like *sukiyaki*. Even MacArthur's G-2 Intelligence chief Maj-Gen Charles Willoughby visited Ishii's home to attend a dinner party.

"The chief interrogator was a man named Arvo T. Thompson, who said he had come as an emissary for President Truman," Ishii's daughter recalled.

"He literally begged my father for top secret data on germ weapons. At the same time, he emphasized that the data must not fall into the hands of the Russians."[7]

Thompson, on February 5th, was presented with an assembly of

---

* Not the NYK (Nihon Yūsen Kaisha, Japan Steamship Company) building which was G-2's headquarters in the Maranouchi area of Tokyo.

145

information; a completed questionnaire on field trials, and in a series of charts Ishii gave details of institutions and personnel connected with BW research, as well as the titles of experiments and work carried out at Pingfan.[8] Next, Thompson was given a demonstration of four water purification appliances. Then, with the assistance of technicians from a nearby Japanese military hospital, probably the Army Medical College, Ishii explained the working of the culture cabinet he had personally designed for the mass-production of bacteria. Thompson was told, however, that the cabinet had been developed primarily to meet the demand for mass vaccination. At no time, Ishii said, were bacterial agents produced and stored in quantity or available for tactical employment.

"You did no BW work except at the Army Medical College and at Heibo?"* asked Thompson.

Ishii replied that the Army Medical College was responsible for general preventive medicine science, and that BW was only researched at Pingfan.

"Was any work done at the Kyoto Imperial Institute?" Thompson continued.

"The professor there did not like that kind of work so none was undertaken," was Ishii's response.

Thompson reiterated the question. Ishii again stressed that Pingfan was the sole location.

It is surprising that Thompson did not press harder, since there was multiple intelligence including Naitō's secret testimony to Sanders, linking Ishii's Nanking Unit to BW.

Next, in a moment of high bluff, presumably designed to pre-empt and forestall awkward questions, Ishii declared that many false allegations had been maliciously circulated about his unit.

"A lot of men in my unit, and others who do not know anything about it, have been spreading rumours to the effect that some secret work has been carried on in BW, and they have gone as far as saying an attack with BW was planned by my unit and that a lot of bacteria were being produced, large quantities of bombs manufactured, airplanes gathered for that purpose. I want you to have a clear understanding that this is false."

"In other words, no work was conducted in BW except at the Heibo Institute," Thompson double-checked.

"That is correct," returned Ishii.

The interrogation record shows no disbelief on Thompson's part. He opened a new line of inquiry.

---

* Heibo was another name for Pingfan.

"Did you expect the enemy to use BW?"

"In my opinion, some countries might," Ishii replied vaguely.

"Which countries did you expect to use it?"

"Soviet Russia and China. They had used it previously and I expected them to use it again."

Ishii continued to state that he did not think America would have used BW.

"Why?" asked Thompson.

"I believed since the United States had money and materials, they would use more scientific methods," he replied, subtly belittling the Japanese effort.

Thompson inquired whether Ishii thought BW was practical.

"You have to have much money and materials to create conditions favourable to BW," he replied.

"Do you think BW is something that nations will have to contend with in the future?"

"In a winning war," replied Ishii, "there is no necessity for using BW and in a losing war, there is not the opportunity to use BW effectively. You need a lot of men, money and materials to conduct research into BW. There is little data on the effectiveness of BW as a weapon. I do not know whether BW can be used effectively on a large scale. It might be effective on a small scale."

"It might be effective under these conditions?"

"I believe," said Ishii, "that such methods could be controlled by my methods of water purification. I heard over the radio that Russia had completed its preparations for BW and it frightened me, but I did not know whether it was an actual fact or just was printed in *Red Star* or some other paper as a 'scare'. I do not know how far they have advanced in BW and have wondered what they would use if they attacked with BW."

Thompson was inquisitive about which bacteria the Russians might use. Ishii suggested tularemia, typhus fever, cholera, anthrax and plague.

"What makes you believe that the Russians would use these organisms?"

"I heard reports from people returned from Russia that the Russians had been using these organisms in their preparation for BW."

"Would it not be difficult to produce typhus organisms on a large scale?" Ishii was asked. Thompson was gently probing to find out what Ishii knew about mass culturing of bacteria.

But Ishii delicately side-stepped the question, alluding in hypothetical terms to the mass breeding of insect vectors. "If you could produce a lot of lice you might be able to produce a lot of typhus," he said. "German and Polish vaccine is prepared from lice. Trouble with lice is that you have to have human infectious blood to infect the lice. Weil's disease is produced in the same manner and it is very hard to get large quantities. If a country was rich enough, it might be able to make that disease a dangerous weapon."

It apparently never occurred to Thompson to establish whether, indeed, human blood had been used. He turned abruptly to plant BW research.

Ishii denied any involvement. "Our work was to protect soldiers," he said.

"Did anyone else concern themselves with BW against crop plants?"

"I do not know," replied Ishii.

His interrogator made no effort to pursue the matter. Thompson, a veterinarian by training, turned to questions of BW against animals.

"We did not do any experiments on large animals," said Ishii. "We used small animals as test animals. Besides, we had no veterinarians."

"Did veterinary laboratories do any research on BW?" he was asked.

"I do not know. It was such a secret that there was no communication between units. Even personnel working on experiments in my unit did not know what they were working on. Only myself, Colonel Masuda, and one or two persons knew."

"Who were the other persons?"

"There were some who suspected what was going on, but did not know. Colonel Tomosada Masuda and myself knew."

"What section of the BW institute did the BW work?"

"When those experiments came up, a number of men from each group were picked out to do the work. They were only together temporarily and were disbanded when the experiment was completed."

"Were all the people in such groups informed of the nature of the work?"

"They were not informed of what they were doing," said Ishii. "They protested that they could not carry on with their own experiments and that their regular work was being interfered with."

"Would not more progress have been made if those working on the experiment had been told what it was all about?"

"If they had known what they were working on they would have shrunk up from fright and asked for more pay. They were not well-trained men and were usually picked from the ranks."

Thompson found the answer incredible and pressed Ishii about his

General Shirō Ishii, the commander of
Unit 731

Ishii and his family in 1938. In the back row, left to right: the brothers
Takeo, Mitsuo and Shirō.

Pingfan from the air, showing the Ro block

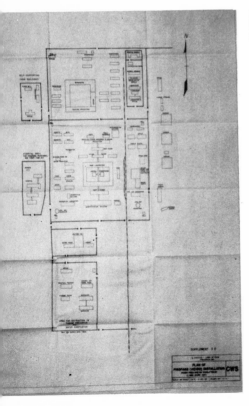

Ishii's plan of Pingfan, from the
Thompson report

Recreation at Pingfan – a staff tug-of-war

中日親善的結果

A Japanese propaganda poster of 1940, addressed to the
Chinese: prosperity if they co-operate with Japan, death if they
do not

A Japanese balloon bomb

A plane of the 731 Air Unit

Uezono in wartime uniform

Kitano in 1944

Naitō in 1980

Yoshimura in 1982

Okamoto as director of Kinki University, Osaka

Ishikawa, Unit 731 pathologist

Tanaka, the flea expert

Yagisawa, the plant expert

12.

information ...." I beg you to ~~make~~ keep ~~secret~~ this information secret, not only to General staffs, but even to General KAMBAYASHI.

I ask you to understand that I am staking my life doing this information; I shall be killed if any one knows that I have done this information. My only hope is to rescue this poor, defeated nation.

Here, in this information, must be many discourtesy because of language difficulty. In such case I ask your large-minded pardon.

I have asked Dr. Naitō whether prisoners were ever used as experimental "guinea pigs". He "vows" that this has not been the case. M. Sanders Lt. Col.

Last page of the Naitō report

Official Japanese list of members of Units 731 and 659, found at the Ministry of Health and Welfare and confiscated by GHQ

Relief supplies arriving at Mukden PoW camp

Pingfan in ruins

The last picture of Ishii in military uniform, 1946

Murray Sanders

Left to right: Arvo Thompson, Ishii's wife Kiyoko and Weber from GHQ's Legal Section, at Ishii's home in 1946

reply: "A soldier is a soldier, and could you not have ordered them to do the work?"

Somewhat flustered, Ishii replied: "They were not soldiers. They were reservists. Those in the branch units were soldiers, but not those in the main unit. I could not order them."

Implausible as the answer may have been, Thompson decided to switch subjects again.

"How much research co-operation was given by the Navy on BW?" he asked.

"There was no co-operation whatsoever," Ishii replied blandly.

"Did not some Naval medical officers attend your lectures at the Army Medical College?"

"No," said Ishii. "Naval officers are too proud. They do not have any brains, but their noses are high."

"From captured documents," insisted Thompson, "we are given to understand that certain Naval personnel received additional pay for hazardous work which included work with bacteria and certain poison gases. Evidently, the Navy must have had some part in it. Why did some personnel receive extra pay?"

"I received no reports from the Navy and I heard nothing about it," said Ishii. "The number of medical men in the Navy is less than 10 per cent of those in the Army and I doubt if they had any men capable of conducting experiments."

"What training in BW was given to the *Kenpeitai*?"

"There is a Military Police unit in Nakano-ku which was given training by some medical officers from the Army Medical College. It was just a basic information course on how to discover and report BW incidents."

Not the slightest glimmer of information was shed by Ishii on the *Kenpeitai*'s role in supplying human guinea pigs.

"Who conducted these courses?" asked Thompson.

"Colonel Tomosada Masuda and Colonel Ryōichi Naitō," said Ishii.

"Would it be possible to obtain copies of their lectures?"

"I will try and find out," promised Ishii.

The day's work with Ishii concluded on this innocuous note. The following day it was again Kitano's turn to be cross-questioned.

At this interrogation, Kitano handed over extensive information about protective ointments developed against BW agents.[9] Thompson had decided to take a tougher line.

"It is inconceivable that BW research was limited to a single institution, Heibo, when other research in Japan, equally as classified, was conducted at many institutions," Thompson stated.

"BW is a restricted subject, prohibited by the Geneva Convention and this was not an authorised activity," Kitano replied passively.

"Who authorised initiation of BW research?"

"Ishii," replied Kitano.

"What support was given BW research by the General Staff?"

"I don't know," said Kitano. "It was started before I came to Heibo. As it was secret, I don't know. Allotment of the necessary money was made by the Kwantung Army."

"Was the Emperor informed of BW research?" asked Thompson.

"No," replied Kitano. "Had the Emperor known, he would have prohibited such work."

"What support did the medical profession in Japan lend to BW research?"

"None," said Kitano.

Again, incredibly, Thompson accepted this statement despite much evidence to the contrary. Without making an attempt to ensnare his subject, Thompson modified his question. "How did the medical profession regard the BW activity?"

"Their opinion was divided, some for, some against it."

"What support was given BW by the Surgeon General?"

"None," said Kitano. "He was opposed to it."

Kitano's interrogations were now over. But two days later Ishii was again visited for a lengthy session.[10] Thompson wanted information about plague experiments.

"What field tests were made with the plague organism?" he asked.

"Due to the danger of it, there were no field experiments with that organism. There were a great many field mice in Manchuria and it would have been dangerous to conduct field experiments with plague because the field mice would very easily carry the organisms and start an epidemic. We conducted experiments with plague in the laboratory," said Ishii.

"What kind of experiments?" Thompson inquired.

"We put rats in cages inside the room and sprayed the whole room with plague bacteria. This was to determine how the rats became infected, whether through the eyes, nose, mouth, or through the skin."

"What did you find out?"

"The results were not too favourable. We usually got 10 per cent infection."

"By which way?"

"That was the total," said Ishii, misunderstanding the question.

"What route was the most effective?" Thompson repeated.

"Through the nose," said Ishii. "Also, through an open wound.

Animals were shaved and it was found that they would become infected through the microscopic abrasions caused by the shaving. We found that the lymph nodes became inflamed. That is how we knew if the animal had been infected."

"Was this spray test conducted in a special chamber or in an ordinary room?" asked Thompson.

"It was not a special chamber," said Ishii. "The windows were double-plated and paper was put all over the walls. The room was made as airtight as possible. Human beings did not enter the room. They conducted the test from an outside corridor."

Thompson must have been surprised at such crude facilities. Camp Detrick had a sophisticated cloud chamber. But like most of his fellow Americans he may have held Japanese capabilities in sceptical disregard. In any event, he continued to allow Ishii to develop his story.

"Was there not any danger in handling the animals after the experiment?" Thompson asked. "And also was it not dangerous because of the bacteria still being in the air?"

"After the experiment, we sprayed formalin in the room and did not enter it for one day," said Ishii.

"How were you protected while handling the animals?"

"We wore protective clothing, masks, and rubber shoes. Before we touched the animals, we put the cages, animals, and all, into a solution of creosol."

"How long after the experiment?"

"After one day."

"The bacteria could have spread all over the room during that day," Thompson observed.

"Yes," agreed Ishii, "there was a danger of that. We put the cage with the animal into a small container smaller than the culture medium [cabinet, perhaps] to transport it."

"Did you have any accidents in the laboratory or nearby as a result of the experiments?"

"Yes," said Ishii. "A person who handled the animals after the experiment got infected and died."

Thompson wanted to know if any people outside Pingfan had become infected.

"No," replied Ishii. "The person who handled the animals went into the room and I believe he caught it from handling the animals," he added, gently side-tracking Thompson's question. "I do not believe the theory that bacteria can be floating in the air after one day."

"Was plague ever tested in bombs or shells?"

"We did not try it because it is too weak. It would be destroyed in five minutes in the sunlight."

His reply was carefully measured. If "bare" bacteria were being spread, Ishii's answer was correct, and he would have known Thompson would have been aware of that. But his reply omitted any mention of the possibility of using an insect vector such as a flea.

"Do you believe the plague organism has any value as a BW agent?" asked Thompson.

"Due to its weakness, I do not believe there is any value in it," said Ishii, backing up his previous answer.

Ishii was wise to be suspicious of Thompson's line of questioning, for Thompson was next to put to him allegations of the use of plague BW in China.

"We have heard from Chinese sources that plague was started in Changteh, China, in 1941, by airplanes flying over and dropping plague material and a plague resulted. Do you know anything about this?" Thompson challenged him.

Ishii flatly denied the accusation, and went on: "It is impossible from a scientific point of view to drop plague organisms from airplanes."

"But," said Thompson, "rats, rags and bits of cotton infected with plague were dropped and later picked up by the Chinese and that is how it was to have started."

"If you drop rats from airplanes," retorted Ishii, "they will die. There is no chance of a human being catching plague as a result of dropping organisms from an airplane."

Thompson's reaction to this scathing remark is not recorded, but once again he abruptly changed his line of questioning, asking about yellow fever experiments. Ishii denied such experiments, stating such work was unnecessary because the particular species of mosquito carrier did not exist in Japan.

"Would not yellow fever virus be a good BW agent?" asked Thompson.

"There is no virus in Japan," said Ishii.

"No culture anywhere?"

"None."

Thompson momentarily became more insistent. "We have evidence that Japan tried to obtain the yellow fever virus from the Rockefeller Institute," he accused.

Ishii was well prepared for that. With equanimity he replied: "I heard that somebody from the Japanese Infectious Disease Institute was sent to try and obtain the yellow fever virus from America, but was refused. This person was a representative of the Imperial Japanese government."

(On the intelligence report of that incident,[11] if Thompson had read it carefully, was the name of Ryōichi Naitō. Naitō had tried to get the virus from the Rockefeller Institute. He was a member of Unit 731, not an emissary from the Imperial Japanese government.) Thompson went on to ask why this representative wanted to obtain the virus if no preventive measures were necessary.

"It was probably to be used in preparation of a vaccine to inoculate persons who were to travel south through infested areas," said Ishii. "I had no concern in this."

In fact, as the Intelligence file on the Rockefeller incident had made perfectly clear, yellow fever was completely unknown in south-east Asia and the south-west Pacific.

"Were attempts made to obtain the virus from other countries?"

"There is probably no yellow fever virus in other countries," Ishii replied. "It must be the United States alone so there were no other attempts."

Thompson made no further attempt to force the issue. "Have you ever been under the control of the Russian authorities during the last year?" inquired Thompson.

"No. I am afraid some members in the branch departments have been captured by the Russians. However, those members do not know anything of importance."

"Who first authorised the beginning of BW research in Japan?"

"There were no orders giving consent to research in BW," said Ishii. "If there were, we would have received all the money, personnel and materials we wanted to carry on this research. Since there were no orders, we only conducted the BW research on a very small scale (1 to 2 per cent) in the Water Purification Bureau."

It was a reply rich in irony and revealed Ishii's complete contempt for his interviewer.

Thompson plainly did not believe him. "Who in the War Ministry gave official approval to permit the work to be carried on?" he asked.

In a misleading reply, Ishii deprecated the scientific bent of members of the War Ministry.

"Most of them were of the old school which depended upon the spirit of the Japanese people and not scientific methods to win the war. They did not listen to any of my requests. I did not ask for help directly from the War Ministry. I had to go through channels which meant through the Kwantung Army."

Obviously dissatisfied with the answer he had been given,

Thompson followed up with the blunt demand whether the War Ministry had been the source of finance.

"I would hand in my request for funds," Ishii replied calmly. "There was no appropriation entitled BW. It all came under preventive medicine and water purification."

"When was official approval first given to start work on BW and by whom?"

"There was no official sanctioning."

"That is hard to believe," said Thompson.

"If I had labelled my request 'BW' it would have been cut off by the higher-ups. It was all under preventive medicine and water purification. When I received the money I used it at my own discretion."

"Would not better progress have been made if official approval had been obtained?"

"Yes," said Ishii. "If the higher-ups had brains and scientific know-how, a great deal of progress could have been made. They believed too much in faith."

Thompson was by now exasperated. "I want information on who was informed of BW work," he demanded. "Was the Minister of War informed?"

"On the whole I do not know he knew about it," was Ishii's carefully-worded response.

"As far as you know, was the Minister of War informed?"

"I never reported to the Minister of War personally about BW," said Ishii, again evading the question.

"Did the Minister of War have access to BW reports?"

"I personally did not speak to the Minister of War and I do not know," said Ishii, reiterating his previous answers.

"Was the Chief of the Medical Bureau of the War Ministry, the Surgeon General, informed?"

"I think he knew," admitted Ishii.

"How was he informed?"

"Through connections with the Kwantung Army."

"Did you have personal contact with the Surgeon General on BW matters?"

"Not in public," said Ishii. "But at private discussions I mentioned it once."

"Did he co-operate in BW research?"

"He was opposed to it because there were not enough medical officers and he could not spare any for this type of work."

"Was the Kwantung Army Commander informed of the progress of the work?"

"I have not met that person to talk to him," said Ishii. "Reports concerning BW were considered so highly secret that they were not reported to the Kwantung Army directly. It may have gone by oral methods.''

By now Thompson had gone beyond exasperation. He was openly incredulous. "But any Army commander would know what was going on under his command. Was he not informed as the work went along?''

"The work was delegated to the Water Purification Bureau and that was water purification and prevention of diseases. There was no sense in giving reports of such a technical nature to a person who would not understand. Most of the work was of a defensive nature. If it was to be used as a weapon, it would come under the infantry and I would have to report it, but this was confined to medical research.''

"Who gave the authority to manufacture the BW bombs?''

"There was no official consent,'' said Ishii. "All we used were some left-over bomb shells which the Kwantung Army got from some source. The casing was just plated with another iron plate and that became the *Ha* bomb. We did not require much money.''

"Was the Commander of the Kwantung Army in favour of BW research?''

"I never met that man and I do not know what his opinion was,'' stated Ishii.

"I cannot see how this work could be done without anybody's approval?'' said Thompson.

"I could not achieve what I had planned due to the fact that I did not receive approval.''

"I am led to understand that you started this work under your own initiative and carried it out on your own responsibility,'' Thompson summarised, in an attempt to put some vestige of logic into Ishii's incredible answers.

Ishii merely replied, 'Yes.''

"Was the Emperor informed of BW research?''

"Not at all,'' replied Ishii. "The Emperor is a lover of humanity and never would have consented to such a thing.''

"Why were you relieved of your command and why was General Kitano put in as chief?''

"In my opinion, my being sent to the 1st Army was due to the fact that higher-ups did not want me to continue BW research. But, in order to be promoted to Lieutenant-General, I had to do some service in the field as head of a unit. I could not be promoted to that grade if I were in the laboratory. After I had been promoted, I could go back to the laboratory in my new grade.''

"Which position was most important?'' asked Thompson.

"Surgeon General of the 1st Army was the most important because I was responsible for the health of a division, 100,000 men."

"Were any BW bombs manufactured at the Mukden arsenal?"

"I do not know," said Ishii. "I just requisitioned them and they were provided."

"The *Uji*-type bomb was specially made for BW," said Thompson. "Who made them?"

"The old laboratory in Harbin, which manufactured the water filters, had the facilities for baking the porcelain and the same equipment was used for making the bombs as was used for the manufacture of water filters. Most trouble I had was trying to get technicians for baking porcelain. The technicians occupied a separate room in the factory and they made a small inner-factory for the manufacture of the porcelain bombs."

"Why was not the assistance of regular ordnance officers used in making the bombs?"

"In ordnance they deal only with iron bombs," said Ishii. "They would not take the responsibility for making porcelain bombs. It does not take too much trouble to make the bombs. We could manufacture the bombs as we pleased and make any changes or improvements which we felt were necessary."

Thompson asked why Ishii had not tried to get official approval for his munitions work. Ishii replied that he had tried, but failed.

Thompson rounded on him: "Who did you try to get approval from?"

"I had to go through channels," said Ishii, cautiously. "The first agency, the Kwantung Army, turned my requests down several times. If BW had been a weapon which was very good, it might have been different. But it was more or less some kind of scientific imagination and was still in the theoretical stage. In the Japanese Army, you have to prove over a period of years that a thing is good before it will be accepted."

"Why did you not go to your friends in Japan who had friends in high circles?"

"It was difficult," said Ishii. "There were not enough men who were scientifically-minded to go to for assistance. If it was a proposition that would make them some money they might help, but not with this."

"Had they no patriotic feelings?"

"If there was such a person as Rockefeller who had the cash and the spirit there might have been some chance."

"What work was done at Pingfan Institute with the trans-oceanic balloon?"

"None," replied Ishii. "I think it was carried out in a scientific laboratory in Japan."

"Are you acquainted with the 9th Army Technical Laboratory at Noborito?"

"I heard that the experiments on the balloon were being carried out in Japan but I do not know where."

"Did you have any connection with that work?"

"None," said Ishii.

Thompson concluded the interview with some questions about Ishii's long-standing friend Tomosada Masuda, wanting to know whether he might know more about bomb trials than his commander. Ishii replied that he believed not.

Thompson completed his interrogations with Ishii by February 25th. But the movement of American officers in and out of Ishii's house continued long afterwards, observed by many local residents.

"About ten o'clock at night I would see American officers and young Japanese hostesses go into Ishii's house and, very frequently, I would see them leave early in the morning," said local barber Kiyoshi Fijino.[12]

Two days after Thompson had finished his interrogations with Ishii, *Pacific Stars and Stripes* followed up their first story with a front page article, about Ishii's interrogation. Though the emphasis was on Ishii's preventive work, the article disclosed his admission that he had invented the porcelain "plague-bomb" and described him as "a determined, almost ruthless individual".[13]

Thompson continued his interrogations until March 11th.

Unit 731 pharmacy officer Major Yoshiyasu Masuda, a trained pilot, was interviewed about bomb trials.[14] Masuda denied involvement, although he admitted such trials had taken place. He also denied meeting Ishii. In fact, according to Issue 283 of the *Japanese Army Medical Journal*, Masuda and Ishii had worked together on preparations for the fiftieth anniversary celebrations of the Army Medical College on November 7th, 1936.

Thompson next travelled to Kyoto, interviewing Lt-Col Yoshitaka Sasaki on February 20th.[15] Sasaki admitted involvement with the construction of Pingfan and its Songo branch, briefly serving as the sub-unit's chief in 1940.

Thompson immediately challenged him about human experimentation. "Have you heard whether the Chinese or PoWs were used in BW experiments?" he demanded.

"I do not know," Sasaki replied, although involvement in construction would have acquainted him with Pingfan's prison blocks. He told

Thompson he had only worked in water purification, and went on to produce the by now familiar answers to all the American's awkward questions.

Thompson had heard enough. He turned to Sasaki and asked him frankly what other men thought of Ishii.

"A famous man with great executive ability and a good head on his shoulders, smart," replied Sasaki.

"Did he have any enemies?"

"I think he had a lot of enemies and a lot of friends. He was an important person."

Thompson wrote the following note after the interrogation:

It is obvious from the answers Lt-Col Sasaki gave us to all the questions on BW that he knew nothing whatsoever about the investigation being carried out in this field at Pingfan. Since such work was top secret and on a relatively small scale compared to the greater part of the work being carried out at Pingfan, men in Sasaki's capacity were not likely to be in a position to know about BW.

Two further interviewees, Admiral Shigetarō Shimada, Navy Minister from October 1941 to July 1944, and Naitō, also yielded little information.[16] Shimada explained captured documentation on the Mark 7 bacteria bomb as having been created "by personnel responsible for drafting Navy regulations who possibly imagined BW with an eye to the future". Naitō claimed his work on *fūgū* toxin had failed because the poison could not be concentrated.

Like his predecessor Colonel Sanders, Thompson had been duped by the Japanese. This can be seen from the report he submitted to Camp Detrick. It should not escape attention, however, that in his conclusions, Thompson expressed some deep reservations. A key sentence read: "It is evident from the progress that was made that BW research and development in all its phases was conducted on a large scale and was officially sanctioned and supported by the highest military authority." Among the conclusions were the following:

The information regarding Japanese BW activities obtained from presumably independent sources was consistent to the point where it seems that the informants had been instructed as to the amount and nature of information that was to be divulged under interrogation . . .

Some of the information, especially sketches of the bombs, was in such detail as to question the contention that all documentary evidence had been destroyed.

It was evident throughout the interrogations that it was the desire of the Japanese to minimize the extent of their activities in BW, especially the effort devoted to offensive research and development . . .*

Thompson's doubts were scattered throughout his report in remarks like:

On the subject of BW research and development, Ishii's replies to questions were guarded, concise and often evasive. On the subject of preventive medical research, water supply and purification, Ishii spoke freely. It was apparent throughout the interviews that he desired to emphasize the activities pertaining to preventive medicine, water purification and supply, and to minimize the BW aspects of the organization he directed.

Elsewhere Thompson wrote, "Ishii estimated this diversion of funds for BW research to be about 1 to 2 per cent of the appropriation . . . His estimate, however, is not in conformity with a later admission in which Ishii stated that about 20 per cent of the research was devoted to BW. Throughout the interrogation Ishii endeavoured to leave the impression that BW research was conducted only on a very small scale . . ." And on another page he stated: "Regardless of Ishii's contention . . . it is evident that BW research and development in all its phases was conducted on a large scale, was officially sanctioned, and was supported by the highest military authorities."

Thompson was doubtful whether all BW information had been destroyed.

In all probability [wrote Thompson], much of the information Ishii presented was compiled with the assistance of his former associates at Pingfan, several of whom were present in Tokyo and vicinity at the time. He had ample opportunity to consult his former associates since the interrogations were intermittent and much of the information was presented by charts and written answers to questionnaires.

Judging by the reports Sanders and Thompson completed, the Japanese appear to have carried off the most extraordinary feat of sustained collusion. This was achieved despite the fact that evidence of war crimes lay scattered everywhere. It is true that the Americans

---

* For the text of Thompson's report summary, see Appendix C.

were unwilling forcibly to extract information or confessions from the Japanese. But it still seems incredible that the Camp Detrick men as well as MacArthur's Intelligence Service performed so poorly.

If it is untenable to accept that the Americans fared so badly – in the Soviet Union at this time the Russians were having much more success with their captured Japanese PoWs – then perhaps another explanation could be entertained. Suppose Sanders, and more particularly Thompson, were prevented by some of their own compatriots from uncovering the full story. Perhaps the two men were "cocooned" to a certain extent. It must remain a hypothesis until pertinent records appear. However, certain puzzling, disparate and contradictory pieces of information would fall into place if it was accepted.

First, Sanders asserted that he was given evidence of human experimentation while still in Japan. That evidence was never included in either of his reports, although it would have given considerable leverage to future American investigators attempting to gain more information from the reluctant Japanese. Why was it not included? What was done with it?

Second, there is evidence of an extraordinarily high, and early, degree of co-operation (not a lack of it) between some American Occupation forces and certain members of Unit 731. For example, a document recently returned to Japan's National Archives in Tokyo entitled *On Frostbite, October 26, 1941, 731st Unit, Manchuria, Army Technician, Hisato Yoshimura*, a special lecture at the Harbin Branch of the 15th Manchurian Medical Academy Conference, bears a date stamp in English, "October 17th, 1945". The remarkable feature of the document is that, with a reasonable degree of deduction, evidence of human experimentation could have been discerned from its contents.[17]

To add to the mystery, a number of strange incidents occurred around the time of Thompson's visit. According to the recollections of former members of Unit 731, Kitano later revealed to a former subordinate with whom he was intimate, that "just prior to the American Army inquiry, GHQ gave Ishii and myself a hearing and granted us permission to consult with each other in order that we could arrange not to contradict each other over items which were to be kept secret."[18]

Another account about this period states:

The Americans knew that Ishii, Kitano, etc, had secretly fled back to Japan after the end of the war and they planned to make secret contact with them. Between the end of 1945 and the early months of 1946, the Americans held secret meetings with Ishii and ranking officers (Maj-Gen to Lt-Gen), a total of five persons, in a restaurant in Kamakura.

During these meetings, Ishii revealed all of the information about the experimentation and the bacteriological weapons. In return for providing the data that he had brought back from Manchuria, he asked that none of the unit members would be indicted for war crimes. The Americans accepted this condition and the secret contract between them was thus made. I was told these facts by a former military physician, a Lt-Col (born in 1902), in Osaka, who had been a member of the 731st. This former Lt-Col said: "When I met Ishii after the war, he would boast, 'It is I who helped you guys out!' The persons involved in these secret meetings called them the 'Kamakura Conference'."[19]

These pieces of information do not appear to rest easily inside the mould of either the Sanders or Thompson reports. But if other Americans were involved, as seems possible, then who were they? If a certain section, or sections, of the American forces in Japan did not wish full public revelations about the activities of Unit 731 then why did they also want the matter kept secret from Washington? Some interacting factors can be considered.

BW was known to have incredible potential, sufficient, perhaps, for MacArthur and his men to worry that if the Japanese data fell into Soviet hands, then this might jeopardise national security. They would also have known that a full-scale public war crimes trial, likely to have been precipitated by the moral outrage in Washington at the discovery of human experimentation, would have been inconsistent with that need for security – better to prevent Washington from knowing.

There perhaps existed a strong community of interest between MacArthur's Intelligence men and the Chemical Corps – both were suspicious of Washington – which could easily have made this possible.

MacArthur defended the independence of his Occupation of Japan vigorously. Tokyo was a long way from Washington, and he and many trusted subordinates were deeply suspicious of the politics of Capitol Hill. Most saw themselves as "realists" out in the field, not weak-kneed "moralists" sitting back at home. They regarded Japan as a front line bastion against Russian expansionism and a crucial battleground for democracy and a free world.

The Chemical Warfare Service was likewise alienated from Washington. Throughout the Second World War President Roosevelt had opposed the CWS's activities, holding, unlike

Churchill, a particular aversion to poison gas warfare. He regarded it as barbaric and inhuman. His attitude was well expressed by Admiral Leahy, his senior naval adviser and later President Truman's Chief of Staff. Using gas, said Leahy, would "violate every Christian ethic I have ever heard of and all the known laws of war".[20] Right up until Roosevelt's death, the CWS complained that any proposal it put forward would not be "seriously considered" but "immediately rejected due to personal bias" by the President.[21]

Camp Detrick's relationship to the nation's top policy makers may have been much more intimate, for biological warfare service founder George Merck had become the Secretary of War's special consultant on BW. The more hardened officers of the Army Chemical Corps presumably viewed the Detrick "academics" with some suspicion.

Dr Riley Housewright, who worked at Detrick during the war, becoming branch chief for antibiotics research in the immediate post-war period, remembered something of that relationship.

> They didn't take us very seriously. We were the new kid on the block. They didn't have much respect. We were essentially civilians. I came from Chicago. We were not in any way connected with the old line Chemical Corps and its old boy network. Although the work was done at Detrick under the aegis of the Chemical Corps, they had no people trained in the biological sciences, the infectious diseases area.[22]

Supporting evidence of a more general conflict between Washington and those running the day-to-day activities of the BW service is to be found in a briefing given to the British Chief of the Imperial General Staff, Field Marshal Montgomery. On August 14th, 1946, just before he was to visit Canada and America his deputy chief wrote:

> Enclosure "C" deals generally with the question of interchange of information with the Americans.
> You will note from Enclosure "D" that over Biological Warfare we get the fullest possible information from the American Department concerned, but, unless you are specifically asked, it might be best not to state this fact, as it is always possible that a higher American authority might discourage the Biological Warfare Department concerned from being too forthcoming. As is stated in Enclosure "C", the amount of information we get depends entirely on the views and personality of the officer concerned, and they all ask us not to make any official approach on this question of the

interchange of information as they are all frightened of agreeing openly to a definite policy, owing to the suspicious and uncertain attitude of Congress.[23]

If it is *not* to be believed that America performed so abysmally in its BW intelligence operation, then it is possible to entertain an alternative: this is, that MacArthur's Intelligence chiefs unified their interests with senior members of the 1,000-strong Chemical Section troops in Japan in order to withhold information, for their own interests and their perceived notions of the interests of national security.

This would have been a moderately simple task to accomplish. G-2 could easily have debriefed Thompson's interviewees on a daily basis, before he talked to them. Furthermore, through its control over interpreters G-2 could ensure that the "right" story was being told by the Japanese.

According to the February 27th *Pacific Stars and Stripes*, Thompson conducted all his interrogations "under the supervision of Lt-Col D. S. Tait, Technical Intelligence, and with the help of Lt E. M. Ellis of the War Department Intelligence Section". Ellis was, in fact, the interpreter. In his full report, Thompson noted that many of his interviewees had already been interrogated. His report stated that ". . . personnel associated with this activity [BW] became available for interrogation and were interviewed in Japan by personnel from War Department Intelligence Targets: G-2, GHQ, Allied Forces Pacific Area Command, and from the Chemical Warfare Service."

It is worthy of note that of the large volume of records about Unit 731 now acceded to public archives in America, none belongs to the BW activities of precisely these three sections – G-2 Technical Intelligence, Chemical Section and War Department Intelligence Targets. These sections would have been responsible for the day-to-day management of important Intelligence targets like Ishii. Vigorous requests through the Freedom of Information Act have also failed to locate these crucial record groups.

Thompson finally completed his report on May 31st, 1946. It materially added to knowledge of the construction of Unit 731's bacteria bombs and mass culturing techniques, but little more. Already, another man was on the trail of Unit 731. His name was Lt-Col Thomas H. Morrow, a member of the bar of the State of Ohio on leave from the Court of Common Pleas in that state, and attached to the International Prosecution Section (IPS) of the Tokyo trial. His special concern was the preparation of the prosecution's case concerning Japanese military aggression in China.

Chapter 12

Evidence and Trials

Brilliant photo floodlights dazzled the auditorium of the old Japanese War Ministry building. Carefully remodelled, it looked more like a Hollywood movie set than a courtroom. Here, at Ichigaya Garrison, Tokyo, on May 3rd, 1946, the International Military Tribunal for the Far East was opened. The world's press and film cameramen were in attendance. The alterations to the auditorium had been made especially to facilitate photographic and press coverage, and to heighten the sense of dignity surrounding the trial. On a high bench were seats for eleven justices, one for each Allied country that had helped defeat Japan. Two seats were empty, waiting for court members to arrive in Japan. The high bench looked directly across and down at the dock. There sat twenty-eight defendants. Stripped by MacArthur of their titles and uniforms these men – once the most powerful in Japan – included one Field Marshal, nine full Generals, four Lt-Generals, one Colonel, one Fleet Admiral, one Admiral and one Vice-Admiral. Five of these military men had once been War Ministers, and two had held the post of Navy Minister. Eleven of the defendants could be described as bureaucrats, five of whom were career diplomats. Fifteen of them had at one time in their career held ministerial rank; eight were known to have strong militarist views; three were extreme nationalists and eight belonged to the nobility. Towering over the accused stood American military police, chosen especially for their height and muscular build, somehow underscoring the Allies' intention to mete out "stern justice".

Sir William Webb, a somewhat coarse, abrasive and opinionated Australian named by MacArthur as President of the Tribunal, opened the proceedings by describing an affirmation, signed minutes before by all the nine judges present, to "administer justice according to law and without fear, favour, or affection".[1] "To our great task," he continued, "we bring open minds both on the facts and on the law." On behalf of the prosecution chief counsel Joseph B. Keenan read the indictment. Late that afternoon all the defendants pleaded not guilty. The trial began. It would last fully two and a half years.

In the summer of 1945 the Big Four had met in London to draw up the charter for the trial of Germany's major war criminals, a court which in due course would sit in Nuremberg. At this conference it was decided that Nazi Germany's leaders would be tried not only for conventional war crimes, but also for two new types of crime. The term "war criminal" referred before 1945 to men found guilty of *conventional* war crimes. But now the Allies proposed to cast the net of criminality wider to include crimes against peace and against humanity.

Crimes against peace were defined as ". . . planning, preparation, initiation or waging a war of aggression, or war in violation of international treaties, agreements or assurances, or participation in a common plan or conspiracy for the accomplishment of any of the foregoing". Crimes against humanity were defined as ". . . inhumane acts committed against any civilian population, before or during the war . . ."[2]

While this conference in London was still in session, the Allies publicly announced their intention to prosecute Japanese war criminals. In the Potsdam Declaration of July 26th, the Allies called "upon the Government of Japan to proclaim now Unconditional Surrender of all Japanese armed forces and to provide proper and adequate assurance of their good faith in such action. The alternative for Japan is prompt and utter destruction." They announced that: "We do not intend that the Japanese shall be enslaved as a race or destroyed as a nation but stern justice shall be meted out to all war criminals, including those who have visited cruelties upon our prisoners . . ."[3]

Unlike the war crimes trials in Germany, however, only one country, America, was charged with setting up military tribunals within Japan. Acknowledging United States' military supremacy in Japan proper, the United Nations War Crimes Commission rested the responsibility of trying the Japanese major war criminals with the American Supreme Allied Commander in the Pacific. General MacArthur received his instructions from America's State-War-Navy (Departments) Co-ordinating Committee (SWNCC). In the latter part of October these instructions to MacArthur were communicated to the other members of the UN War Crimes Commission and to the USSR. No equivalent of the London conference was held to draft the Tokyo trial charter, a fact which considerably annoyed Britain, Australia and Russia.[4]

MacArthur's powers were sweeping. In the communication to the UN War Crimes Commission MacArthur "requested the designation by the interested Allied Nations of suitable individuals for appointment to the international courts to be established for the trial of Far Eastern war criminals".[5] The Supreme Commander was empowered to appoint special military courts and prescribe and approve rules of procedure for such courts. He was required to establish, promptly, an agency acting under his command which would collect and analyse evidence, arrange for the apprehension and prompt trial of suspects, prepare, supervise and conduct the prosecution of individuals and organisations before military courts or tribunals and to recommend back to him which individuals and organisations should be prosecuted, before what courts they should be tried and what persons should be secured as witnesses.[6] MacArthur was also given the responsibility for carrying out judgments. He had "the power to approve, reduce or otherwise alter any sentence imposed by such a court or tribunal, but not to increase the severity thereof . . ."[7]

Like MacArthur, Chief Prosecutor Keenan also derived his powers directly from the decisions of the US government. In this, and in many other matters relating to the Tokyo trial, other nations were forced into reluctantly ratifying the unilateral actions of the US government. The only alternative facing these nations was to cease involvement with the trial. On November 27th, Keenan was appointed by President Truman as the chief prosecutor at the IMTFE. A fortnight later he arrived in Tokyo with an assortment of forty-five lawyers and a similar number of clerical assistants. Keenan's appointment was a purely political act designed to give him the publicity profile he would need to win a future US Senate race against "Mr Republican", Robert Taft of Ohio.[8] Prior to his appointment by Truman, Keenan had been a New Deal bureaucrat and politician. President Franklin D. Roosevelt had called him "Joe the Key", presumably for his liaison work on Capitol Hill. Criminal law was his forte. Before the war he had written the Lindbergh kidnapping law and served as gang-busting head of the Criminal Division of the Department of Justice. *Time* magazine suggested a resemblance, with his florid face, to W. C. Fields.[9]

"The day after I arrived," recalled Keenan, "I met with the Supreme Commander, whom I found tremendously interested in the subject matter of the prosecutions and who emphasized the avoidance of delay, because, as he explained, certain aspects of the Occupation could not be dealt with until after the successful completion of the trials."[10]

Soon after this – much to the disgust of some of his senior aides who tried unsuccessfully to restrain him – Keenan handed control of the whole International Prosecution Section (IPS) to MacArthur. Keenan's authority derived directly from the President of the United States and he was not required to take this course of action. MacArthur's power had swollen yet again.[11]

*   *   *

166

Japan was a bewildering place for most of the American prosecution team, and for Keenan himself. A glimpse of the confusing world into which they were thrown can be seen from a record of one of their first briefing meetings. On December 10th, the prosecutors met at the Meiji building, Tokyo, to discuss at length the term "international tribunal" and to be given assignments. Lt-Col Henry Sackett, head of IPS's document section, then addressed the meeting. "The Japanese government is intact. Therefore, we [the American Occupation] are not a military government."

Sackett outlined some of the practical problems.

The Japanese Government surrendered on August 17, 1945, after which the Jap Government ordered all records to be destroyed. The first Occupation Forces arrived on September 2, 1945, two weeks after this order was issued. The Occupation Forces did not put guards on buildings or take over the functions. General MacArthur never issued any orders to departments or individuals – he told the Emperor what orders he wanted issued and then the Emperor issued the orders to the Japanese people.

No Allied officer attached to this Headquarters had access to any Government files nor could interview any person connected with the Jap Government; could not go into War, Navy Department or Foreign Office and look at any records.

Sackett explained that, until the previous week if any Occupation personnel wanted information from the Japanese, it was not obtained through investigations but by submitting a questionnaire to a Japanese central organisation which acted as a liaison office between General MacArthur and the Emperor. But this method had proved useless, he said, because in response to every question the answer had been "so sorry, no records".

We don't know what is in the government departments, he said. We don't know how much was burned and how much is left here by way of documents to be examined. Particularly within the last few months, Sackett explained, the Japanese had had plenty of time to burn them since the arrest of the so-called Japanese criminals and the publicity about the war crimes trials.

Now, said Sackett, the policy had changed. The Emperor had acquiesced in a request from SCAP headquarters and had signed a pass entitling entry to any government department, and to interview officials and look at records. The pass had gone into effect about a week ago.

We will go into the records of the Foreign Office first, then Cabinet meetings, high Army, Navy and Planning Council of the Cabinet, etc and things of that nature which will be of value [the memorandum recorded]. We can assume that the top Japanese people have destroyed their personal records. Japs are diary keepers. They will say they have none. The thinking of the top man is similar to the German in charge: "I am an authority, I am responsible, no purpose questioning my subordinates." They attempt to stop investigation at the top because they feel they are smarter and can cover up more successfully. The Jap will talk and as long as a man talks, he will talk himself into jail. The Jap has a phobia relative to implicating others – doesn't want to say anything to implicate others. If you ask who else was responsible at that time, he will say he doesn't know. If you ask "How may I corroborate this?" he will give you the information. When he is surprised, he will suck his breath and sometimes the nerves under his ears will twitch . . . If the Japs can justify a lie in their own minds, they will do so.[12]

Gradually, documents began to emerge. Some had been moved to caves 10 to 20 miles outside Tokyo. Although prosecutors had no way of guessing whether documents existed or not, persistent requests frequently brought results. Information rapidly swelled to a torrent.

On January 19th, 1946, as General Order No 1 issued by GHQ, MacArthur promulgated the first charter of the trial. Nine countries were named as having an active part in the prosecution and judgment. They were Australia, Canada, China, France, the Netherlands, New Zealand, the USSR, the UK and the US. Shortly after this announcement prosecution teams from the other Allied countries began to arrive in Tokyo to work with their American counterparts. Later, on April 26th, 1946, only three days before the lodging of the indictment against the accused, the nine countries named in the original charter were joined by India and the Philippines.[13]

The eight-man British delegation to the Tokyo trial had been quickly thrown together. Five had legal qualifications – Sir Arthur Comyns Carr, KC, David Scott Fox of the Foreign Office, Rex Davies, Maurice Reed of the Attorney General's Office and Christmas Humphreys (President of the Buddhist Society in London for more than two decades).

"The party was led by Comyns Carr, KC, a Counsel with an enormous practice in the High Court, particularly in rating appeals," recounted Humphreys.

168

I had appeared in one or two cases against him, but hardly knew him as a man, and the same applied to the third of our team, Rex Davies, who later died so tragically in an air crash in Hong Kong. Maurice Reed of the Attorney General's Office came with us to help on the administrative side, and David Scott Fox of the Foreign Office to smooth our way at Washington, and to introduce us to our Embassy and its amenities in Japan.

Because Fox returned to his official duties in London before the end of March 1946, and as Humphreys spent much of his time enriching his understanding of Japanese Buddhism, after barely six months in Japan the British team was seriously under strength. In any event, as Humphreys wrote rather defensively, "No team of lawyers ever left for court with less instructions. We knew literally nothing about the form of the indictment, the men to be charged or the place or duration of the trial, and it was only when we arrived in Tokyo that we realised that the whole prosecution shared our ignorance."[14]

A foot of snow lay on the ground on February 3rd, the day the British contingent arrived. News that Keenan had a list of no fewer than 100 potential accused had added urgency to their dispatch.[15] While still en route, Keenan's behaviour caused even more anxiety. He had raised the question of a possible Japanese share in the prosecution of war criminals, thereby causing great consternation in Allied circles.[16] This ludicrous suggestion perhaps reflected Keenan's inability to comprehend the nature of the Japanese situation.

Every Western-style hotel surviving the destruction of Tokyo had been taken over for billets by the Allies. The city's famous Imperial Hotel became home for the trial's eleven judges. The British team, together with all the other Commonwealth prosecutors, were housed in the luxurious Canadian Legation. But, despite the pleasant life of the Legation, the British team found the trial's preparation in a mess. The task of organising the prosecution and indictment had been too much for Keenan. Comyns Carr quickly realised that the American efforts were in disarray. In a furious letter to the Attorney General in London, Comyns Carr complained that he had found everything in total chaos on his arrival, with enormous stacks of documentation left untranslated.

Comyns Carr's complaints earned him a reward. He was appointed chairman of an executive committee to sort out the mess. Comyns Carr's committee was the linchpin in the prosecutors' endeavours to bring together the trial indictment. It determined matters of general policy, co-ordinated and directed the work of all other committees, settled questions of international law relating to the trial, the terms of the indictment, the evidence supporting it and the defendants to be tried.[17]

The British were struck by the complexity of the Japanese situation as it led up to the Pacific War. Maurice Reed wrote in a letter on April 16th: "The difficulties of drafting and agreeing the defendants have been much greater than over the Nuremberg indictment in that Japan never had any consistent party like the Nazis, and out of a plethora of possible defendants responsible since 1931, only a few can be picked from a very competitive bunch."[18]

The executive committee set about its work. Compiling the list of defendants went on side by side with the accumulation of evidence against them. A dossier was prepared on the case against some fifty or sixty men. Week by week these dossiers were considered by the executive committee, who voted them "in" or "out" or "deferred for further consideration". In the early stages some prosecutors thought fifteen defendants would be sufficient to represent those who had led Japan into war. But as prosecutors from each of the ten countries arrived more names were added until the "ins" reached twenty-eight. Significantly, General Umezu's name was only added at the last minute on the insistence of the Soviets who had been late in arriving. Umezu's name had originally figured on the British, American and Chinese lists but had been dropped for lack of evidence.[19]

Keenan declared that all the defendants had been selected by "a truly democratic prosecution, in the sense that all the accused were selected by a majority vote of the prosecutors from the various nations". Yet patently this selection procedure was a highly political process of "give and take".[20]

The drafting of the indictment was almost entirely Comyns Carr's work. It was a difficult job. Crimes against peace and humanity, new concepts so recently articulated at the London conference, did not fit neatly into the Anglo-Saxon legal framework of the trial. Comyns Carr was forced to rely on the somewhat questionable and wide-ranging concept of "conspiracy" in drawing up the indictment; that is, that all the accused had participated in the formulation or execution of a common plan and were responsible for all acts performed by any person in execution of such a plan. Such a concept, however, fitted nicely with the then current vogue for conspiratorial theories of history.[21]

There were fifty-five counts in the indictment.[22] Counts one to thirty-six dealt with crimes against peace, conspiracy to wage, planning, preparing for, initiating or waging a war of aggression. Counts thirty-seven to fifty-two were crimes of murder and conspiracy to murder, such as the attack on Pearl Harbor and other activities immediately preceding the declaration of war in 1941, together with the slaughter of ordinary civilians as acts of murder. The last three counts were for other conventional war crimes and crimes against humanity. The indictment covered events spanning the years 1927 to 1945.

To build up a charge of conspiracy the prosecution had to cast its net so wide that almost every nook and cranny of Japanese public life was investigated.[23] Stacks of documentation were translated for the prosecutors.

Initially only one area of Japanese life was explicitly forbidden. The Japanese Emperor was not allowed to be tried as a war criminal, and the Imperial family surrounding him remained enshrouded in a grey mist. At Potsdam the Allies had stated that they did not intend that the Japanese should be enslaved as a race or destroyed as a nation. To most of the Japanese the Emperor had a quasi-divine status and he was the embodiment of Japan. To classify him as a war criminal would have been to bring about an implosion of Japanese society. China, Russia and Australia strongly opposed this decision but finally acquiesced to the wishes of the British and Americans.

It was not until as late as March 15th that the Australians accepted that the Emperor would not stand as a defendant. The Russian government signally failed to place the Emperor's name for consideration as a suspect before Comyns Carr's executive committee although the Russian press continued to clamour about the issue until well into April. However, in the end, all the participating countries consented to the terms of the indictment despite any private reservations they may have continued to feel.[24]

While Comyns Carr struggled, under pressure of time, to put his "conspiracy" indictment together, another conspiracy had begun to take shape. There is evidence of a systematic effort to conceal from the IPS investigators, and so from the Tokyo trial, evidence about Japanese atrocities in biological and chemical warfare. The politics of the Cold War had begun to supervene. It is clear, though, that certain members of the IPS wished to bring BW and CW matters before the Tokyo trial, one of whom was American IPS investigator Colonel Thomas H. Morrow.

There is no question that Ishii as an individual, and many of his associates, were guilty of serious war crimes. As a Lt-General, Ishii undoubtedly possessed sufficiently high military rank to be classified as a Class "A" war criminal. He was the top of the tree in his own field. His actions as the head of Unit 731 qualified him as a criminal on many counts of the indictment. Not only was BW considered extra-legal by most countries, but Ishii was also guilty of outrageous conventional war crimes. He had carried out calculated human experimentation on prisoners-of-war, a conventional war crime that had long been proscribed in the manuals of military law of every major power. He had carried out similar research against innocent civilians, clearly a crime against humanity. Ishii had taken his biological weapon out of the research laboratory and used it in the field. He had sought autonomy and independence of action for his BW forces throughout the war zones. He had done nothing to restrain the conduct of his subordinates. They, themselves, had also committed sufficiently heinous crimes to be classified as "B" and "C" class war criminals, of whom the Allies prosecuted no fewer than 5,570. There is no doubt that Ishii was a major conspirator against the customary and conventional laws of war. But there is no mention of his name on the list of those accused, nor on any lengthier list of those considered as possible Class "A" defendants. Neither do the names of any of his subordinates appear as Class "B" and "C" defendants.

What is perhaps even more remarkable is that it appears that neither BW nor CW received anything more than passing mention at any of these major and minor trials, despite the fact that Japan had frequently resorted to both such methods of warfare. Mention of BW and CW is noteworthy by its absence in the voluminous annals of war crimes trials in the Far East. Not only did Ishii and his associates fail to appear as witnesses or defendants, but neither was biological warfare considered as a topic at any of these trials. This becomes all the more surprising when Ishii's connections with so many of the Class "A" defendants are taken into account.

Ishii had pressed the accused General (Baron) Sadao Araki to support his BW efforts when Araki was War Minister. Later, in 1938 and 1939, Araki became Education Minister. The accused Field Marshal Shunroku Hata had been Commander-in-Chief of the Japanese Armies in China when Ishii launched his large-scale ground contamination attack in 1942. The accused General Seishirō Itagaki knew of Ishii's work when he was Chief of Staff of the Kwantung Army in 1936 and 1937. Itagaki later became War Minister (1938 –39), Chief of Staff of the Japanese Expeditionary Forces in China (1939–41) and Commander-in-Chief of the 7th Area Army at Singapore in 1945. The accused General Heitarō Kimura had been Chief of Staff of the Kwantung Army from 1940 to 1941, becoming Vice-Minister of War (1941–43) and then in 1944 Commander-in-Chief of the Japanese Army in Burma. The accused General Hideki Tōjō who had almost certainly known of Ishii's work ever since the days when he was *Kenpeitai* Commander of the Kwantung Army from 1935 to 1937, became the Kwantung Army's Chief of Staff (1937–38); Vice-

Minister of War (1938–39); War Minister (1940–41); Prime Minister and War Minister (1941–44), and Chief of the Army General Staff (1944). The accused General Yoshijirō Umezu who, as Commander-in-Chief of the Kwantung Army (1939–44), had authorised consignments of human experimentees and agreed to Ishii's BW raids on China, became chief of the Army General Staff from 1944 until the end of the war. Defendants who could have been cross-examined about BW during the course of the trial were in ample supply.

Furthermore, most prosecuting nations had evidence of Japanese BW crimes, including China, Britain, America and the Soviet Union. Yet, at the outset of the trial, none of these countries appears to have been willing to raise the subject in open court.

Nonetheless, Colonel Thomas Morrow, the man in charge of preparing the prosecution phase of the trial concerning Japanese military aggression in China, did at least initially begin systematically preparing evidence about BW and CW crimes.

The prosecution case was eventually divided into fifteen distinct phases. Each day prosecutors laboured under terrific pressure to get the trial started as soon as possible. They were weighed down by mountains of translated and untranslated documentation, and by the sheer expanse of the wide-ranging needs of the indictment. Despite such problems, it can be seen, from what has emerged into public archives today, that the IPS did uncover sufficient evidence of BW war crimes to be able to raise the matter fully before the court.

On March 2nd, the day Comyns Carr's executive committee was formed, Morrow wrote to Chief Prosecutor Keenan about the expected scope of the case involving the Sino-Japanese War.

The last quarter of an extensive report was devoted to outlining information about Japanese use of chemical and biological warfare, and the last page was addressed solely to the subject of BW. It ended:

This matter, as well as the poison gas episodes, assumes importance because of the obvious impossibility of developing such methods of warfare on the field of battle or through the resources of an army general in the field, and indicates that such prohibited methods of warfare were carried on by the Tokyo Government and not the field commanders.[25]

On March 4th, two days after Morrow submitted his report, Comyns Carr's eleven-strong executive committee met for the first time. Judge Hsiang, chief procurator of the Shanghai Supreme Court, was a member. So too was British assistant prosecutor Christmas Humphreys and an American prosecutor called Frank

Tavenner. Tavenner, an able yet aggressive and cynical lawyer from Virginia, on leave from the US Department of Justice, was later to play a fateful role in the story of Unit 731. Comyns Carr started by devolving responsibilities to sub-committees – one for drafting the indictment, another to look into incidents and treaties, and one dealing with evidence and defendants. Although there was some discussion about new investigations, the meeting agreed that all interrogations on major matters should be completed by March 12th, details to be filled in later if necessary.[26]

Much of the IPS's evidence came from these interrogations, especially those of potential defendants.

Part of the evidence, [recalled Humphreys] and in some cases the major part of the evidence against each defendant, was the result of his own interrogation. So full were the confessions obtained by American lawyers from most of the defendants in this way that I made it my business to attend one or two to see if, in fact, an inducement or threat was used. Nothing of the sort occurred, and indeed most of these Japanese one-time national leaders were grateful for the chance to express, at inordinate length, their own part in national affairs for the last 15 years, and many of them, indeed, boastingly took upon themselves a responsibility greater than warranted by the facts.[27]

On March 8th, Morrow updated Keenan on the progress of interrogations in the Sino-Japanese phase of the case. In a three-page report he informed the chief prosecutor which IPS members were interviewing which defendants and witnesses.[28] He returned once again to the subject of BW, having followed up his initial investigation.

"The undersigned [Morrow] saw Lt-Col Thompson and Col D. S. Tait, G-2 Technical Intelligence, GHQ, in regard to Bacterial Warfare and the statement of activities of Lt-Gen Ishii, as reported in the recent *Stars and Stripes*," wrote Morrow. "This points to a connection with the alleged Bacterial Warfare reported in the *China Handbook, 1937–42*."

The meeting, he explained however, had proved fruitless. "The interview was negative in results," his report records. Morrow was referred by Thompson to a Colonel Marshall, GHQ's Chief Chemical Officer based on the fifth floor of the Mitsubishi Shōji building.

It is not known whether Morrow ever met Marshall. The document trail of Morrow's investigation into BW on the Japanese mainland ends with this ambiguous statement that the interview with

174

Thompson and Tait was "negative" in results. Morrow, however, was to continue his searches in China.

Three days later the results of the various interrogations were submitted to Comyns Carr's committee. Morrow was present. Although Chinese matters were discussed, the minutes record no mention of BW or the Thompson incident. The following day, accompanied by associate prosecutor Hsiang, secretary Henry Chiu and American assistant counsel David Nelson Sutton, Morrow left for China.

Morrow and his party arrived in Shanghai that afternoon. Their mission in China was to collect war crimes evidence by interrogating witnesses, and to screen and analyse documents. Five days later, Keenan and his party followed on. While Morrow, Hsiang and Sutton set off for Peking, Chungking and Nanking, Keenan paid calls upon Chiang Kai-shek and Dr Wellington Koo.

Morrow had by then decided that out of all the matters concerning Japanese aggression on China, eight separate issues were worth investigating. Biological warfare was one; chemical warfare, another. The three men arrived back in Shanghai almost one month later with an impressive array of information.

One section in Morrow's report was devoted entirely to the subject of BW. "The bacteriological warfare charge is based upon a report in the *China Handbook* 1937–43, made by Dr P. Z. King," he wrote. "Dr King and his associates have been interviewed by Mr Sutton, who is submitting an attached report on them." It was Dr King's report that Koo had handed over to the Pacific War Council in the summer of 1942.

Morrow completed his report on April 16th and submitted it to Keenan on the 23rd. On April 17th, four days after the Russian IPS delegation made its belated appearance in Tokyo, Comyns Carr presided over a meeting of the associate Prosecutors (the heads of each national component represented in the IPS) to present the indictment which he had drafted. Keenan informed the meeting that he was under great pressure from the US government to begin proceedings in the very near future. It was only at this meeting that Umezu was included as a defendant, upon Russian insistence, as already noticed.[29]

The trial opened on June 3rd, and days passed by as the tribunal rejected successive defence challenges to its jurisdiction, competence and authority.

Then, during the afternoon of August 29th that summer, during the China phase of the prosecution case, BW made its sole appearance during trial proceedings.

175

The official transcript of the proceedings recorded an exchange between the court and David Nelson Sutton of the IPS.[30] Sutton, it will be recalled, had been one of Morrow's colleagues on the evidence-gathering trip to China. The transcript read:

Mr Sutton: The enemy's *Tama* Detachment carried off their civilian captives to the medical laboratory, where the reactions to poisonous serum were tested. This detachment was one of the most secret organisations. The number of persons slaughtered by this detachment cannot be ascertained.

The President: Are you going to give us any further evidence of these alleged laboratory tests for reactions to poisonous serums? This is something entirely new, we haven't heard before. Are you going to leave it at that?

Mr Sutton: We do not at this time anticipate introducing additional evidence on that subject.

President Webb was alert to the importance of this new revelation. But no sooner was the matter raised than it was dropped. Two American defence attorneys, Captain Alfred Brooks and Michael Levin, objected that Sutton had not provided sufficient information. It might just have been, they suggested, a vaccination programme carried out by the Japanese for the benefit of the Chinese populace.

The Nanking allegations were thrown out of court with no murmur of protest from either Sutton or any of his colleagues.

Sutton almost certainly introduced this piece of information inadvertently. At this point in the trial Sutton's concern was with one of the most ghastly atrocities of the Second World War – the Rape of Nanking.

Recently, further evidence has been found in the archives suggesting IPS's awareness of the BW issue. Listed as IPS Evidentiary Document 1896, and lodged in the Files Unit of IPS's Document Division, the document bears the title "Affidavit of Osamu Hataba, on Bacterial Warfare carried on by *Ei* 1644 Force in China, 1943". It clearly corroborates intelligence gained during the war that Ishii, in waging BW during the Chekiang Campaign in the summer of 1942, suffered a serious reverse in his fortunes when his weapon backfired.

Hataba, a former member of Ishii's Nanking *Sakae* 1644 Unit who defected to the Chinese during the war, had signed the document in Shanghai on April 17th. Sutton himself had departed from Shanghai on April 12th, but, according to Morrow's report to Keenan, two men were left behind "to get additional information and to await a special plane expected to be set up for the China investigation".

After summarising the official duties of the unit and making general affirmation that "infectious germs" were also being manufactured by it, Hataba declared:

In September 1943, I was in the Army Hospital in Hangchow, and even at that time this hospital was still then overfilled with epidemic sufferers (Japanese soldiers) and each day three to five of these people died. In August of that year it was said that they had made an enclosure in the exercise yard of the same hospital in which several thousand patients were isolated.

Furthermore, I have the oral testimony of Tadao Tachizawa (who comes from Tokyo), the hygiene squad leader of the No 1644 Detachment, whereby he said that he was active in disease germ application duties at the front by airplane.

The corps had certainly more than two specially assigned airplanes. I, myself, was assigned duties from May 1942, to March 1943, at the anti-epidemic section of the anti-epidemic and water supply division and I know that the above described inhuman acts were carried out under the euphemism of "the Holy War", and I am one of those that deserted from the corps. Furthermore, in the scientific section they were also carrying out research on poisons.[31]

Hataba's name is not listed in various indexes to names and subjects at the trial, and his testimony was not tendered in evidence during the proceedings. That evidence could have been available in translation had Sutton wished to substantiate the allegations about BW before the court.

It is likely, however, that Sutton did not wish such allegations raised, and may indeed have been acting as a filter preventing them from reaching the court. At this time Sutton may well have headed IPS's Document Division, the very organisation holding Hataba's affidavit. Certainly, a year later, he is recorded as holding this position.[32] Sutton had set up the Scanning Unit through which documents passed for translation to gain a quick idea of their contents. It is interesting to note that in his capacity as head of the Document Division, Sutton was empowered to approve any request by attorneys for documents to be processed (translating, mimeographing, circulating, etc) during the cross-examination of defence witnesses and also during the rebuttal stages of the trial.

Another chance to call Ishii and his associates to justice had passed. But the prosecution case still had many months to run, and the Allies had stated that even after the end of the IMTFE, subsequent war crimes trials were envisaged.

*   *   *

177

Inside MacArthur's headquarters a special section had meanwhile been established charged with investigating "B" and "C" Class war crimes cases, as already mentioned. Headed by Colonel Alva C. Carpenter, Legal Section was entirely separate from the IPS. With offices throughout Japan, Legal Section's investigation and prosecution divisions amassed and carried out proceedings against these so-called minor Japanese war criminals.

Military commissions to try these "B" and "C" Class cases began to be appointed by the commanding general of the American 8th Army, following authorisation by MacArthur in December 1945. Some tribunals were held in China, the Philippines and the Pacific Islands, but most, a total of 314 cases, were held at Yokohama, Japan.[33]

At these courts a sufficient number of medical atrocity cases were heard for them to be considered as a special category. The most well known and worst case presented by Legal Section at Yokohama concerned the fate of captured American fliers held by the Japanese Western Army in Kyūshū after April 1945. The appalling experiments to which they had been subjected included vivisection and the substitution of sea-water for their blood.

For this gross act of barbarism, on August 27th, 1948, the nine Japanese involved were convicted and sentenced either to be hanged or to serve life imprisonment.[34] One, Professor Ishiyama of Kyūshū University, committed suicide in prison.

Legal Section had mounting evidence of atrocities on PoWs at many Japanese hospitals. Communications from various sources to MacArthur reflected that nine hospitals in or near Tokyo had been conducting experiments on PoWs, some of which could be traced directly to the activities of Unit 731.

Legal Section's Investigation Division opened case files on each of these hospitals. It also began investigating the Infectious Disease Research Laboratory (*Densenbyō Kenkyū-jō*, "*Den Ken*" for short) at Tokyo Imperial University. As we have seen *Den Ken* had been involved in the abortive attempt to get yellow fever virus from the Rockefeller Laboratories in New York. Tokyo Imperial University was also Unit 731's primary recruiting ground for microbiologists during the period of Kitano's stewardship.

Legal Section opened case file 1117 on *Den Ken* after a letter sent to MacArthur alleged that PoWs had been subjected to bacterial experimentation there. Although inquiries at the Japanese Board of Education, which formerly had jurisdiction over *Den Ken*, showed that no PoWs were ever confined there, and that there was no information on the matter, investigator Smith found that two of the doctors accused

178

in the letter had died. One had committed suicide and the other had died in an irregular way.[35]

However, Smith was never allowed to bring the case to fruition, possibly because it was too closely involved with Unit 731. Certainly there was a connection with the notorious *Tama* Detachment–Ishii's headquarters during the abortive Chekiang BW campaign of 1942.

Moreover, at the Yokohama trials no reference whatsoever appears to have been made either to bacteriological warfare or to microbiological experimentation on prisoners-of-war – even though Legal Section's investigators had discovered that nine hospitals in the Tokyo area alone had been doing so.

Chapter 13

SOVIET INTERROGATIONS AND INFORMATION

Meanwhile, across the Japan Sea in the Soviet Union, vigorous investigations were being carried out.

By the time Japan capitulated on August 14th, Soviet forces had crossed the Khingan Mountain ranges and were moving on Tsitsihar. Russian advance airborne detachments swiftly occupied Harbin, Hsinking, Mukden, Dairen and Port Arthur.[1] Russian casualties were given as 8,219 killed and 22,264 wounded; Japanese losses were put at 80,000 killed.[2] An estimated 600,000 were taken prisoner, including Yamada and his operations chief Maj-Gen Tomokatsu Matsumura.

Great effort had been made by the Japanese to obscure the crimes of Unit 731. Pingfan was so thoroughly destroyed during the hurried withdrawal from Manchuria that cameramen of the invading Russian Army decided the ruins were not worth photographing.[3] Unit 731's satellite units along the border had also been put to the torch before the Japanese positions were overrun. Damning evidence was uncovered, however, in *Kenpeitai* archives. A manual on sabotage warfare tactics found at the Japanese Military Mission in Mutan-chiang in a file labelled "Russian Whiteguard Unit in Hantaohětzu" dated January 20th, 1944, listed bacteria and pistol-type diffusers as weapons for killing enemy civilians.[4] It stated:

> The means for destroying enemy personnel in the course of military operations include chemicals, bacteria, or explosives with delayed fuses. It is best to eliminate all after a given operation. If this is impossible it is necessary to achieve the maximum effect in the very first operation.[5]

Next, instructions concerning the establishment of a special military zone around Pingfan were discovered, signed on June 30th, 1938, less than a fortnight after Tōjō's departure as Kwantung Army Chief of Staff, by his successor Maj-Gen Rensuke Isogai.[6] So too was a secret circular from the Kwantung Army's General Staff now un-earthed by the Russians which revealed that villages near the same area had been subjected to frequent searches. At Kwantung

Army Headquarters the Russians read about secret weapons dispatched to China in the summer of 1940 on orders from C-in-C Umezu.[7]

But the most ominous revelations were in documents referring to *Tokui-Atsukai* (special consignments) found in a "miscellaneous correspondence" file belonging to the 1st Division of Kwantung Gendarmerie Headquarters. The fate of captured spies, saboteurs and ideological criminals at Unit 731 could be pieced together from one document dated March 12th, 1943,[8] and this, together with the service diary of a Gendarme Unit codenamed *Hirano* dated July 17th to September 19th, 1939, revealed that these "special consignments" were taken, bound and fettered, to Harbin, "to be handed over to the chief of the Ishii Detachment". The order, originating from *Kenpeitai* Headquarters, stated that "the chief of the Harbin Gendarme Unit is to establish close contact with the chief of the Ishii Detachment and ensure at Harbin Station and along the route all measures of precaution against foreign espionage and the necessary surveillance measures."[9]

From such documents the Russians learned the names of some victims – old railwayman Sung Chao-Sang from Mutanchiang, carpenter Wu Tien-Sing, repairman Chu Chih-Men, Chinese patriot Wang Ying from Mukden. They read that Chinese Communist Chih Tieh-En from Huan County, Shantung Province had not yielded to the *Kenpeitai*'s torture, and that Dairen commercial clerk Chun Ming-Chi had been sent to Unit 731 because he was suspected of sending through the post an article to a newspaper denouncing Japan's occupation of Manchuria.[10]

Like her British and American allies Russia's Intelligence services had gained information about Japanese BW activity both before and during the Second World War. Before the war she had tried Japanese servicemen for putting bacteria aboard troop trains, and during the 1940s, according to information from Kasahara, some of his own secret scientific papers were stolen from a safe and taken to the Russian Consulate General in Harbin.[11] Unfortunately, however, the files of the NKVD, the forerunner of the KGB, are not open to public inspection so it is impossible to gauge the extent of Russian information.

Among the half a million or so PoWs, the Soviet authorities began searching for members of the elusive Epidemic Prevention and Water Supply Unit. They soon found and interrogated Pingfan's bacteria production chief Major Tomio Karasawa. By early 1946, perhaps even before, Karasawa had made a startling confession. At the time the IPS in Tokyo was still carrying out its preliminary investigation

181

prior to the full trial, Karasawa had already revealed to the Soviet Union nearly the full extent of Unit 731's war crimes.[12]

Interrogated by Captain Peters, a member of staff of the office of the Ministry for Internal Affairs for the Khabarovsk Territory in early 1946, Karasawa began unfolding the story of the top security world of Unit 731[13] – the oath of secrecy, the study of bacteriological method under Ishii: "I hereby certify on my responsibility that experiments were conducted in the Ishii Corps in which living human bodies were sacrificed . . . I participated in this work so I hate to say anything about it, but I will explain it because it will be a burden on my mind if I don't . . ."

The worst admission over, Karasawa provided a complete, and accurate, outline of the organisation, structure and personnel of the Ishii Unit.

Questioned on more detailed scientific matters, Karasawa made a more startling association.

A research was conducted in the unit, to decide the reaction of an immunizing serum inoculation according to races. To accomplish this purpose, a small party from the 1st Section headed by Mr Utsumi, a technical expert, was dispatched to Inner Mongolia at the beginning of 1943 and Mr Minato, a technical expert, examined the blood of American prisoners of war who were near Mukden about the summer of 1943. About this Minato told me that as a result of the study of blood which was started simultaneously with the experimental research of strengthening the power of bacteria, no distinction had been found in serum immunity between races.

Karasawa went on to reveal that Ishii had told him that as early as 1933 or 1934 experiments had begun with cholera and plague on the mounted bandits of Manchuria. He told of bomb burst and spray tests on humans at Anta, of BW raids on China, of the massive production of anti-plague serum in 1941. He also mentioned the exchange of scientific literature on bacteriology between Germany and Japan.

Among their captives the Russians found another senior figure of Unit 731, Maj-Gen Kiyoshi Kawashima. On September 12th and 16th, 1946, he was interrogated in the Siberian city of Khabarovsk.[14] Russian interrogator Captain Nikitkin found him an evasive character on the first day of questioning. Nikitkin desired to know whether Ishii's personal friend and head of the Kwantung Army's Medical Administration Lt-Gen Ryūiji Kajitsuka, now also in Russian hands, had been aware of or even directed Unit 731's work. Kawashima's replies were ambiguous, but he admitted that, as Chief Medical

Officer, Kajitsuka ought to have known of the work being done. He maintained, however, that the work of the Unit was preventive.

But at the next interview, at which Nikitkin was joined by Colonel Kudoryavtsev, more information-producing questions were asked.[15]

"We are questioning you as an important witness in regard to major Japanese war criminals by request of the Soviet representative of the IMTFE. Who in the Kwantung Army directed and supervised the work of the Ishii Unit?"

"The sanitation duties of the Ishii Unit were supervised by the Chief of the Medical Department of the Kwantung Army," replied Kawashima. "Maj-Gen Ishii reported directly to the Medical Affairs Bureau [War Ministry] and the section in the [Army] General Staff on matters concerned with research and experiments. The budget and materials were supplied by the Kwantung Army."

"What kind of experiments were carried out by the Ishii Detachment regarding the use of plague-bacilli-infested fleas? State also when and where."

Kawashima replied: "I myself remember once having seen . . . the spreading of fleas from an airplane and the dropping of bombs containing fleas . . . Experiments were carried out on animals and human beings."

"Under whose leadership were the experiments conducted . . . ?" he was asked.

"The experiments were conducted under the leadership of Colonel Ōta, who was chief of the Epidemic Prevention Section at the time . . . The experiments were made on rats and human beings, the latter comprised about 20 Manchurian capital punishment convicts."

Kawashima was warned that his evidence was required for the IMTFE. But the Russians' information was never brought forward at the trial. Why not?

The Russian prosecution team arrived late in Tokyo. Nonetheless, they signed an indictment sufficiently far-reaching to incorporate the crimes of the Ishii Unit. At that late date they even insisted that former Kwantung Army C-in-C Umezu be included as a defendant, a perfect target for BW accusations. The interrogation of Karasawa clearly shows they had gained evidence of BW crimes by this time. There were many stages of the trial when such evidence could have been admitted.

During the Manchurian phase of the prosecution case, which opened on Monday, July 1st, 1946, and closed on Tuesday, August 6th, not one shred was put forward. Likewise, on August 29th, during the China phase, when Sutton made his startling revelations about Unit 731's Nanking *Tama* Detachment, the Russian prosecutors said

183

nothing. Even during their own, the Russian, phase of the trial, from October 8th to October 21st, no mention of BW was made.

Such opportunity lay open even in the last phases of the prosecution case, phases XIII and XIV in January 1947, which dealt with atrocities against civilians and PoWs. The prosecution case closed on Friday, January 24th. The very last matter to be dealt with, written on the same page of the official transcript as the one on which Judge Higgins formally closed the prosecution's evidence in chief, concerned the individual responsibility of Umezu. Virtually no new evidence, none from the Russians and certainly none on BW, was added at this date.

Such behaviour seems strange when the Russians' subsequent and internationally proclaimed outrage at Japan's BW atrocities is taken into account.

The Russians have since claimed they did make efforts to have the matter raised at the IMTFE. Colonel Mark Raginsky together with colleague Colonel Lev Nicholaevich Smirnov arrived from the Nuremberg trial in early 1947 to join their country's large, approximately fifty-strong, prosecution contingent in Tokyo. Raginsky said in Moscow in 1985:

The Soviet delegation presented Mr Keenan with a lot of evidence. For instance, the Soviet Prosecutor Sergei Golunsky suggested putting on trial members of the *zaibatsu* [large Japanese financial and industrial combines], like the Minister of Arms Supply Fujiwara [Ginjirō] and the like. They also lay behind the aggressive policy of Japan. But all the suggestions of the Soviet side were rejected by Keenan.

He was also given evidence that the Japanese Army had a special BW unit. The Soviet side suggested that the case should be investigated. He was given this information in September 1946. However, for three months Mr Keenan kept this information all to himself and seemed not to pay any attention to it. Then MacArthur's GHQ itself issued a statement claiming that an investigation had been undertaken and no proof had been found. This was deliberate disinformation.[16]

Raginsky's assertion that it was decided in December 1946 not to raise the BW issue at the trial is correct. This decision, reportedly taken by the IPS, not by the direction of MacArthur's headquarters, was made "on the basis of information then available that these witnesses [Unit 731 members] should not be produced, as evidence

184

was not sufficient to connect any of the accused with Ishii's detachment's secret activities".[17]

There is no question that the Russians presented transcripts of the Karasawa and Kawashima interrogations to the Americans. These may well have been given as early as September 1946, and there is corroborative evidence that the Americans most certainly had received them by January 1947, at a time before the prosecution case was concluded.

Cold War tensions had been increasing throughout 1946. On March 5th, 1946, on the same platform as President Truman at Westminster College, Fulton, Missouri, Winston Churchill had made his famous "Iron Curtain" speech. The desire to mete out stern justice at the Tokyo trial was increasingly subsumed if found in conflict with the interests of national security. Japan was in the front line. So too now was biological warfare. On July 24th, 1946, Washington cabled MacArthur ordering him to protect intelligence, especially scientific, which might jeopardise America's national security. It read: ". . . Under present circumstances Intelligence relating to research and development in the field of science and war material should not be disclosed to nations other than the British Commonwealth."[18]

BW intelligence seems by this time to have become much too sensitive to be brought into the glare of a massive international trial. Throughout 1946 both Russia and America appear to have been reluctant to reveal their hands. In Japan, America appears to have taken some extra precautions to prevent information falling into Soviet hands.

Soon after the Russians allege they handed over the Karasawa and Kawashima interrogation transcripts, GHQ interviewed two more senior Unit 731 members, Colonel Kiyoshi Ōta and Major Nobukazu Hinofuji, both mentioned in the Soviet reports. The purpose of the interviews seems to have been to determine their political allegiance. Both men were asked a few half-hearted questions on Japanese BW activities, and both responded with the standard evasive replies. But Major Owen Keller of the CWS went on in both instances to question the two about their attitudes to Communism (which both declared they detested) and to the US Occupation (which both considered to be reasonable and rehabilitative).[19]

From these interrogations it is clear that considerations of national security had become much more important than war crimes. Both men appeared compliant, not likely to want to talk to the Russians.

Early in 1947, the Russians once again raised the matter. They made a low-key approach to one of the IPS's backroom men, D. L. Waldorf, with a request to interrogate Ishii, Ōta and Kikuchi.[20]

G-2 was quickly informed, and asked the Russians to re-submit their request in writing, setting forth reasons for wishing to carry out the interrogations. The Russians lost no time in replying: two days later on January 9th, Russia's IMTFE Associate Prosecutor Maj-Gen A. N. Vasiliev delivered his formal submissions to G-2. His reply was relayed directly to Willoughby. Vasiliev had written:

At the disposal of the Soviet Division of the IPS there are materials showing the preparations of the Kwantung Army for bacteriological warfare. To present these materials as evidence to the Military Tribunal it is necessary to conduct a number of supplementary interrogations of persons who worked previously in the Anti-Epidemic Group (Manshu) N731 of Kwantung Army . . .

These persons [Ishii, Ōta and Kikuchi] are to testify about research work on bacterias carried out by them for the purpose of using bacteria in warfare and also about the cases of mass murder of people as the result of these experiments.

Aware of the potential importance of such information Vasiliev had added:

I believe that it would be expedient to take preliminary measures preventing the spreading of information concerning this investigation before the investigation is completed and the materials are presented to the Tribunal, that is, to take from those witnesses certificates to the effect that they promise not to tell anybody about the investigation of this matter and to conduct the preliminary interrogations not in the premises of the War Ministry building.[21]

Time was fast running out before the close of the prosecution's evidence in chief, which finally wound up on January 24th. The Russians were anxious for information. G-2 stalled. The Russians were told that G-2 officer Lt-Col Robert McQuail would confer with them on the subject at 9 a.m. on January 15th in the War Ministry building.

Both sides assembled, the Americans represented by McQuail, Keller and Waldorf and the Russians by Colonel Smirnov, the man recently arrived from Nuremberg. McQuail asked Smirnov for some background.

"Shortly after cessation of hostilities," said Smirnov, "Gen

Kawashima, 4th Section, Manchu 731, and his assistant, Maj Kurasaba* were interrogated."

McQuail noted the phonetic rendering of the names, but took care not to reveal America's keen interest, and even went through the motions of asking Smirnov the exact spelling. The Russian interrogators had disclosed information on the programme at Pingfan and the numerous "field experiments" – information found "so preposterous" that experts had been called in.[22] Kawashima and Karasawa were re-interrogated and Pingfan's ruins checked. The initial information was confirmed.

McQuail seemed mildly curious about the fate of Pingfan, asking how well the Japanese had destroyed it. "The Colonel said 'ruins of Pingfan'. Was it bombed or destroyed as a result of fighting?"

"Pingfan was completely destroyed by the Japanese who attempted to cover up all evidence," replied Smirnov. "All documents were also destroyed; our experts did not even bother to photograph the ruins, so thorough was the damage."

Smirnov continued: "The Japanese committed a horrible crime killing 2,000 Manchurians and Chinese and Gen Ishii, Col Kikuchi and Col Ōta are involved. Also the quantity production of fleas and bacteria is very important!"

Smirnov hinted at a possible sharing of information. The Russians were obviously dissatisfied with the amount of technical data they had so far acquired in Manchuria, and were aware that the key personnel and documents had been returned to Japan.

McQuail reported back to Willoughby, noting that Smirnov's information corresponded "with knowledge previously in possession of the United States, or suspected by previous investigators". "Information that Pingfan was destroyed with documents, confirms previous information," added McQuail.[23]

G-2 stalled again. The IMTFE prosecution case was just about to end. From their earliest interrogations of Ishii, almost a year previously, G-2 felt confident that the Russians were unlikely to gain useful technical intelligence from the few Unit 731 members in their hands, and they certainly had no wish to give the Soviets any opportunity to enlarge on what they had already learned.

Washington was cabled on February 7th for a decision about the Russian request.[24] Meanwhile, orally through IPS, the Russians were told the request was being considered. The Americans' delaying tactics drove the Russians to exasperation. Each day they plagued the Americans with inquiries which reportedly became highly

---

* Karasawa.

"unpleasant".[25] Vasiliev demanded to see Willoughby in person later that month, reiterating that the evidence was wanted solely for war crimes. He offered to make Soviet documents available and to bring Russian experts to assist if required. Again Willoughby parried. The Soviet general was notified that when a decision was reached he would be notified by IPS.

In Washington, where the matter was being dealt with urgently, the Joint Chiefs of Staff (JCS) passed the decision to the State-War-Navy Co-ordinating Committee (SWNCC).

On March 5th, the SWNCC agreed the JCS's recommendations, and after some delay MacArthur was cabled on March 21st:

Part I
Subject to following conditions permission granted for SCAP controlled Soviet interrogation Gen Ishii, Cols Kikuchi and Ōta . . .

a) Cols Kikuchi and Ōta to be interviewed by competent US personnel. Subject your concurrence, War Department prepared to dispatch immediately especially trained representatives to conduct interrogation and monitor subsequent interrogation by Soviets.

b) If any information brought out by preliminary interrogation considered of sufficient importance that divulgence to Soviets should not be permitted, Kikuchi and Ōta are to be instructed not to reveal such information to Soviets.

c) Prior to interview by Soviets the Japanese BW experts should be instructed to make no mention of US interview on this subject.

Part II
Since there is no clear cut war crimes interest by the Soviets in acts allegedly committed by the Japanese against the Chinese, permission for the interrogation should not be granted on that basis, but rather as an amiable gesture toward a friendly government. It should be made clear to the Soviets that the permission granted in this instance does not create a precedent for future requests, which shall be considered on their individual merits.[26]

Lt-Gen Kusma Derevyanko, the Russian member of the Allied Council for Japan, finally received Willoughby's reply on April 10th. It stated:

. . . former Japanese Gen Ishii and Col Ōta cannot be turned over to USSR as there appears to be no clear cut war crimes interest by the Soviets in acts allegedly committed by the Japanese on Chinese or Manchurians . . . Personnel referred to . . . are already under consideration for interrogation in conjunction with IPS, SCAP in cooperation with the Associate Prosecutor for the USSR, IMTFE. It should be noted, however, that joint interrogation is not granted on a basis of war crimes investigation nor does permission granted create a precedent for future requests.[27]

Other matters, Willoughby explained, would be dealt with in a separate communication at an early date.

On April 1st, Washington cabled MacArthur. Camp Detrick expert Dr Norbert Fell would leave America on April 5th to conduct the debriefings.

Chapter 14

FURTHER INTERROGATIONS

After arriving in Japan, Dr Norbert Fell held a conference on April 21st with Dr Kan'ichirō Kamei, the man who had assisted Niizuma during Sanders' investigations. Kamei, then a director of a firm called the Scientific Research and Propagating Institute for Modernising People's Life and Economy, had since the Americans' first BW investigation been interviewed by IPS during its preparations for the IMTFE. Fell, chief of Detrick's Pilots-Engineering Division, accompanied by McQuail of G-2 and interpreter Tarō Yoshihashi, asked Kamei and his American-educated secretary Hiroto Arakami why the Japanese had been withholding information about offensive BW. New information, it was explained, had come to light.

"Interrogations were carried out too soon after the surrender," explained Kamei. "The Japanese were uneasy and would not talk freely. Since then, the Occupation has gone well, Japan has settled down, and I believe you can obtain more information if the Japanese concerned are assured that their information will not be used for war crimes prosecution . . ."[1]

The Americans, joined by Keller of the CWS, assembled the following day to interrogate Ishii's deputy Tomosada Masuda. Kamei offered to act as Masuda's spokesman, and asked permission to relate a conversation that he had had with the former Unit 731 officer earlier that day. Once again, the point was made that the Japanese would divulge secret information in return for immunity. The BW trials against the Chinese Army in Central China were admitted, and two further names – Naitō and Kaneko – were offered as possible informants on these trials.[2]

Just as the meeting concluded, out of Masuda's earshot, Kamei whispered a dramatic revelation to Fell.

"Masuda admitted to me that experiments were carried out on humans. The victims were Manchurian criminals who had been condemned to death. The personnel involved in carrying out these human experiments took a vow never to disclose information. However," he added, "I feel sure that if you handle your investigation from a scientific point of view, you can obtain detailed information."

190

For the moment, the Americans did not pursue the matter. Two days later Kamei was summoned to report his progress.

Kamei made a startling revelation. "Information about Japanese BW was given fully to Germany, and a large German laboratory was captured intact by the Russians. Thus, the Russians may be well informed on Japanese BW activities. The Japanese have a tendency to feel that continued silence is advisable."[3]

No comments are recorded about this startling revelation on the extent of Axis collaboration, and Kamei was allowed to expand on the subject of Masuda's technical knowledge. Kamei then returned again to the Japanese fears about disclosure.

"Masuda, Kaneko and Naitō know the most about BW. If transported to US territory, they can reconstruct all records from memory," said Kamei. Again, no response to this statement was recorded.

Following the interrogations by Lt-Col Sanders [continued Kamei], the Japanese were relieved that their evasive and incomplete answers were accepted. Lt-Col Sanders did not know enough about the technical side of the subject. The human experiments were extensive enough to reach scientific conclusions. The methods of infection I mentioned were thoroughly explored and the results and conclusions are in no way based on imagination. Kaneko knows the results of the trials against the Chinese, and these trials included the use of plague.

At a later meeting to question Masuda along with Kaneko and Naitō, Fell finally made a breakthrough. At first they were unhelpful. Then Fell produced the Kawashima and Karasawa testimonies revealing the human experiments. After some parrying, Masuda let slip that he had heard of human experiments but had never seen them. Fell let him continue.

I never heard that a total of 1,500–2,000 humans were used [said Masuda]. I cannot estimate the number involved and can only give you effects. I do not know about experiments in which subjects were administered vaccine and then infected. It was not done – we had no vaccine and knew no immunization. Ishii directed the experiments, and those in charge were shifted frequently.

The three men talked quietly among themselves for a moment, and interpreter Yoshihashi overheard Naitō say: "We might as well tell all, as Dr Fell already has a good idea." The others were unsure.

191

Naitō turned to the expectant Americans and said:

We want to co-operate and know we owe it to GHQ, but we have a responsibility to our friends. We took an oath never to divulge information on human experiments. We are afraid some of us will be prosecuted as war criminals. We do not know how much others will be willing to give us. If you can give us documentary immunity, probably we can get everything. The subordinates, not the section chiefs, know the details. If we contact someone who is a Communist, he is liable to tell the Russians.

The Japanese were given assurances that war crimes would not be involved. Fell then instructed them on the extra information that was needed, and discussions started again. Naitō revealed the name of Unit 731's epidemic haemorrhagic fever expert, Masuda gave details of a plague flea attack in China, and Kaneko provided information about typhoid spray tests.

That night Fell dispatched a letter with news of the breakthrough, via air courier, to the chief of the CWS, Maj-Gen Alden Waitt.

The following day the three offered to co-operate with full information.

Fell wrote a note: "The outlines submitted this date gave a fair amount of detailed information and indicated that the required information eventually would be forthcoming. Highlights of the papers were: a) Masuda, minimal infectious dose of anthrax and plague on humans, b) Naitō, methods of coating bacteria, c) Kaneko, methods of measuring particle size."

In order to bring all the information together, Masuda offered to visit ex-colleagues in the Tokyo area, and Naitō likewise in the Kyoto-Osaka region. Naitō also inquired if Fell was interested in anti-crop agents. If so, he said, the Yukimasa Yagisawa of the Penicillin Society in Tokyo should be found.

Masuda, perhaps in an attempt to unburden himself somewhat told Fell that personnel engaged in offensive BW work had been carried as medical men to gain protection under the League of Nations Covenant. He had complained about this practice, and was sent to Burma as punishment.

"I was only ordered out of Burma because I was badly needed at Pingfan," he continued.* "We completely destroyed

---

* On October 9th, 1945, Masuda had told Sanders he had worked on malaria control in Burma from March 1943 to December 1944. The authors have seen Masuda's own 8 mm home movie of this trip. It probably had a far more sinister purpose. See p. 111 for the Far Eastern evidence.

Pingfan. I had 400 kilos of dried organisms which I destroyed by burning."

Fell must have been surprised at this gigantic figure – potentially sufficient to wipe out the human race. He made a note to check the amount at a later date.*

Masuda continued: "The four Japanese the Russians will interrogate† should know a great deal about offensive BW. Since you want their information and do not want me to contact them, I will write a letter for you to show them. I will tell them to let you know all."

On May 1st, all three were given a detailed questionnaire of information required. To make the questionnaire more "acceptable" to the Japanese, Fell amended all references of human to "animal" experimentation.[4] The same day, Fell interviewed one of Unit 731's most senior figures, Maj-Gen Hitoshi Kikuchi, chief of 731's 1st Section from 1942 to the end of the war.

Kikuchi was told that under the terms of the Japanese surrender he was liable to "penalties" if he did not reveal full information.

Fell asked for a description of Unit 731's organisation, and about the work of its 1st Section. Kikuchi volunteered nothing. So Fell produced the Kawashima and Karasawa affidavits. In answer to every question, Kikuchi pleaded ignorance and denied knowledge.

Fell jotted down: "It is apparent that Kikuchi was excited and afraid."[5]

Interpreter Yoshihashi stepped in to calm him down, pointing out that the interview was to gain scientific information, not for war crimes. Other Japanese were co-operating, he explained.

The next day Yoshihashi again urged Kikuchi to co-operate, pressing him to reveal "all information for use in medical sciences". Kikuchi admitted knowing about human experiments, but only through rumour. He denied having detailed information. Fell handed him Masuda's letter. Its contents were sufficient to change Kikuchi's mind, and the former Major-General agreed to do his best to help the United States. Questioning commenced on the Kawashima and Karasawa testimonies, to which he made guarded and reluctant replies about the anthrax experiments on animals.

". . . To the best of my knowledge, humans were not used in any of these experiments."[6]

Kikuchi was told he would be interrogated by the Russians. Deeply shocked, he cut short the interview and requested permission to

---

* Masuda later amended the figure to 40 kilos, stating that 400 kilos was the total production during the life of Pingfan.
† Ishii, Ōta, Kikuchi and Lt-Col Takashi Murakami.

collect himself and return the following day. As he left the office, Kikuchi let Yoshihashi into a peculiar and surprising confidence.

He confided that he was afraid to say anything more at present because he might be accused of lying by the "other interrogators".

Who were these "other interrogators"? Unfortunately for posterity, Fell appears to have let the comment pass, and made no effort to follow it up. Perhaps he assumed that these "other interrogators" were just those responsible for the security of top Intelligence targets like Kikuchi, and no more. It does not seem to have struck Fell as odd that Kikuchi could have "other interrogators" when the former Major-General had stated that Fell's interview was the first contact he had had with US personnel.

As a Major-General, Kikuchi would, in all probability, have been one of those top Unit 731 men who secretly met with American Intelligence officers at the Kamakura restaurant in late 1945 or early 1946 to bargain for war crimes immunity. If such a bargain had indeed been struck at that time without Washington's knowledge, then it would have been highly embarrassing for MacArthur's men to be discovered, more than fifteen months later, by Fell as having known all along about such things as human experimentation. It must remain a speculation whether Fell, like Thompson, was allowed to discover only what he, with the indirect aid of the Russian evidence, could uncover independently for himself. Perhaps the only secret remaining by then was the existence of this early covert co-operation between GHQ and Unit 731.

Kikuchi returned for another meeting on May 5th, and was instructed not to reveal any information to the Russians about human experimentation, trials against the Chinese Army, mass production of fleas, the chain of command of the Unit and, naturally, any instructions given to him by US personnel.

The following day, MacArthur sent a five-part radio message to Washington, showing the extent of his knowledge. Paragraphs 3B and 5 were subsequently to cause considerable anxiety and debate in America's capital. The core of the message read:

Part 2 Experiments on humans were known to and described by three Japanese and confirmed tacitly by Ishii; field trials against Chinese Army took place on at least three occasions; scope of program indicated by report of reliable informant Masuda that 400 kilograms of dried anthrax organisms destroyed at Pingfan in August 1945; and research on use of BW against plant life was carried out. Reluctant statements by Ishii indicate he had superiors (possibly General Staff) who knew and authorized the program.

194

Ishii states that if guaranteed immunity from "war crimes" in documentary form for himself, superiors and subordinates, he can describe program in detail. Ishii claims to have extensive theoretical high-level knowledge including strategic and tactical use of BW on defense and offense, backed by some research on best BW agents to employ by geographical areas of Far East and the use of BW in cold climates.

Part 3A Statements so far have been obtained by persuasion, exploitation of Japanese fear of USSR, and desire to co-operate with US. Large part of data including most of the valuable technical BW information as to results of human experiments and research in BW for crop destruction probably can be obtained in this manner from low echelon Japanese personnel not believed liable to "war crimes" trials.

B Additional data, possibly including some statements from Ishii, probably can be obtained by informing Japanese involved that information will be retained in intelligence channels and will not be employed as "war crimes" evidence.

C Complete story, to include plans and theories of Ishii and superiors, probably can be obtained by documentary immunity to Ishii and associates. Ishii also can assist in securing complete co-operation of his former subordinates.

4 None of the above influences joint interrogations to be held shortly with USSR under provisions of your radio W-94446.

5 Adoption of method in Part 3B above recommended by CINCFE. Request reply soonest.[7]

It is clear from part 5 of the message that MacArthur favoured gaining the BW technical information by offering the assurance that such data would not be employed at war crimes trials.

Exactly when Fell first interrogated Ishii is unclear, but it appears to have been held at the former Lt-General's home at 77 Wakamatsu-chō, Tokyo. Ishii was bedridden and appeared to Fell to be in ill-health.

Fell explained that Kawashima and Karasawa had told the Russians all that they knew. Ishii was then asked to reveal information he had previously withheld, specifically on human experimentation and trials against the Chinese. The information was for scientific not war crimes purposes, said Fell.

"I will not reveal information to the Russians," replied Ishii. "I told Lt-Col Sanders that I wouldn't. * I have recently received another warning not to talk to the Russians."[8]

* Sanders did not meet Ishii.[9] Ishii presumably meant Thompson.

Willoughby had sent this warning through one of his G-2 agents.

Anyway [continued Ishii], I cannot give detailed technical data. All the records were destroyed. I never did know many details, and I have forgotten what I knew. I can give you general results.

Japan was forced into the study of defensive BW as a result of use by Chinese and Russian agents. I never heard of Anta until I returned to Pingfan in 1945. I did not visit the location.

I am responsible for all that went on at Pingfan. I am willing to shoulder all responsibility. Neither my superiors or subordinates had anything to do with issuing instructions for experiments. If you ask me specific questions, I can tell you general results. Major Hinofuji was in charge of experimental work in anthrax. I read about the Ningpo incident in the Chinese paper *Shinko*. I was in Manchuria and do not know anything about the matter.*

I am wholly responsible for Pingfan. I do not want to see any of my subordinates or superiors get in trouble for what occurred. If you will give documentary immunity for myself, superiors and subordinates, I can get all the information for you.

The advisability of complying with Ishii's bargain – war crimes immunity *in written form* in exchange for scientific data – was to occupy some of Washington's most senior minds throughout the summer of 1947. Ishii continued:

Masuda, Kaneko and Naitō, whom you say you know, can give you a lot of information. I would like to be hired by the United States as a BW expert. In preparation for the war with Russia, I can give you the advantage of my twenty years' research and experience. I have given a great deal of thought to tactical problems in the defence against BW. I have made studies on the best agents to be employed in various regions and in cold climates. I can write volumes about BW, including the little-thought-of strategic and tactical employment.

The day's business with Ishii was concluded. As Fell, McQuail and Yoshihashi left Ishii's house, they discussed among themselves whether Ishii's sickness might be used as an excuse to refuse inter-rogation by the Russians. They resolved to explore the possibility.

On May 8th, the three Americans returned with Captain Penton, a medical officer from the 361st Station Hospital, to assess Ishii's

---

* Ishii, in fact, commanded this raid.

physical condition. Penton conferred with Ishii's personal physician first, then announced that "poor health" was insufficient reason to deny joint interrogation with the Russians.

After his medical examination Ishii was in a highly co-operative mood, and what had been intended as a short visit lasted for two hours. Ishii was notified that no decision had been reached about a written immunity deal. He was then presented with Masuda's letter.

> I will tell everything needed [he responded]. But it is such a broad field that I would like to know what aspects Dr Fell is interested in. I know very little about the experiments which went on at Anta after I left. I suggest that Kitano be contacted and questioned about humans getting pulmonary anthrax as a result of bomb bursts. I do not think the Germans got much information from the Japanese. The Germans were eager to get the data, but were always stalled off.[10]
>
> The free balloons were a secret project, and I did not know of their existence until I read about them in the newspaper. I do not know if their use as a BW agent was contemplated on high level information. It is such a problem that I can write a book on the subject. I used to think up a problem, assign experts to follow down on the defensive and offensive aspects, and submit a report. For this reason, I do not know the details of experiments.

Ishii was asked about the most effective BW agent.

"With regard to anthrax, I considered it the best agent because it could be produced in quantity, was resistant, retained its virulence, and was 80 to 90 per cent fatal. The best epidemic disease I considered to be plague. The best vector-borne disease I consider to be epidemic encephalitis."

Asked about Unit 731's final days in Manchuria, Ishii replied: "As to responsibility for the destruction of Pingfan, I do not know of formal instructions. I was in Harbin until August 9th when I found out officially that the Japanese were at war with the USSR. When I returned on that date, Pingfan was already burning. I was unable to get even my personal documents from my office."

Ishii was given detailed instructions to limit the scope of his answers to the Soviets. Fell noted that more briefing would be needed.

The following day an outline technical questionnaire was carefully read out to the former Lt-General. Ishii interrupted occasionally, asking questions and injecting ideas, but there was obviously still doubt about full co-operation without a written pledge of war crimes immunity. He meticulously avoided any direct reference to human

experimentation. However, it appeared to Fell that Ishii was prepared to do some work in the interim. Ishii requested to be interrogated in future at his home rather than the NYK building, because of
poor health and the fact that he was afraid to leave his house.

At this meeting Ishii revealed data on plague and cholera. The
minimum infectious dose (MID) of cholera, finally attained after
constant increases in the virulence of the best strain, he said was
about 3,000 organisms, 10^{-4} of an original liquid culture. For plague,
the MID was approximately 10^{-7}.

"Ishii did not specifically state that his technical discussion per-
tained to humans, but it was obvious," noted Fell.

On the subject of liaison between Unit 731 and Unit 100 (Kwantung Army Stables), Ishii stated: "I was in no way connected with the
Stables and know nothing of their activities."

As the interrogations continued with Ishii, Dr Kamei was still
supplying Fell and G-2 with a steady flow of information.

"I contacted Mr Miyamoto, a friend and associate of Ishii's," he
told McQuail. "Miyamoto is in the medical supply business, and was
awarded many war contracts through Ishii. He gives Ishii financial
assistance in gratitude. I convinced him of the necessity of seeing Ishii
and advising him to co-operate fully with Dr Fell."[11]

Fell also interviewed others of Unit 731's personnel and Unit 100's
commander Maj-Gen Yujirō Wakamatsu. Some were warned that
interrogation by the Russians might follow. All of them stressed their
lack of detailed knowledge and their lack of documents to refer to, as
well as a surprisingly uniform need of a few days "to prepare mentally
for interrogation".[12]

An element of mystery still surrounds the Soviet-American interrogations. No transcripts have yet come to light and the Russians
deny any such joint interrogations. Raginsky, who came from
Nuremberg to Japan in February 1947 to compile the BW information, has categorically stated they were never held.[13]

However, Ishii's daughter Harumi has recalled the Russian visits to
their home.

One day I was told by the Americans that Russian officers were
to visit my father and they warned me not to betray any hint of
the friendliness we had shown toward the American officers
accompanying the Soviets even if I recognized anyone.

We had at our home a pet monkey I had brought back from an
earlier trip. The animal took a liking to the khaki-clad American
soldiers. Once he jumped at an American officer in a playful

manner and all the Americans present were apparently embarrassed by the incident and shot glances at the Russian officers' faces. This was because they deliberately left the Russians out of the picture despite their repeated requests to interrogate my father.

The Soviet officers visited our house only twice. One was a female soldier who was apparently a stenographer. During their interviews with my father, American officers were present at all times. I presume further requests by the Russians to interview my father were rejected by the Americans.[14]

Correspondence recently discovered between Fell and G-2 refers directly to the joint interrogations. A letter from Fell to Willoughby stated: "We [Camp Detrick] received . . . together with Col McQuail's final report including transcripts of the joint interrogations."[15]

Another from McQuail to Fell stated:

We finished the last joint interrogation 13 June, and Ishii says since then he has been so nervous he can't think or sleep . . . Ishii has received threats from various unknowns and I called on CIC for help. Thus far nothing has developed . . . Yoshihashi has had an awful time with the transcripts. He has done a great deal of them himself. "Our Friends" [the Russians] wrote a letter to me pointing out to me that one and a half months had gone by and requested them at once. I sent them what we had to call them off, but it will take weeks before all of them are finished.[16]

By the time the joint interrogations took place, the Russians probably regarded them as of minor significance. It would not have escaped Soviet attention that the Americans had created sufficient time for experts to debrief the Japanese interviewees. Also, the Russians would have been aware that the Americans could gain valuable intelligence about Soviet BW from their line of questioning. The Americans, however, were still extremely concerned over whether the Soviet information would be produced at the Tokyo trial. But by then, the Soviet Union, in all likelihood, had shaped other plans to deal with the Japanese BW war criminals. Smirnov and Raginsky were later to play leading roles in those plans.

Newly returned to America, Fell submitted a report to CWS chief Maj-Gen Alden Waitt. It stated that:

nineteen key figures in the Japanese BW programme had spent almost a month assembling largely from memory a sixty-page report on BW activities against humans;

a botanist with Unit 731 was submitting a ten-page report covering research on crop diseases;

an interesting report had been received on the theoretical and mathematical considerations involved in particle-size determinations, and on droplet distribution of BW materials dispersed by bombs or aircraft sprays;

a summary of twelve field trials against Chinese civilians and soldiers as well as a map of the villages and towns involved had been submitted;

a short report had been received on the balloon bomb project;

an original printed document representing a series of leakages to spies and saboteurs had been obtained;

twenty members of Unit 100 were preparing a report into veterinary BW.

Fell's report also disclosed that 8,000 slides of pathological sections from more than 200 human cases of various diseases had been hidden in temples and buried in the mountains of southern Japan. The pathologist who directed the work, he said, was currently recovering the material and photomicrographing the slides. A report would soon be available.

Finally, Fell wrote that Ishii was preparing a treatise on the whole subject. "This work," Fell reported, "will include his ideas about the strategical and tactical use of BW weapons, how these weapons should be used in various geographical areas (particularly in cold climates), and full description of his *Do* theory about biological warfare."

None of these reports has yet come to light in public archives, and requests under the American Freedom of Information Act have proved fruitless. Camp Detrick, however, has admitted that the photomicrographs were until recently in their possession, although they have now been misplaced.[17] Considerable effort was made to get the pathological slides. McQuail wrote to Fell:

Yoshihashi and I are going to see Ishikawa [the Unit 731 pathologist who had kept the slides] next week. Masuda wrote me a letter in which he stated they had 50% more slides than estimated, or a total of 15,000. Also, some of the work must be done in Tokyo because the qualified photographer in Kanazawa* is a Communist.

* Dr Ishikawa was a professor of Kanazawa University.

I shipped Ishikawa four boxes of supplies, after a most difficult time obtaining certain chemicals he needed.[18]

McQuail's successor at G-2, Infantry Corps Major W. D. Drake, later updated Fell:

On August 6, Dr Masuda and Dr Ishikawa contacted Mr Yoshihashi and requested a conference with me . . . Dr Ishikawa had with him a portion of his report which he desired to show to me . . . I was impressed with the meticulous care evident in the preparation of this report . . . The doctor tells me that it will be the end of September before the report will be finished."[19]

Wakamatsu and his colleagues produced their report on veterinary BW on July 1st. Ishii, after a spell of poor health, was scheduled to complete his report by the end of August. Drake assured Fell that he was "keeping after" Ishii to ensure completion prior to Fell's return to Japan.

Fell himself never returned to Japan. The final round-up was left to two Camp Detrick pathologists, Dr Edwin Hill and Dr Joseph Victor.

However, there still survives a summary Fell made of the sixty-page Japanese report, included in the information sent to Waitt. It contained many revelations for the Americans.

It noted that during anthrax bomb trials "in most cases the human subjects were tied to stakes and protected with helmets and body armour". Fell wrote that anthrax immunisation experiments in humans with live spores were "followed by such violent reactions that it was concluded it could not be employed except in emergencies". The plague-spraying experiments, the glanders experiments and the flea bombs were all reported.

Willoughby congratulated Fell on the report. "Your letter and the report you made to the Chief of the Chemical Corps were most interesting to me," wrote Willoughby. "I brought it to the attention of the Commander-in-Chief [MacArthur] and the Chief of Staff." He also complimented Fell on his "proper technique" and the "discreet use" of Military Intelligence Division Confidential funds in gaining the BW information.

Fell's successful work, however, left Washington with two major problems: firstly, the politically sensitive issue of a written guarantee of war crimes immunity for the Japanese, and secondly, the danger that this embarrassing pact might be exposed by the Russians at the Tokyo trial. These problems were to occupy the Americans through until 1948.

Chapter 15

US Secret Knowledge

Even by the time Dr Fell had arrived in Japan, Legal Section had begun to realise that the ramifications of Case 1117 and some others were connected with another file, number 330. File 330 named Ishii in its title, and dealt directly with atrocities committed by Units 731 and 100. It was this file that the Russians had been aware of, and appear to have been alluding to, when Lt-Gen Derevyanko raised the BW issue at the Allied Council for Japan. Now that the Americans feared exposure by the Russians at the Tokyo trial, G-2 was forced into making some quick decisions about closing down cases 1117, 330 and others.[1] It required some careful co-ordination and planning, notably with the IPS, to do so.

An open admission about human experimentation, allegations about the use of BW, even hints about the connection between Unit 731 and a member of the Japanese Imperial family, were all contained in the files of Legal Section's Case 330 by the middle of 1947. How had this come about, and why was nothing done about the files' contents?

Case 330 was made up from dozens of pieces of disparate evidence. The file's long narrative title bears witness to the number of suspects thought to be involved. When Lt Neal Smith summarised the case that spring, the unwieldy title read: "Motoji Yamaguchi, alias Honji Yamaguchi, Yujirō Wakamatsu, Yasazuka, Yasutaro Hosoka alias Yasutara Hozaka, Shirō Matsushida alias Shirō Yamashita, Shirō Ishii alias Hajime Tōgō". Smith's summary described how the file had opened:

> This investigation was originally predicated upon the receipt of an undated letter from a person giving his name as Nishimura which reflects that members of the Imperial Japanese Army infected PoWs with glanders and then dissected their bodies as an experiment. Named as responsible for the experiments were: former Maj Honji Yamaguchi, former Maj-Gen Yujirō Wakamatsu, former Lt-Gen Yasuzaka (fnu)* and Capt Shirō Matsushida.[2]

* fnu = "first name unknown".

Received by GHQ as early as autumn 1945, Nishimura's letter accused former graduates of the Tokyo Military Veterinarian School. Its contents clearly refer to Unit 100's activities. Legal Section discovered later that the human experiments had been carried out in an open field near Mokotan [Mukden].*

Next, Legal Section had acquired information about Ishii. It is clear from Smith's report of April 1947 that as early as February 1946, at the time of Thompson's investigation, Legal Section had been given extensive allegations, some by the Counter Intelligence Corps, about Ishii's criminal acts. His report for the period summarised the accusations of research into bacteriological warfare, with corroborative details of place and supplies, and specifically named Ishii as one of those responsible for experimentation on human beings.

Despite the gravity of the allegations, Legal Section had not held any interrogations until June 26th, 1946 when former Unit 100 member Kino was interviewed. Kino admitted he had heard of experiments, but was unable to recall whether they were performed on PoWs or Chinese coolies. Interrogated at a later date by Smith, twenty-nine-year-old Kino revealed his suspicion that the experimental subjects were Russians, and that their death had been caused either by injection of bacteria or by germs added to food. Kino named Motoji Yamaguchi as head of Unit 100's human experiment section.

In August, Yamaguchi was found and interrogated. He denied the charges. But later that month, he was again accused in another letter to the Occupation authorities which read:

The above veterinary surgeons [Yamaguchi, Wakamatsu, Hozaka] dissected many war prisoners of the Allied Forces at the outdoor dissecting ground of No 100 Army Corps at Hsinking (Changchun), Manchuria, as their inspections of the cattle plague. If you would investigate these criminals, you will find many other persons who have participated in the dissections. There are a number of witnesses to the inspections.[4]

Ishii was again named as a war criminal in October in a letter from Hiroshi Ueki of Kyoto. Smith recorded:

Ueki alleged that during the present war Lt-Gen Shirō Ishii, an army medical doctor, established a large scale human experimental

---

*Unit 100 buried the bodies of human experimentees in trenches in the cattle cemetery at the back of the detachment's premises.[3]

station in the suburbs of Harbin. He allegedly acted as commander of the fictitious *Kamo* Unit and executed brutal experiments on many Allied PoWs. According to Ueki it was no secret that he destroyed the experimental station and evidence of his activities. Ueki further alleged that Ishii considered the placing of his name on a war crime suspect list as inevitable and has been using bribes to escape the consequences of his acts.[5]

But perhaps the most startling accusations were made in an anonymous letter to GHQ which reached Legal Section in November. It read:

> . . . A repatriate from Manchuria reported in a newspaper that he [Lt-Gen Ishii] was shot to death, but this is not a fact, this article was made by the order of the [Japanese] government and nothing else. He was a well known militarist and enemy of humanity . . . I was once attached to his corps, so I know quite well about his work. Militarists are afraid of his summons [by GHQ], as secrets will be revealed by it. His summoning will provide evidence and data against "A" class war criminal suspects and even one Imperial family member will be affected. So the cabinets, especially the Foreign Ministry, ex-Army Ministry, De-Mobilization Board and Liaison Office have endeavoured to make this case lost in oblivion. I believe that it is utterly necessary to judge him and those who planned and worked with him fairly for the establishment of a truly peaceful country.[6]

The informant suggested he could be contacted if a specially-worded advertisement was placed in the *Nihon Keizai Press* within three days. But as the letter was not translated in time, no contact was made.

In December, Unit 100 Commander Lt-Gen Yujirō Wakamatsu was interrogated. Like his colleague Yamaguchi, he also denied all accusations. He claimed, however, that it was common knowledge that an "unknown" number of Manchurians had died of glanders after herding diseased animals. The Legal Section interrogator noted that Wakamatsu appeared to be withholding information.

It was Lt-Col Ryōichi Naitō, the man who had been Sanders' interpreter and who had also been interviewed by Thompson and Fell, who made the most damaging revelations.

> . . . Naitō said that it was common knowledge among the microbiologists in Japan, all of whom were connected with Ishii, that

humans were used for experimentation at the Harbin installation, and that Ishii used the alias of Hajime Tōgō during the course of the experiments, as did all of his officers connected with the laboratory during their tour of duty.[7]

By March 1947, Legal Section's Case 330 investigation was in full flood. Allegations were received that photographs had been taken at Unit 100 of dissected PoWs. Masuda was interviewed, then Kitano.

The following month in his summary of the case, Smith was able to conclude that "the trend of the research reflects that this was a part of a large scale plan for the initiation of strategic bacterial warfare."[8]

Legal Section's file had, however, by then become a security risk. G-2 first reclassified the case "confidential", then "secret". G-2 also curtailed the Legal Section investigation and took it over. It had become a "security threat" because the Russian delegation in Japan appear to have had some sort of access to Legal Section files. This is evident from the references to Legal Section contained in the irate memorandum submitted by the USSR member of the Allied Council for Japan when, on March 7th, he demanded that Ishii and Ōta be handed over to be tried by the Russians.

Meanwhile in Washington, the SWNCC continued its agonising deliberations about Ishii's demand for a written guarantee of war crimes immunity. The Army's War Crimes Branch cabled Legal Section Chief Alva Carpenter for advice:

It is imperative that you furnish this office by cable soonest detailed information on all possible war crimes evidence or charges against Ishii or any number of groups . . . for consideration in conference here concerning this matter. Specifically that evidence of war crimes is now in possession of US authorities against Ishii or any member of groups for whom he has requested a guarantee of immunity. Which of our Allies have filed war crimes charges against Ishii . . . ? Is Ishii or any member of groups included among major Japanese war criminals awaiting trial? Please co-ordinate with Tavenner of IPS.[9]

Carpenter's carefully worded response was an exercise to reassure Washington. It is interesting to note that he avoided any direct admissions that Legal Section had gained about human experiments or the use of BW. It read:

1 The reports and files of the Legal Section on Ishii and his co-workers are based on anonymous letters, hearsay affidavits and

rumors. The Legal Section interrogations, to date, of the numerous persons concerned with the BW project in China, do not reveal sufficient evidence to support war crimes charges. The alleged victims are of unknown identity. Unconfirmed allegations are to the effect that criminals, farmers, women and children were used for BW experimental purposes. The Japanese Communist Party alleges that "Ishii BKA" (Bacterial War Army) conducted experiments on captured Americans in Mukden and that simultaneously, research on similar lines was conducted in Tokyo and Kyōto.

2 None of Ishii's subordinates are charged or held as war crimes suspects, nor is there sufficient evidence on file against them. Ishii's possible superiors, who are now on trial before IMTFE, include Umezu, Commander, Kwantung Army, 1939–44, Minami, Commander, Kwantung Army 1934–36, Koiso, Chief of Staff, Kwantung Army 1932–34, Tōjō, Chief of Staff, Kwantung Army 1937–38.

3 None of our Allies to date have filed war crimes charges against Ishii or any of his associates.

4 Neither Ishii nor his associates are included among major Japanese war criminals awaiting trial.

5 This matter co-ordinated with Tavenner of IPS, who reports as follows:

A. Maj-Gen Kiyoshi Kawashima and Maj Tomio Karasawa, subordinates of Ishii, are held by the Soviets, presumably as war criminal suspects. No subordinates are charged or held by US as war crimes suspects. Affidavits of above-mentioned subordinates and of Lt-Gen-Hikosaburo Hata, Chief of Staff, Kwantung Army, and Doctor Peter Z. King, are on file in IPS.

B Kawashima affidavit alleges detachment had secret duty of research of virus for the purpose of using them in war and experiments were conducted. Ishii called attention of his staff to instructions from General Staff in Tokyo to improve virus war researches.

C Karasawa affidavit states that Ishii detachment experimented as to most effective virus, germ cultivation, the way of infection, dispersing germs as means of attack, large-scale production of virus, preservation of virus and discovery of preventive materials.

D Hata affidavit states that Ishii was very anxiously controlling detachment under the instruction of General Staff in order to find out new virus and preventive materials, but it does not state that the General Staff intended to resort to bacteria warfare.

E The affidavit of Doctor Peter Z. King reflects that Japanese planes scattered wheat grains at Ningpo October 29th, 1940, and Changteh on November 4th, 1940, and shortly after each occurrence bubonic plague appeared.

F Since certain of Ishii superiors are now on trial for major war crimes before IMTFE, use of this material was considered by IPS and decision was reached by IPS in December 1946 on the basis of information then available that these witnesses should not be produced, as evidence was not sufficient to connect any of these accused with Ishii's detachment's secret activities, the tribunal having announced prior thereto that evidence relating to atrocities and prisoners of war would not be received in the absence of an assurance by the prosecution that the accused or some of them could be associated with the acts charged. The Soviet prosecutor probably will endeavour in cross-examination of one or more accused to lay foundation for the use in rebuttal of the above-mentioned evidence and the evidence which may have resulted from their independent investigation.[10]*

This reply, however, failed to put Washington at ease. Two weeks later, Carpenter was again radioed:

Request soonest clarification and further details . . . particularly IPS opinion as to whether evidence now in its possession warrants opinion that Japanese BW group headed by Ishii did violate rules of land warfare. We are satisfied evidence now in possession Legal Section, SCAP, does not warrant such charge against and trial of Ishii and his group. Must have information re all possible proof re Ishii group participation in activities that could be considered war crimes under rules of land warfare before reaching decision re 3B and 5 [MacArthur's recommendation of written immunity from war crimes for Ishii group (see p. 195)] dated May 6, 1947.[11]

In perhaps a pragmatic attempt to forestall further concern in Washington, MacArthur stepped in and issued a curt reply: "Any pressure will endanger present status of valuable BCW [biological and chemical warfare] intelligence. Refer to Dr Fell now returned to CWS."[12]

A few days later, Carpenter reported a new and more worrying opinion to Washington after further liaison with Tavenner. He explained this had come about because IPS had only just translated the full contents of the Kawashima and Karasawa affidavits. It is

---

* It is interesting to note that the Tribunal *did* admit evidence on atrocities where the connection with the accused was far more remote or even non-existent.

difficult to believe the truth of this statement, and one must be suspicious of a ploy on Carpenter or Tavenner's part. IPS and G-2 had held the two affidavits since at least January 1947, and even if the Russians are to be believed, since September 1946. Such important documents were unlikely to have remained untranslated and out of circulation, unless G-2, which controlled the translation agency ATIS, had desired such restriction. In any event, McQuail of G-2 and Waldorf of IPS had been present when the Russian Smirnov had made his allegations about human experimentation and the use of BW.

Carpenter's reply to Washington hinted that the matter could be skated over at the trial:

> IPS of the opinion that foregoing information warrants conclusion that Japanese BW group head by Ishii *did violate the rules of land warfare, but this expression of opinion is not a recommendation that group be charged and tried for such* [Authors' italics]. Karasawa affidavit would necessarily need collaboration and testing for trustworthiness by a thorough investigation before prosecutive action is decided upon.
>
> . . . IPS did not include any evidence reference BW in its Case in Chief because at time of closing case it could not assure the Tribunal under its rulings that the Accused or some of them would be known to have been associated with acts of BW group. Since seeing translation of Karasawa affidavit IPS more certain than before that Soviet Prosecutor will endeavour in cross examination of one or more of the Accused to lay foundation for the use in rebuttal of some of the evidence above recited and other evidence on this subject which may have resulted from their independent investigation in Manchuria and Japan.
>
> Copies of pertinent affidavits are being forwarded for your information.[13]

In Washington, the SWNCC's sub-committee for the Far East prepared a report in conjunction with the CWS, the War Department's Intelligence Division and War Crimes Branch, the Office of Naval Intelligence and the Air Chemical Office, after noting Carpenter's comments. The sub-committee also drew an international comparison:

> Experiments on human beings similar to those conducted by the Ishii Group have been condemned as war crimes by the International Military Tribunal for the trial of major Nazi war criminals in its decision handed down at Nuremberg on September 30, 1946.

This Government is at present prosecuting leading German scientists and medical doctors at Nuremberg for offences which included experiments on human beings which resulted in the suffering and death of most of those experimented on.[14]*

This argument was balanced against the high value of the Japanese BW information:

Data already obtained from Ishii and his colleagues have proven to be of great value in confirming, supplementing and complementing several phases of US research in BW, and may suggest new fields for future research.

This Japanese information is the only known source of data from scientifically controlled experiments showing the direct effect of BW agents on man. In the past it has been necessary to evaluate the effects of BW agents on man from data through animal experimentation. Such evaluation is inconclusive and far less complete than results obtained from certain types of human experimentation . . .[15]

On balance, the sub-committee felt it was desirable to avoid a war crimes prosecution:

Since it is believed that the USSR possesses only a small portion of this technical information, and since any "war crimes" trial would completely reveal such data to all nations, it is felt that such publicity must be avoided in interests of defense and security of the US. It is believed also that "war crimes" prosecution of Ishii and his associates would serve to stop the flow of much additional information of a technical and scientific nature.

It is felt that the use of this information as a basis for "war crimes" evidence would be a grave detriment to Japanese co-operation with the United States occupation forces in Japan.

For all practical purposes an agreement with Ishii and his associates that information given by them on the Japanese BW program will be retained in intelligence channels is equivalent to an agreement that this Government will not prosecute any of those involved in BW activities in which war crimes were committed. Such an understanding would be of great value to the security of the

---

* A number of token prosecutions were held, notably for high altitude and freezing experiments. However, a parallel round-up of German scientists, code-named "Operation Paperclip", had also secretly taken place.

American people because of the information which Ishii and his associates have already furnished and will continue to furnish. However, it should be kept in mind that there is a remote possibility that independent investigation conducted by the Soviets in the Mukden Area may have disclosed evidence that American prisoners of war were used for experimental purposes of a BW nature and that they lost their lives as a result of these experiments, and further, that such evidence may be introduced by the Soviet prosecutors in the course of cross-examination of certain of the major Japanese war criminals now on trial at Tokyo, particularly during the cross-examination of Umezu, Commander of the Kwantung Army from 1939 to 1944 of which army the Ishii BW group was a part. In addition, there is a strong possibility that the Soviet prosecutors will, in the course of cross-examination of Umezu, introduce evidence of experiments conducted on human beings by the Ishii BW group, which experiments do not differ greatly from those for which this Government is now prosecuting German scientists and medical doctors at Nuremberg.[16]

The sub-committee concluded that:

. . . c) The value to the US of Japanese BW data is of such importance to national security as to far outweigh the value accruing from "war crimes" prosecution.

d) In the interests of national security it would not be advisable to make this information available to other nations as would be the case in the event of a "war crimes" trial of Japanese BW experts.

e) The BW information obtained from Japanese sources should be retained in intelligence channels and should not be employed as "war crimes" evidence.[17]

The SWNCC was urged to agree to MacArthur's proposal. It was recommended that the Japanese involved be told that all information would be retained in "top secret" Intelligence channels and not be employed as war crimes evidence.[18]

Only the State Department's representative disagreed with this course of action. And in a prophetic warning he outlined the dangers of making such a promise: "It is believed . . . that it is possible that the desired information can be obtained . . . without these assurances, and that it might later be a source of serious embarrassment to the United States if the assurances were given."

The State Department's fears were later to be fully justified. Instead, the Department recommended that information be gained without formal commitment, and only retained in Intelligence channels "unless evidence developed at the International Military Trial presents overwhelming reasons whereby this procedure can no longer be followed".[19]

The Army's Civil Affairs Division objected to the State Department's proposal pointing out that:

> ... it is apparent from a reading of the entire message [MacArthur's original May 6 recommendation to Washington] that it is the wish of the CINCFE to make the most expeditious arrangements possible with the Japanese BW group ... for the desired information and that in his opinion this [assurance about war crimes immunity] is the least possible offer that can be successfully made.
>
> It is recognized that ... this government may at a later date be seriously embarrassed. However, the Army Department and Air Force members strongly believe that this information ... is of such importance to the security of this country that the risk of subsequent embarrassment should be taken ... it is believed that, in the final analysis, the security of the United States is of primary importance.[20]

Consideration was given as to whether the SWNCC could be presented with a split report. But in the end, the matter was postponed by an agreement that representatives of the Chemical Corps, about to depart for the Far East, would investigate to determine whether MacArthur had made the best possible bargain with the Japanese BW group.

Meanwhile, in Japan, GHQ was taking a keen, but discreet, interest in the Washington deliberations. McQuail wrote to Fell on July 2:

> We are worried about the war crimes aspect due to two recent radio inquiries from War Crimes in Washington ... We are hoping that you have been conferred with and have been able to present the true picture. We sent a couple of radios to MID [Military Intelligence Division] suggesting that you be called in to see War Crimes.
>
> Yesterday, I went over to IPS to see the Chief Prosecutor to get the true picture. It appears that "our friends" [the Russians] will attempt to get in some of the affidavits. Also, I was shown for the first time the Chinese affidavits. It appears that the Chinese had a medical investigation. The dates tie in, and copies would probably

supplement the chart which you got. I got a promise that copies would be given to me as soon as typed. I will send them to you when available.[21]

Again, this is clear evidence that the Chinese and IPS had put together a coherent BW case against the Japanese, although such evidence was never, saving the brief Sutton incident, presented before the court.

McQuail added: "Would like to hear from you as to what they think of the material you took with you, and what is really behind the radios from War Crimes."

On July 22nd, Willoughby wrote to tell Fell that funds for Camp Detrick's Japanese BW Intelligence investigation had ceased at the end of June. Perhaps in the hope of once again putting some distance between Washington and Tokyo, he wrote:

Thus, I will be unable to support Dr Ishikawa's work, Ishii's report, and the supplementary report on crop destruction with confidential funds as I did during your stay. What I am seeking is some support from your end, specifically, that "someone should suggest" the unrestricted use of MID authorized and allotted funds for this purpose instead of hamstringing us?[22]

Fell replied:

Since receiving your letter . . . we have been exploring the possibilities of obtaining some solution of the problem you mentioned. However, the feeling of several staff groups in Washington, including G-2, is that this problem is more or less a "family" affair in FEC [Far East Command]. Nevertheless, we have continued to stress the importance of obtaining all possible information by any reasonable methods.[23]

What exactly he meant by such a "family" affair inside Far East Command is unclear. Again one is drawn towards speculating that FEC had already set up an organisation and procedures for full-scale technical liaison with Unit 731's former members.

It is interesting to note that, in August 1947, US Naval Intelligence circulated a document that, almost incidentally, hammered home the fact that human beings were indeed known to have been used by the Japanese in experiments. A summary of this document, the Inglis Report, is reproduced in Appendix D.

Fell had been dispatched to England, and he did not return to Japan. His place was taken by Camp Detrick pathologists Dr Edwin V. Hill, chief of Basic Sciences, and Dr Joseph Victor. They were sent to Japan to examine and find suitable protocols for understanding Dr Ishikawa's pathological material, and generally to complete the BW investigation.

When Hill and Victor arrived at Kanazawa University, however, they found Ishikawa's specimens in complete disorder. As they began preparing an inventory of specimens from the approximately 500 human cases, only 400 of which were found fit for study, it became obvious that much material was being withheld. "However," wrote Hill, "it required only slight encouragement to obtain an additional collection of specimens which was considerably more than first submitted."[24]

Assisted by Unit 731 pathologist Kōzō Okamoto, they produced a results table.[25]

Disease	Human Cases Adequate Material	Total
Anthrax	31	36
Botulism	0	2
Brucellosis	1	3
Carbon Monoxide	0	1
Cholera	50	135
Dysentery	12	21
Glanders	20	22
Meningococcus	1	5
Mustard Gas	16	16
Plague	42	180
Plague Epidemic	64	66
Poisoning	0	2
Salmonella	11	14
Songo	52	101
Smallpox	2	4
Streptococcus	1	3
Suicide	11	30
Tetanus	14	32
Tick Encephalitis	1	2
Tsutsugamushi	0	2
Tuberculosis	41	82
Typhoid	22	63
Typhus	9	26
Vaccination	2	2
	403	850

As well as assembling the pathological information, Hill and Victor throughout November interviewed many participants in the Japanese BW programme, including researchers from academia. They spoke to Shirō Ishii, Kiyoshi Ōta, Jun'ichi Kaneko, Kōzō Okamoto, Tomosada Masuda, Yukimasa Yagisawa, Masaji Kitano, Shirō Kasahara, Tachiomaru Ishikawa, Kiyoshi Hayakawa, Masahiko Takahashi, Yujirō Yamanouchi, Yoshifumi Tsuyama, Masaaki Ueda, Saburō Kojima, Shōgo Hosoya, Kanau Tabei, Senji Uchino, Kaoru Ishimitsu, Hideo Futaki, Masayoshi Arita and Toyohiro Hamada.

Additionally, they were given research data on botulism, brucellosis, gas gangrene, influenza, meningococcus, mucin, smallpox, tick encephalitis, tuberculosis, tularemia, tsutsugamushi fever (scrub typhus), *fugū* toxin and about decontamination procedures.

Ishii was particularly reticent about providing information, and restricted himself to providing only the briefest outline on the numbers of human experiments, the mortality rate and infection method in the diseases he had researched. However, he revealed that influenza virus had been derived from "American sources".

Ōta stated that anthrax experiments had begun before 1937 in the laboratory of the South Manchurian Railway Company in Mukden. Takahashi described to the Camp Detrick men the octagonal-shaped aerosol chamber used for human experimentation. Hayakawa and Yamanouchi handed over human experimental data on the brucellosis research that had begun in 1939. It was obvious from Hayakawa, in charge of media preparation at Pingfan from 1937 to 1940, that he had been aware of the human guinea pig tests before he left Japan in 1939 to study for six months at the University of Michigan!

Tsuyama, who had worked at the Army Medical College in Tokyo from 1943 to 1945, explained decontamination techniques. Masuda and Tabei were interviewed about dysentery. Assistant director of the National Institute of Health, Dr Saburo Kojima, although not a participant in human experimentation, was asked about salmonella, dysentery and typhoid. Hosoya described immunisation tests with gas gangrene toxoid on ten subjects.

Ueda and Uchino, the latter a professor in Kyoto University's biochemistry department, told Hill and Victor about their work with mucin which had been "purchased from American sources"!

Kasahara and Kitano were interviewed about epidemic haemorrhagic fever. Kasahara produced some records, temperature charts and pertinent clinical data on three human tests. Kitano and Kasahara admitted that mortality in experimental cases was 100 per cent due to the procedure of sacrificing experimental subjects.

Obviously impressed by the information they had uncovered, Hill wrote to the chief of the Chemical Corps, Gen Alden Waitt, about the findings:

Evidence gathered in this investigation has greatly supplemented and amplified previous aspects of this field. It represents data which have been obtained by Japanese scientists at the expenditure of many millions of dollars and years of work. Information has accrued with respect to human susceptibility to those diseases as indicated by specific infectious doses of bacteria. Such information could not be obtained in our own laboratories because of scruples attached to human experimentation. These data were secured with a total outlay of Y250,000 to date, a mere pittance by comparison with the actual cost of the studies.

Furthermore, the pathological material which has been collected constitutes the only material evidence of the nature of these experiments. It is hoped that individuals who voluntarily contributed this information will be spared embarrassment because of it and that every effort will be taken to prevent this information from falling into other hands.[26]

Hill, perhaps trying to allay fears in Washington, noted that all "information supplied by interviewed persons was admitted voluntarily. No question of immunity guarantee from war crimes prosecution was ever raised during the interviews."

In Washington, the Chemical Corps informed the SWNCC that the problem of MacArthur's written immunity deal had "about solved itself by the passage of time". For the purposes of record the sub-committee reconvened itself on March 4th, 1948, to draft a formal reply to MacArthur. A paper attached to the minutes noted:

It is believed the fact that the taking of evidence in the IMTFE at Tokyo has just been completed will remove one cause of disagreement among the working party. While it is true that an additional six weeks will be devoted to argument in this case, it may be assumed that for the purpose of the matter at issue, the trial is at an end.[27]

The State-Army-Navy-Air Force Co-ordinating Committee cabled their reply to MacArthur:

. . . Reports by technical experts who have returned from your theatre indicate that to date necessary information and scientific data have been obtained to your satisfaction. Suggest your recommendation . . . be resubmitted for further consideration if and when you consider necessary.[28]

Satisfied they had been given the whole story, the Americans were presumably further delighted that the matter was not raised by the Russians at the Tokyo trial. Only in two isolated instances during the defence case did BW raise its head again, only to be lost in the mass of evidence produced at the trial.

On September 10th, 1947, during remarks made by Lawrence McManus in opening the individual defence of Sadao Araki, the man who while War Minister had supported Ishii's BW plans, mention was made of chemical and biological warfare. McManus stated that he intended to introduce evidence which would prove that ever since the First World War, Araki had "condemned the use of poison gas or bacteria as a crime and contended that the destructive power of weapons should be limited and that war damage upon women, children and other non-combatants should be avoided at all costs". The following pages of the trial document, however, show that the tribunal upheld prosecution objections, put by Comyns Carr, that effectively blocked such evidence.[29]

The other incident occurred almost immediately before that. During the fifth sub-division of Division Five of the defence case on September 8th and 9th, James N. Freeman presented evidence designed to show the Japanese Army's humanitarian concern for the welfare of PoWs and civilian internees held in their custody.

During an examination of Colonel Tadashi Odajima, formerly a senior official in the PoW Information Bureau and the PoW Control Bureau at the War Ministry, various reports were tendered which showed that some malnutritional studies had been made by the Army Medical College on PoWs detained in the Tokyo PoW Camp and numbers 1, 2 and 5 Branch Camps, beginning in February 1943.

As Odajima continued his testimony, the trial was given evidence of orders issued by General Umezu on February 1st, 1943, instructing the Chief Supply Officer and Officer Commanding the Kwantung Army's Anti-Infection and Water Supply Main Dept (Unit 731) to improve medical services at the Mukden PoW camp. Then came evidence about the general state of health suffered by 1,485 Anglo-Saxon PoWs transported to Mukden camp "for a certain purpose".[30] The words used in the report "for a certain purpose" have a chilling ring to our ears, although none of the extracts read by the defence make any reference to PoWs being used as guinea pigs in BW experiments.

Also in September, during the section of the tribunal which dealt with the infamous Burma–Siam Railway, the importance of Unit 731's forces in South-East Asia became apparent. In his sworn testimony, Army Medical Colonel Tsuneo Yasuda, once directly responsible for medical and sanitary affairs to the commander of the Southern Army's Medical Administration, stated that the Water Supply and Purification Department "was most powerful in the said army's operation area".[31] In fact, the commander of the Unit, a Colonel Kitagawa, was appointed to direct the Railway Corps Medical Unit and "to launch those medical services into full swing". Yet it was notorious, and remains so, that the Japanese showed the most callous disregard for the health of prisoners-of-war working on the project.

Final arguments before the IMTFE lasted until April 16th, 1948. By that date the trial record covered a staggering 48,412 pages. Seven months later, between November 4th and 12th, the tribunal rendered its judgment in an opinion 1,218 pages long. In it, the judges rejected challenges to the tribunal's jurisdiction, issued findings of fact on the eighteen-year period of Japanese history and rendered judgment and verdicts on the accused. The tribunal upheld the prosecution's interpretation of evidence that there had been a conspiracy to wage aggressive wars; that such wars had been waged, and that the responsible Japanese leaders had shown reckless disregard for the welfare of PoWs.

For all but two of the accused, the verdict was "guilty of conspiracy to wage aggressive war". Seven of the men were condemned to death by hanging, including Tōjō, Itagaki and Doihara. Araki, Umezu, Hata, Minami and Koiso were sentenced to life imprisonment.

The tribunal, however, did not speak with one voice. Six different opinions were returned by the eleven justices, and the majority decision was only signed by nine of them. Justice Pal of India found all the defendants innocent, Justice Bernard of France found the defendants not guilty because of defective procedures at the trial. Justice Röling of the Netherlands found that career diplomat and former premier Hirota, sentenced to death, and four others receiving lesser sentences, were innocent. Even President of the Tribunal Webb had some reservations. He argued that the death penalty was perhaps inappropriate. If deterrence is "the main purpose of punishment for an offence", he stated, then "imprisonment for life under sustained conditions of hardship in an isolated place or places outside Japan . . . would be a greater deterrent to men like the accused than the speedy termination of existence on the scaffold or before a firing squad." He added that it might prove a revolting spectacle to hang or shoot such old men and that, anyway, the "leader in the crime, though available for trial, had been granted immunity". He wrote: "Justice requires me to take into consideration the Emperor's immunity when determining the punishment of the accused found guilty."[32]

The defendants were granted ten days in which to appeal to the Supreme Commander. On November 24th, 1948, MacArthur, after consultation with the diplomatic representatives in Japan of the nations making up the Far Eastern Commission, confirmed the sentences, issuing a proclamation, part of which read:

> No duty I have ever been called upon to perform in a long, public service replete with many bitter, lonely, and forlorn assignments and responsibilities is so utterly repugnant to me as that of reviewing the sentences of the Japanese war criminal defendants by the International Military Tribunal for the Far East . . .
>
> Insofar as my own immediate obligation and limited authority in this case is concerned, suffice it that under the principles and procedures described in full detail by the Allied Powers concerned, I can find nothing of commission or omission in the incidents of the Trial itself of sufficient import to warrant my intervention in the judgements which have been rendered. No human decision is infallible, but I can conceive of no judicial process where greater safeguard was made to evolve justice . . .[33]

The stern justice promised by the Allies at Potsdam was quick to follow the Japanese camp guards and staff at Mukden (Hoten) PoW camp, when compared to the treatment given to the members of Unit 731. By as early as October 1945, no fewer than seventy of them were subject to immediate capture and detention to face lesser war crimes trials. Although almost all were prisoners of the Russians, the Far Eastern and Pacific Sub-Commission of the United Nations War Crimes Commission had ordered that immediately any were apprehended the China Theatre Headquarters of the US Armed Forces was to be informed. The Commission had by then been satisfied that there was, or would be by the time of any trial, sufficient evidence to justify their prosecution.[34]

On November 9th, 1946, the *Army Times* recorded:

> Shanghai – The Chief Medical Officer of the prison camp in Manchuria where Gen Jonathan Wainright was held prisoner was convicted of being a war criminal this week and sentenced to be hanged.

The four-man American Military Tribunal convicted Capt Jiuchi Kuwashima without recommendation for clemency. The Tribunal also convicted Col Genji Matsuda, camp commandant, and sentenced him to seven years in prison.

Kuwashima was hanged on February 1st, 1947.

No member of Unit 731, however, was called before any British or American military tribunal to account for war crimes. And although it had originally been intended to hold further major war crimes trials, the British and Americans announced in December 1946 during the closing stages of the prosecution's case before the IMTFE that they did not wish to carry out such supplementary tribunals. Only the Russians wished such a course of action.

Chapter 16

Six Days at Khabarovsk

Christmas Day 1949 dawned mild and overcast in London, crisp and sunny in Washington and cold and grey in a busy industrial town on the eastern side of the Soviet Union.

The people of Khabarovsk – those of them who could find a place – trooped along to a cavernous courtroom to hear and see Japanese soldiers and scientists stand trial, accused of researching biological warfare and experimenting on human beings to find out whether the diseases they dispensed would prove effective.[1]

The trial lasted six days, from December 25th to 30th. No Western observers attended the hearings; all reports came from official Soviet statements from Moscow. There were twelve accused, all members of the Japanese armed forces, men who, if the propaganda could be stripped away, would tell one of the most extraordinary and brutal stories of the Second World War. They told it without frills and, apparently, under scant pressure save the knowledge of the predicament in which they found themselves. There was an air of resignation in the way they detailed the story, extending even to the most senior figure among the twelve – General Otozō Yamada.

Yamada was commander-in-chief of Japan's vast Kwantung Army when he was captured by the Russians. He was thus directly responsible for the work of Unit 731. On the morning of December 26th, 1949, Yamada admitted in evidence that Unit 731 "was formed with the object of preparing for bacteriological warfare, chiefly against the Soviet Union, Mongolia and China".

It was further intended, he said, "to employ the bacteriological weapons against any other enemy state or enemy army . . . the United States and Britain, in particular".

Beside Yamada in the dock were eleven other men who had failed to flee eastwards quickly enough to avoid being captured by the Russians. They were:

Lt-Gen Ryūiji Kajitsuka, chief of the Medical Administration in the Kwantung Army, a bacteriologist, and a doctor of medical science;
Major General Kiyoshi Kawashima, who had served in Unit 731

220

from April 1939 to March 1943 and who had a number of divisions in that Unit "including the experimental division";

Lt-Gen Takaatsu Takahashi, who from 1941 to 1945 was head of the Veterinary Division of the Kwantung Army;

Major Tomio Karasawa, a Medical Corps officer who had been in charge of a section of Unit 731 that produced in a factory germs on a large scale;

Lt-Col Toshihide Nishi, whose responsibility had been to breed fleas, white rats, mice and guinea pigs in vast numbers, and to catch field rodents, to grow the bacteria Unit 731 needed for the experiments;

Major Masao Onoue, who, like Nishi, had bred laboratory animals, and had trained cadres of bacteriological laboratory assistants in Unit 731;

Maj-Gen Shunji Sato, who had produced the germs while in charge of two of Unit 731's divisions – the Canton Detachment *Nami* 8604 and the Nanking detachment *Tama* or *Ei* 1644;

Lt Zensaku Hirazakura, a bacteriologist researcher, who admitted "producing germs and strong poisons" in Unit 100;

Senior Sergeant Kazuo Mitomo, who admitted manufacturing anthrax, glanders, cattle plague and sheep plague for use in bacteriological warfare;

Corporal Norimitsu Kikuchi, a probationer medical orderly of branch 643 of Unit 731 who tried to produce a medium in which typhoid, paratyphoid, dysentery and tuberculosis germs would grow more quickly; and

Pte Yuji Kurushima, once a laboratory orderly in "branch 162", who had dissected fleas, caught rats, put germs into test tubes and taken part in Unit 731 preparations for germ attacks on China.

The Russian haul of members of Japan's bacteriological warfare machine was small but representative, comprehensive enough to give a clear overall picture of what the Unit was, and what it was trying to do.

As the evidence unfolded, it revealed that there were two units – Unit 731, formed to prepare and carry out bacteriological warfare, and Unit 100, which was "charged with the duty of carrying out sabotage measures . . . infecting pastures, cattle, and water sources with epidemic germs . . . [a unit] closely connected with the Intelligence Division of the Kwantung Army headquarters".

It was during this trial that there emerged many of the details of Unit 731's work that have already been quoted in this book. The setting up of the laboratories and workshops, the appalling experiments on human beings, the BW attacks on China – all were exposed.

On the evening of December 29th, the state prosecutor, State Counsellor of Jurisprudence of the Third Class, L. N. Smirnov, rose to close the case for the prosecution. He had painstakingly assembled a formidable argument. He had seen his country humiliated in its attempt to introduce fabricated evidence at the Tokyo trial but the result of the case before him now was a foregone conclusion. Smirnov chose, however, to launch into a strong attack of Japanese military intentions in the 1930s in that they threatened the Soviet Union and, more importantly, to cast his closing speech at targets far outside the dock. What about those Japanese soldiers and scientists who had escaped the Soviet net? he asked. What about Ishii and Kitano and Wakamatsu? What about Ōta and Murakami, Ikari, Tanaka and Yoshimura who had "mercilessly and in cold blood murdered defenceless people and bred many millions of plague-infested parasites and hundreds of kilograms of lethal microbes for the extermination of mankind"?

Smirnov spelled out a message intended for the ears of an audience thousands of miles from the courtroom in Khabarovsk. These men, Ishii and the rest, "enjoy the protection of those reactionary forces in the Imperialist camp who are themselves dreaming of the time when they will be able to hurl upon mankind loads of TNT, atomic bombs and lethal bacteria . . ."

The accused received sentences as follows:

Twenty-five years in a labour correction camp for Yamada, Kajitsuka, Takahashi and Kawashima;
Twenty years for Karasawa and Sato;
Eighteen years for Nishi;
Fifteen years for Mitomo;
Twelve years for Onoue;
Ten years for Hirazakura;
Three years for Kurushima; and
Two years for Kikuchi.

But what impact would these six days at Khabarovsk have on the world outside the Soviet Union?

The Russians' attempt to disseminate the information contained in the Khabarovsk trial was vigorous. They used diplomatic channels, and the media.

On December 24th, the Soviet news agency Tass, from its Fleet

Street office in London, had issued a lengthy special bulletin.[2] It was headed "Indictment of former Japanese Servicemen: charged with preparing and applying bacteriological weapons". It listed the names of the accused and the nature of the charges. It also summarised the indictment, assembled from testimony given, under the Soviet system of jurisprudence, in a preliminary investigation. It described how the biological warfare units had been established "in accordance with secret edicts of the Emperor Hirohito, the General-Staff and War Ministry of Japan". It went on to set out the organisation and the work of the units, with examples from the evidence on the experiments.

A second Tass bulletin quickly followed.[3] It contained more comprehensively listed details of the Khabarovsk trial – including a section on one of the raids on China.

A third special bulletin[4] appeared from Fleet Street on December 27th. It included an extract from the Khabarovsk court exchanges:

The Prosecutor: Tell us, defendant, owing to what reasons were preparations for bacteriological war conducted in Manchuria and not in Japan?

Kawashima: Manchuria is a country contiguous to the Soviet Union and in the event of war against the USSR it would be easier and more convenient to use the bacteriological weapon from there. Also Manchuria was very convenient for experiments in testing the bacteriological weapon.

The Prosecutor: Convenient, in what way?

Kawashima: There was ample territory in Manchuria and moreover, there was sufficient experimental material.

The Prosecutor: What does it mean, "experimental material?" People who were brought by the gendarmerie to the prison of Unit No 731?

Kawashima: Precisely so.

And the bulletin drew attention to the fact that American prisoners-of-war had been involved in the experiments.

To ascertain the degree of vulnerability of the American Army to combat different infections, members of the Unit No 731 studied, on American war prisoners, the degree of their receptivity to different infections.

Replying to a question of the State Prosecutor, Karasawa testified:

At the beginning of 1943 when I was laid up in hospital in

Mukden, a scientific worker of the unit, named Minato, visited me. He told me that the immunity of American war prisoners to infectious diseases was being studied at Mukden. Minato was specifically sent by Unit No 731 to the camp of prisoners of war to study the immunity of Anglo-Saxons to infectious diseases.

Prosecutor: Was the prospect of using bacteriological weapons against the United States envisaged?

Karasawa: That is precisely so. It was envisaged.

At 11.34 a.m. on Boxing Day, December 26th, 1949, the British Embassy in Moscow sent the following telegram (No 1103) to the Foreign Office in London:

Soviet press on December 24th and 25th give twelve columns to the publication of the indictment of former members of the Japanese Army charged under Clause 1 of the edict of the Presidium of the Supreme Soviet of the USSR of April 19th, 1943 with preparing and using bacteriological weapons against the Soviet Union and other states . . .

2 The indictment opens with a description of the aggressive plans of the Japanese imperialists in the Far East and of their frustration by the decisive intervention of the Soviet Union. Responsibility for establishing the "institute of total war" which outlined the limits of Japan's imperialist designs, is attributed to the Japanese Emperor . . .

3 The indictment continues under five heads. These are:

a) The organisation of special formations for preparing and waging bacteriological warfare. The investigation, it is stated, established that the Japanese General Staff and Ministry of War organised a bacteriological laboratory under Lt General Shirō Ishii, which actively prepared to use bacteria for the mass destruction of peoples and the infection of cattle and crops. Two top secret bacteria formations were set up in Manchurian territory in 1935–6 in accordance with the secret orders of Emperor Hirohito.

b) Criminal experiments on live human beings. Experiments were carried out on a mass scale on Chinese patriots and Soviet citizens with the knowledge and consent of Yamada, Commander of the Kwantung Army. After inhuman torture, dead victims were cremated. Experiments were also undertaken to discover means of combating the freezing of extremities in the course of military operations planned against the Soviet Union.

c) Application of bacteriological weapons in the war against

China. Experiments were made in operational areas in Central China in the summer of 1940 when a plague epidemic was started in the Ningpo district by means of infected fleas dropped from aircraft. Further plagues were started in 1941 and 1942.

d) Increased activity in the preparation of bacteriological warfare against the USSR. Before 1942, in preparation for war against the Soviet Union, bacteriological groups were established along the Soviet frontiers and frontier reservoirs were infected especially in the Trekhreche district. In 1944 manoeuvres were held in the Anta district to test the effectiveness of bacteriological weapons. The Soviet Union, however, disrupted the Japanese plans by invading Manchuria, and on the eve of the capitulation, the Japanese destroyed all buildings, equipment and documents of the bacteriological detachments.

e) The personal responsibility of the accused. The accused are charged individually for their direct responsibility of or connexion with the organisation and conduct of bacteriological warfare against the Soviet Union and other states, for the carrying out of experiments on living persons resulting in the death of at least 3,000 persons and for undertaking bacteriological sabotage against the Soviet Union.

4 Text by bag. Foreign Office please pass to Washington as my telegram No 83 . . .

The Moscow Embassy repeated the information both to Tokyo and to Washington. The telegram was received in London at 1.25 p.m. on December 26th.

December 27th, 1949:[5] From British Embassy, Moscow, to Foreign Office, London: telegram 1105 timed 3.10 p.m.:

Trial of former members of Japanese Army.

Trial began at Khabarovsk on December 25th.

According to press reports the evidence of defendants so far examined has simply followed the indictment and all have admitted full responsibility and have freely described the experimental atrocities etc., which they allegedly conducted or supervised. It looks as though trial may continue on these lines.

2 Please inform me by telegraph if you wish to receive telegraphed summaries of Soviet press reports of proceedings. Otherwise I shall send full accounts by bag and telegraph only if points of special interest arise.

The telegram, routinely, was copied to Washington and Tokyo for the private consumption of the diplomatic staffs. Despite the apparent revelations, it caused no stir. In the Foreign Office in London there were evidently no internal repercussions.

In Tokyo, the minds of General MacArthur and his Allied administrators were taken up with other matters. Four days before Christmas, at the December meeting of the Four-Power Allied Council that supposedly ran Japan, the Soviet delegates had walked out. Led by Lt-Gen Kusma Derevyanko, they had refused to take part in a debate aimed at exploring an American allegation that some 376,000 Japanese prisoners-of-war and civilian detainees captured at the end of the war in 1945 had been allowed to die – and were certainly missing – in areas under Soviet control. Repatriation from the Soviet Union, said the Americans, had "lagged noticeably" behind the return of soldiers and civilians from South-East Asia. US offers to help speed the repatriation "had been spurned".

In the early part of 1949, Japanese and Allied sources had estimated 376,000 prisoners still in Soviet hands. The Soviet estimate was 95,000 – plus an unspecified number of war criminals. The discrepancy was enormous. It was of deep concern to the Japanese, and to the Allies who, as they continued to nurture the growth of a democratic state in Japan, needed to be seen to be supporting the genuine anxiety of a people who, at both personal and political levels, sought reassurance over the fate of soldiers and civilians alike.

But the Soviets refused to discuss the issue. In Tokyo, the Japanese reaction was noisy, the emotions raw. Numerous petitioners badgered the Japanese government to seek a satisfactory answer. On December 22nd, 1949, crowds had besieged the Soviet Embassy in Tokyo, clamouring for a reply.

On New Year's Day, 1950, the Associated Press world wire service carried an item on the trial of Japanese war criminals in Khabarovsk. All twelve accused had been convicted and sentenced to between two and twenty years. All defendants, added AP, had pleaded guilty on all counts – with the exception of one, who had been found guilty anyway.

The Japanese press fell upon the information eagerly and used it interestingly.[6] Coverage in three large Tokyo dailies, *Yomiuri*, *Asahi* and *Mainichi*, indicated that the non-Communist press was inclined to view the Moscow story with caution, if not scepticism. Neither the daily nor the evening editions of the *Yomiuri* on December 25th carried the Soviet indictment. *Asahi*, which received the December

23rd dispatch from London's Associated Press bureau, printed it on the third page of its Christmas Day morning edition, side by side with an account of an Upper House hearing on Japanese prisoners-of-war held in the USSR. *Mainichi* ran a twenty-nine-line story prominently on its front page, juxtaposed to a United Press dispatch on Mac-Arthur's request to the State Department for a neutral investigation of Japanese internees still under Soviet control. It added coverage of a statement made in Washington by Joseph P. Keenan.

The Japanese, said Mr Keenan, had *not* planned to use bacteriological warfare in the last war.

The newspapers which were politically on the left pursued the story all week. *Akahata*, the Communist Party daily, followed its publication of the indictment, in full, with two interviews supposedly obtained from men who at one time or another had been directly connected with the installations and operations of the "Administration of Water Supply and Prophylaxis for the Kwantung Army". One of the two men interviewed, Hideo Takeyama, claimed that he had been staff writer of the *Nippon Shinbun* (Japan Times) in the USSR and that, during his detention in Siberia, he had obtained information on the germ units from one of the accused, Tomio Karasawa, in August 1948. Two more interviews printed by *Akahata* on December 31st and January 5th were with former soldiers who claimed direct knowledge of the activities of Units 731 and 100 in Manchuria.

The right-wing press gave the affair scant coverage but smaller, district newspapers wrote editorial criticism of the Soviet Union.

The *Gifu Times* questioned Soviet motives:

The real intention of the Soviet authorities in taking up this problem independently is puzzling. If evidence had been gathered and the crimes established, should not an international military crime of this sort be tried according to procedures followed by the International Military Tribunal held in Tokyo and be handled by an Allied Military Court? . . . It is desirable that Japanese attorneys be allowed to plead for the accused to show fairness of the Soviet court to the world.

Chugoku Shinbun on December 20th editorialised briefly that:

. . . it is beyond our comprehension why this sudden announcement should appear as a new phase in the war crimes trial when a movement for the release of Japanese internees has just been initiated.

. . . Since the war's end, secrets and historical facts of the war

227

have been made public and discussed considerably, and the secrets of the Japanese army revealed by returning soldiers, but stories of germ warfare are new to us . . . Mr Keenan has said that he has not found information covering all aspects of Japan's war efforts . . . If the Soviet Union has taken up this trial as a means of checking public discussion of the repatriation problem, this is undoubtedly a very serious matter.

Generally speaking, outside Japan and the Soviet Union, the story was ignored. It made a tiny paragraph in a couple of Britain's national daily newspapers – apart from the Communist *Daily Worker* which castigated the US across three columns for "jumping to the defence of the twelve high Japanese officers who have admitted the most atrocious war crimes . . . including tying victims to iron posts . . . while bombs containing disease germs were exploded near them". There was even less press reaction in the United States.

For when the press cared to investigate on either side of the Atlantic the briefing in diplomatic circles was the same: the whole Khabarovsk trial should be seen as a confidence trick.

A secret US District Field Intelligence report[7] dated February 3rd, 1950 best summed up the Allied public reaction to all that had been revealed at Khabarovsk. The trial, says the report, was an attempt to distract attention from the *really important* matter – where were the 376,000 Japanese still in Soviet hands?

The document goes on:

The Moscow technique had been unmistakably applied in all its variations. There was little doubt that the Kremlin had prepared this interlude well beforehand and in preparation for an inevitable showdown on the repatriation issue. Without previous announcement, the would-be spectacular trial was thrust upon the world to fill an accusing silence created by the Allied Council. News of the trial was startling enough to leave few audiences complacent, for the implication of germ warfare was sufficiently grisly to rival atomic warfare rumors.

Charges were selected purposefully [sic], since the prosecuting authorities claim they held all documentary evidence to substantiate their accusations, although there was no means for determining the authenticity of these official writs.[8]

Not only was such evidence in the hands of the USSR but the choice of twelve victims was up to Soviet accusers who also selected "witnesses" who would support the tribunal.

The Khabarovsk trial depended almost solely upon the "confessions" of the accused who willingly expanded upon their guilt and described at length their participation in a diabolic plan for mass slaughter with bacterial weapons. The single instance of protest from Kajizuka Ryūiji, who pleaded guilty only in part, was swiftly and "fully exposed by the testimony" of the others accused, as well as the sworn statements of selected "witnesses" and in this the standard Communist technique of "justice" was completely on display. Finally the Khabarovsk legalistic burlesque stood out as a remarkably blatant piece of histrionics. It seemed to deceive no one outside the Iron Curtain.

On February 2nd, 1950, the Soviet Ambassador in Washington formally demanded additional trials of alleged Japanese war criminals, such as Ishii, Kitano, Yoshimura and others, who, he said, were being protected by the Americans. The evidence was there for all to see, from the Khabarovsk testimony. The indictment would be that they were involved in biological warfare. Emperor Hirohito himself should be so charged.

The secret US document typifies the United States' responses. A simple groundswell of disbelief was built on a mistrust of the Soviet Union and faith in the individual integrity, however misplaced, of men such as Keenan and MacArthur – both of whom had something to hide. This war crimes counter-attack, said US Intelligence, was further evidence that "the USSR was seriously concerned over the world-wide unfavourable reaction to the unfinished story of the Japanese POW repatriation." The USSR, says the document, was prepared to pay "a stiff penalty" to make the world forget its callous cruelty to Japanese prisoners-of-war.

The British, however, did not believe there was a link between the two issues. The timing made nonsense of the US and Japanese assertions. On December 27th, 1949 a cable was sent from the British Embassy, Moscow, to the Foreign Office in London at 3.10 p.m. It read:

TRIAL OF FORMER MEMBERS OF JAPANESE ARMY

The indictment was foreshadowed nearly sixteen months ago in an article in Red Star – see Mr Harrison's telegram no 56 of 1948 (not repeated to Tokyo or Washington). It is tempting to see a connexion between the trial and the discussions in the Allied General Council in Tokyo last week about missing Japanese prisoners of war; but the time factor makes this improbable unless

229

the Russians have known for some time that this latter subject was going to be raised.

Foreign Office please repeat to Tokyo and Washington as my telegrams No 8 and 84 respectively.

Received 7.06 p.m. . . .

This view, echoed in Foreign Office minutes, rapidly gained credence in the British government over the next few days.

This trial in Khabarovsk of twelve members of the Japanese biological warfare machine lasted six days.

To speculate why it took place at all is fascinating. In a matter as sensitive and dramatic as germ warfare, little is as simple as it seems. Did the Soviet Union decide to prosecute simply because they had finally given up hope of persuading the West to allow them access to Ishii and the other Japanese scientists? If so, they had nothing to lose and perhaps something to gain in trying to embarrass the US government into revealing that they had given safe haven to Japanese scientists guilty of germ warfare experiments on human beings.

For the Americans, the trial *was* an embarrassment. They were forced to lie in an effort to conceal. But conceal they did, diverting attention away from the questions posed at the end of the trial, by ignoring them.

For the British, it was a much less pressing matter; probably the scientists at Porton Down had access to the information contained in the Unit 731 research but the British government was not likely to be directly embarrassed however much – or little – consultation had gone on over the decision whether or not to prosecute Ishii and his men. None of the scientists was apparently in British hands; no Briton, as far as we know, had been involved in the interrogations.

In the next few years, the Soviet Union urged through diplomatic circles and, increasingly shrilly, in the Communist-controlled press, that Ishii, Kitano, Kasahara, Wakamatsu and the rest, should stand trial. Eventually, even these protests faded into silence.

The trial at Khabarovsk has for thirty-five years been dismissed in the West as an exercise in propaganda. Yet the evidence recorded there was, we now know, accurate in most details.

The fact that it was ignored, obscured by a fog of Cold War bitterness and laid to rest because it suited the Allies to do so, is one of the scandals of the Second World War. The interests of justice were not served.

For the "revelations" of Khabarovsk – challenged so bitterly, undermined so methodically by the Allies – were in reality, no revelations at all. The Allies already knew the substance of what the Japanese on trial were saying. They'd known it for years – pieced together from their own Intelligence officers, assembled from the stories of prisoners-of-war and civilian internees, and confirmed by the members of Unit 731 and Unit 100 who had fallen into their hands in the months of chaos that marked the end of the Second World War.

The guilty men had now been publicly named. But to their shame, those who were protecting them did nothing to make them pay for their crimes against humanity.

On December 27th, 1949, three years after Murray Sanders' investigations and the resultant deal between General Douglas MacArthur and the Japanese, the following story appeared in the *New York Times*,[9] datelined Tokyo:

NO KNOWLEDGE, MACARTHUR SAYS

General Douglas MacArthur's headquarters said today there were no known cases in which the Japanese used American prisoners in germ warfare experiments . . .

The headquarters added that the Japanese had done some experiments with animals but that there was no evidence they had ever used human beings.

As far as is known here, no Americans held prisoner by the Japanese at Mukden ever accused their captors of having used them as "guinea pigs" in biological warfare tests . . .

To this day, Russia has allowed itself to bask in feelings of moral superiority over America, and not without some justification, in respect of the way it brought its Unit 731 criminals to justice. But Raginsky denies that Russia ever attempted, via his colleague Smirnov, to negotiate an exchange of technical information with the Americans in early 1947. He also denies that any joint interrogation of Ishii was held that summer.[10]

Recently, some evidence has emerged from the US Department of Defense which suggests that the Russians themselves may have been engaged in BW experimentation on humans in Mongolia. The evidence is contained in a report written for the CIA several years after the end of the Second World War by a former German Intelligence expert on Russia. A source of information that is not above suspicion, the "Hirsch Report" cites the interrogation of a Captain Von Apen on Russian BW plans and experiments. It states:

231

He [Von Apen] said that Prof Klimeshinski had carried out in 1941 experiments on human beings, too, in Ulan Bator and other sections of Mongolia, using pest [plague], anthrax and glanders. The subjects for the experiments were political prisoners; Japanese prisoners of war were also used in some cases. The prisoners in chains were brought into an 8-man tent, on the floor of which were kept, under wire nets, a number of rats infected with pest fleas; the latter transmit the infection to the subject of the experiment. The experiments were positive in most cases and the infection ended in bubonic plague. Besides the rats, ground squirrels and other rodents also proved efficient intermediary hosts. The escape of a prisoner infected with bubonic plague started a great plague epidemic among the Mongols in the summer of 1941. To check the further spread of the epidemic, a chase was unleashed with the participation of many air units, during which some 3–5,000 Mongols met their death.

Glanders may be spread by guerillas, secret agents, or airplanes in regions in the possession or under the occupation of the enemy. It is said that in 1939/40 in Moscow, a group of investigators (code name: "War College") tried anthrax on men (prisoners of war) isolated in experimental cells, using infected food.

Best results are obtained by infecting herds or pastures; or letting loose infected animals; dissemination by aircraft has not proven satisfactory.

Other thorough experiments have been made with highly effective infection-producing agents, e.g. with the germs that cause encephalitis, by using ticks . . .[11]

Elsewhere in this unconfirmed and undated report was contained a summarisation of Russian BW intentions during the Second World War:

Stalin will not initiate BW so long as it is not absolutely necessary. Only as a last resort in case the German troops penetrate deep into the country and an anti-Soviet revolution breaks out in the land, will he order the use of BW agents, alleging, for propaganda purposes as an excuse that it was first started by the Germans.

Original installations and the most important centres of BW are located certainly in the Ural regions . . .

PART 3

CONSEQUENCES

Chapter 17

FORTY YEARS ON

It is forty years and more since the events that make up this chronicle. Many of the principal actors in the drama are now dead; but many are not – otherwise it would have been impossible to have reassembled the jigsaw. For some, little has changed in their circumstances during these turbulent years; the Emperor of Japan, Hirohito, is still, as we write, the Emperor of Japan. For others the affairs of Unit 731 and the repercussions of their actions have remained both tragedy and mystery, matters privately to be assessed and reassessed in the intervening years. For too many, Chinese, Manchurian, American, British and Australian, the deeds of those Japanese scientists cost them their health, even life itself.

After the war, most of the scientists of Unit 731 prospered. Protected by the deal struck between General MacArthur and their leaders they resumed their places in a reconstructed Japanese society and were, and are, numbered among the most senior and respected names in the Japanese scientific community.

The success that these senior members achieved may seem surprising today when considering the extraordinary efforts that have gone into tracking down Nazi war criminals such as Mengele, Barbie and Bormann. Much is explained by the clear complicity on the part of United States' authorities in the war crimes of Unit 731. There is no question that the American government corrupted the workings of the Tokyo trial by offering its immunity deal in exchange for the scientific data acquired by Unit 731. But on a wider perspective, after the conclusion of the proceedings of the IMTFE, no judicial system for prosecuting war criminals has ever been established in Japanese law. At Nuremberg, by contrast, the criminal nature of specific groups such as the Nazi Party, the SS, the German Secret Police, and the German High Command was clearly recognised, and the German court established the bounds for further prosecutions beyond the indictments issued by the tribunal itself. As a result, the prosecution of German war criminals continued after East and West German independence. Both countries established legislation, without statutes of limitation, for the prosecution of Nazi war criminals by the German peoples themselves. Not so in Japan. As British prosecutor

235

Comyns Carr had pointed out while preparing the IMTFE's indictment: "The whole Japanese situation is infinitely more complicated than the German for the purposes of prosecution, as all the politicians, soldiers and sailors were all squabbling and double-crossing one another all the time and it is by no means easy to pick the right defendants."[1] In Japan, there was no clearly identifiable specific group or groups who had perpetrated a conspiracy to wage aggressive war.

In a sense, there is a supreme irony in this. Unit 731 committed atrocities which could truly be described as "crimes against humanity", as much and perhaps more than anything else heard before the tribunal. Yet the principal culprits were at the same time, by virtue of their acts, the most immune from prosecution. They returned to untroubled civilian life, their past, if anything, aiding their future careers.

The Americans appear to have been reluctant in the main for Unit 731's former *military* ranking officers to return to careers in universities, but the detachment's civilian researchers and other associated scientists were quite free to return to academia.

Dr Kiyoshi Asanuma, who visited Pingfan in 1942–43 and identified the tick insect vector of epidemic haemorrhagic fever, went on to work at the Research Institute for Natural Resources.[2] His companion on the entomological trip, Dr Asahina, later became chief of the Entomology Section of the Health and Welfare Ministry's Preventative Health Research laboratories.

Dr Ken'ichi Kanazawa, who performed tests on the Songo ticks, became chief of the research section of the Takeda Pharmaceutical Company.[3]

Dr Kōji Andō, who once headed Unit 731's vaccine-producing detachment at Dairen, became a professor of Tokyo University's Infectious Diseases Research Institute (the successor to *Den Ken*).[4]

Dr Tsunesaburō Fujino, formerly a member of the Singapore Unit, became a professor at the Biological Research Unit of Osaka University.

Dr Tachiomaru Ishikawa, once a pathologist at Unit 731 who had brought home with him thousands of human pathological samples, became a professor at Kanazawa University in 1944, a position he held throughout the 1960s and 1970s. He eventually became President of the university's Medical School. The local newspaper, the *Hokuriku Shinbun*, once planned to award him with a medal for his contribution to society, but after students who knew of his wartime record objected, the award was cancelled.

Professor Ren Kimura, the bacteriologist at Kyoto University

236

under whom Ishii had gained his doctorate and who was jointly responsible for drawing up the *makimono* (scroll) of young medical graduates to go to Unit 731, became director of the university's Medical School for four years beginning in 1944. Afterwards, he became dean of the Nagoya Municipal Medical School, holder of the Japan Academic Institute Prize and a member of the New York Academy of Sciences.[5]

Dr Masao Kusami, leader of Unit 731's pharmacology squad, later became professor of the Showa University of Pharmacology.

Dr Tōru Ogawa, once a researcher at Unit 731's Nanking Department working on typhoid and paratyphoid organisms for poisoning food and drinking water, went on to work with his brother Jirō at the Nagoya Prefecture Medical University.[6]

Dr Kōzō Okamoto, pathology squad leader at Pingfan between 1938 and 1945 who carried out human vivisection experiments, later became a professor of Kyoto University and director of the University's medical department. He went on to become an emeritus professor of the university and then medical director of Osaka's Kinki University.[7]

Dr Kazu Tabei, who researched dysentery, typhoid and paratyphoid at Pingfan between 1938 and 1943 and was involved in feeding typhoid germs in milk to human experimentees, to increase germs' virulence by cultivating them in man – he also tested a buckshot-type germ bomb on one subject – subsequently became professor of bacteriology at Kyoto University.

Dr Takeo Tamiya, Unit 731's talent scout at Tokyo Imperial University, became dean of the university's Medical School in April 1945, and later achieved worldwide fame for his research into contagious diseases caused by rickettsia, notably scrub typhus. He went on to become the first general director of Japan's National Cancer Centre, and president of the Japan Medical Association.[8]

Dr Hideo Tanaka, Unit 731's expert on the mass production of fleas, later became director of Osaka Municipal University's School of Medicine. For his research work he received an Order of the Rising Sun in March 1978.[9]

Dr Yoshi Tsuchiya, leader of the diagnostic group at the Nanking sub-unit, became an honorary professor of Juntendo University.[10]

Dr Toshikazu Yamada, once a director of the first bacteriological unit of Unit 731's related detachment the Manchurian *Den Ken*, became a professor of Kumamoto University and then temporarily held the position as Director of Hygiene for the City of Yokohama.

Dr Taboku Yamanaka, from February 1940 a civilian technician attached to the Nanking Unit, became dean of Osaka Medical School and in 1974 the forty-seventh director of the Japan Bacteriology Association.[11]

Dr Hisato Yoshimura, who directed Unit 731's frostbite experiments, literally freezing people to death, became a faculty member of Kyoto Prefectural Medical College in the 1950s, and later its president. He became an adviser to the Japanese Antarctic Expedition, and in 1973 was appointed as the first president of the Japanese Meteorological Society. He was expelled five years later when word leaked out about his Manchurian experiments. Yoshimura, however, states that he left the society because he was suffering from TB.

For his pioneering work in "environmental adaptation science" and his work as an "educator", Yoshimura was to receive one of Japan's highest accolades: on April 29th, 1978 – the Emperor's birthday – the then Minister of Education presented him with the Order of the Rising Sun – Third Class.[12] He subsequently became president of Kobe Women's University and has served as a consultant to an association that advises frozen food and fishery companies.

Today, Yoshimura does not deny that freezing experiments took place. But he claims that the maruta were paid for their services. A baby that was used for tests belonged to a Japanese woman member of Unit 731 and was "volunteered", he says.[13]

Many former members of Unit 731 joined the Japanese National Institute of Health (NIH) after the war. Dr Shinpei Ejima, a dysentery researcher at Unit 731, joined the NIH, as did the Unit's former bomb expert Jun'ichi Kaneko, who went on to study Sendai virus infection on laboratory mice.[14]

Professor Saburō Kojima, once a director of *Den Ken*'s fourth research department and a visitor to the Nanking Unit for human experiments, worked in the Health and Welfare Ministry's National Preventive Health Research Centre after the war, becoming its director in 1954. Once a pro-militarist in his published writings, he changed his tone dramatically in later years. Writing about his upbringing, and how he failed the entrance examination for the Army Youth Service, Kojima coolly stated that "had the Army taken me then, in later years they would have had a planner who would have done his best to stop Japan's participation in this 'Holy War', and perhaps this would have led to a happier history for Japan."[15]

Yujirō Wakamatsu, once commander of Unit 100, according to American Intelligence sources in 1963, was active in the NIH studying streptococcal infections in primary school children.[16]

Dr Yukimasa Yagisawa, Unit 731's plant disease expert for a

238

decade, subsequently became secretary of the Japanese Penicillin Association, joined the Society of Antibiotics, and worked at the NIH.[17]

Many former members went into general practice or succeeded in business.

Dr Kiyoshi Hayakawa, a member of the Singapore Detachment who had attempted to get yellow fever virus from the Americans, who had been in one of Ishii's water purification units at Nomonhan, went on to become manager of the Hayakawa Medical Company and used vaccine-producing techniques that he had acquired during his wartime work.[18]

Ishii's protégé and deputy Tomosada Masuda took up general practice in Chiba Prefecture after the war. Travelling by motorcycle on his doctor's rounds, one day, Masuda was in collision with a truck. He died on April 5th, 1952, aged fifty-one, from the serious head injuries he had sustained.[19]

Dr Hideo Futaki, who headed Unit 731's tuberculosis research squad, became president of S. J. Company Ltd.

Dr Kiyoshi Ota, one of Unit 731's original military surgeons, the detachment's 2nd Division Chief, and the man who headed the BW raid on Changteh town, returned to the old castle town of Hagi in Yamaguchi Prefecture and entered general medical practice. According to a friend, he committed suicide after his two daughters died.[20]

Dr Masahiko Takahashi, Pingfan's leading plague researcher, became a general practitioner, managing a clinic in Mobara, Chiba Prefecture.[21]

Dr Zen Kawakami, a compatriot of Ishii's from Kyoto Imperial University who initiated research at Pingfan on the differential susceptibilities of races to infectious disease, died while in Manchuria.[22]

Dr Sueo Akimoto, the young serologist drafted at the end of the war to Pingfan, wrote a book on the ethics of medicine, but abandoned his academic career as a result of the traumas at Unit 731. "I will regret it to my death," he says. "I was silent for thirty years and nothing can change that. These people were my friends, and I did not have the courage to condemn them." Akimoto now shuns contact with those former colleagues. "It's astonishing; these people have no shame. Their work in Manchuria had nothing to do with patriotism. It was an elitism that grew like a monster."[23]

Shunichi Suzuki, who served as a lieutenant in the accounting department of Unit 731's detachment in Shansi, became Governor of Tokyo and a leading member on the right of Japan's ruling Liberal

Democratic Party. Although this detachment was not involved in human experimentation, Suzuki has admitted that he knew the grim secret of Unit 731.[24]

Seiichi Niizuma, the man who censored and prevented most of Unit 731's scientific information from reaching the Americans during the Sanders' investigation, entered the Tokyo Research Institute of the Japan Self-Defence Force. In his eighties, he now runs a club for former Army officers.[25]

In the early years after the war, Prince Tsuneyoshi Takeda ran a stock farm in Chiba Prefecture. Under the pseudonym Miyata, Takeda had been the central link man between Kwantung Army Headquarters and Unit 731. By Occupation decree, Takeda, a grandson of the Emperor Meiji, was stripped of his royal title.[26] In October 1951, the Japanese government officially depurged nearly 2,000 former military officers at and below the rank of colonel, including Takeda. He became managing director of the Japan Amateur Sports Association, and in October 1962, he was appointed president of the Japan Olympic Committee.

As president of the Japan Skating Union, Takeda travelled widely overseas including the Soviet Union. In 1963, after Japan hosted the speed skating world championships, Takeda decided to express his feelings of internationalism in an article in the *Japan Times*. At the skating meeting, the International Skating Union and Japanese officials had argued that the display of national flags and the playing of national anthems was contrary to the purpose of the non-political, peaceful international meet. "I am convinced that our 'no national flag, no national anthem' policy at the Karuizawa meet was a definite success," he wrote, "and I want to suggest, in my private capacity, that the forthcoming Tokyo Olympic Games be conducted in the same manner. International sporting meets should be held to promote friendship among athletes of the world. Moreover, the gatherings should definitely not be turned into arenas for diplomatic squabbles."[27]

The *Japan Times* in a personality profile of Takeda the following year wrote of him: "A text by his desk urging adherence to truth, fairness and goodwill in everyday actions suggests the principles by which he is guided in life. If you wanted to espouse the cause of royalty, you need look no further for the perfect model for your argument than Tsuneyoshi Takeda." Despite his adherence to truth, however, Takeda, now retired and living in Tokyo, declines to speak about Unit 731.[28]

After the war, Unit 731's second commander, former Lt-Gen Masaji Kitano, formed a vaccine-producing company under his detachment's erstwhile talent scout Takeo Tamiya. It went bankrupt. Shortly after the outbreak of hostilities in Korea, however, Murray Sanders' one-time interpreter Ryōichi Naitō formed the Japan Blood Bank and asked Kitano to join him. Kitano became chief of its Tokyo branch.[29]

Naitō, who had opened his own surgery before forming the Japan Blood Bank, went on to become prominent in Japan's medical circles. He transformed the blood bank into the highly successful multinational Green Cross Corporation. The Osaka-based international pharmaceutical giant, which employed many ex-Unit 731 members, specialised in the manufacture of interferon, plasma and artificial blood. Naitō became vice-president of the company. Kitano was also a board member. Naitō became the company's president in 1973 and its chairman in 1978. The company's projected profits for 1985 were 6,000 million yen. The company has subsidiaries, the Alpha Therapeutic Corporation with large research laboratories in Los Angeles, California and Alpha Therapeutic UK Ltd in Norfolk, England.[30]

A member of the New York Academy of Sciences, Naitō received an award in 1963 from the Japanese Science Society for his pioneering work in artificial blood. At Pingfan, by contrast, researchers had once pumped human guinea pigs full of horse blood in primitive attempts to find a substitute for human blood.

Green Cross's artificial blood has had a checkered record. In 1982, the company became embroiled in a scandal after press reports spoke of initial tests on its product in January 1970 on a seventy-two-year-old female cancer patient. But in its application to Japan's Health and Welfare Ministry for a licence to manufacture and market artificial blood, the company stated that the test had been implemented in *March* of that year, claiming that the first human guinea pigs were Naitō and other Green Cross executives. Green Cross was accused of testing its product on a sick person in the face of the commonly respected rule that first tests on human beings should be done on healthy volunteers. After the press reports were confirmed, the Ministry simply instructed the company to recheck the data it had submitted and re-apply for government approval.[31]

In April 1977, Naitō received an Order of the Rising Sun. His work often took him abroad, to destinations including the USA. He died in July, 1982. The Green Cross Corporation has plans for a huge new complex in Los Angeles. It will be named after Dr Naitō.[32]

Today, those scientists who are still alive are less than eager to discuss their links with Unit 731 or Unit 100. Naeo Ikeda runs a clinic specialising in blood diseases in a suburb of Osaka. In 1968, Ikeda felt secure enough to publish in a Japanese scientific journal the results of a human experiment that had been carried out in Manchuria with epidemic haemorrhagic fever. Extraordinary as it may seem, Ikeda wrote: "The author examined infectivity of fleas and lice isolated from patients, and acquisition of infectivity on the artificially incubated unsustained louse line by stinging the patients with EHF. Thus, it was confirmed that the healthy persons would develop the disease by stinging of poisoned louse."[33] When we asked about the documentary evidence we had found, and to which his name was attached (see Chapter 1), that indicated that he had supervised injections of tetanus into the heels of prisoners-of-war, he declined. We pressed the need to find out why he had done these things, and he muttered that he was "too old . . . it was a long time ago." He shuffled away, out of our sight into a back room of his dingy clinic.

Some would speak only anonymously. In a Japanese hotel bedroom we talked with a stocky chemist, once a member of Unit 100, of killings and deadly virus and bomb manufacture. Then he left the hotel, walking back into the warmth of the afternoon, a pillar of society, the sunlight glinting on the Rotary Club badge on his lapel.

Shirō Kasahara, who researched Songo fever at Pingfan, published medical papers undoubtedly based on his experiments on human beings at Pingfan. He became emeritus vice-president of the Kitasato Hospital and Research Unit in Tokyo where he agreed to see us, to discuss his published papers. A small man with expressive hands and a fixed smile, gradually drawn into a discussion of horrors far removed from the white-coated world in which he now moved.

". . . I could submit a form to the administration section . . . to get maruta for my experiments . . .

". . . Maybe I could check the blood to see whether the blood would carry the virus to the next one . . .

". . . we tested on a Chinese spy using the blood and liver and kidney of the other dead body."

A secretary and laboratory assistants floated deferentially in and out of the great man's laboratory. The final dialogue:

To experiment on, let alone kill, even one prisoner-of-war is against the Geneva Convention, never mind medical ethics.

Kasahara: Yes. I think it was a contravention. They were soldiers, prisoners-of-war and I think the Japanese Army was wrong.

But what about *your* part in the work of Unit 731? Do you have any conscience about that?

Kasahara: I feel very guilty about what I have done . . . I think I did wrong.

How did Ishii and yourself escape prosecution?

Kasahara: I don't know much but I've heard there was a deal between General Ishii and the American Occupation Army . . .

The Japanese government's efforts to cover up the Unit 731 affair have been considerably aided by the self-censorship of most of the detachment's former members. Ishii, in 1945, had sworn all junior members to take the Unit's secret to the grave, and bound them never to contact each other, or to hold public office. It was an oath that all, for many years, took extremely seriously. Many junior members lived out the rest of their lives in fear. So seriously did some take their secrecy oath that in order to hide their past, they did not register for military pensions, ending their lives destitute.

Gradually, however, junior members began to contact their old companions once again. Old comrades societies sprang up with regular and somewhat clandestine meetings. Memorial services are regularly held and congratulatory telegrams read out. On September 5th, 1981, these societies met together for the first time. The inaugural Kwantung Army Unit 731 reunion was held at a hotel in Sinchu Matsumoto village in Yamabe. The Kwantung Army song was sung:

"Looking into the distance under the dawn clouds, the mornings, the evenings, the mountains and rivers eternal; our power and efficiency is our authority and our force, our allies are content.

"Our Army is glorious . . ."

Sutras were chanted for the Unit's founder "War God", the Honourable Shirō Ishii, and for all former members of the Unit. A memorial to the Unit, called the Seikon Tower, has been erected in Tama cemetery, in a suburb of Tokyo. Around 2 metres high it is inscribed with a few Sanskrit characters. Otherwise, it is anonymous, undated and has no other identifying marks. The detachment's printer, Naoji Uezono, is among those who tend the memorial.

During the early years of the American Occupation, Uezono hid in Kagoshima in the south of Kyūshū Island, but later returned to continue his trade in Tokyo. For two or three years after the war he suffered nightmares. Unlike most former members, he now feels it is his duty to talk about Unit 731 "so that young people know what happened". He keeps in touch with Unit photographer Tadashi Yamashita, and Masakuni Kurumizawa, once a technician assistant at the live vivisections. Yamashita became a radiographer, and is now

243

retired in Chiba Prefecture. Kurumizawa became a farmer after the war.

Naokata Ishibashi, who saw the malnutrition experiments, is now a caretaker in a block of flats in the seaside spa town, Atami. Deeply remorseful, he attends meetings to discuss questions of medical ethics and science.

At Kamo village, Ishii's home, the people avoid answering questions about the war and Manchuria. "I have nothing to say concerning the military secrets of the Honourable Shirō Ishii," was the villagers' customary reply to our questions about Unit 731.

The scientists sentenced by the Soviet Union at Khabarovsk in 1949 served their time in prison and labour camps – and many survived. In February 1956, the Soviets allowed Tsuneyoshi Takeda, the Emperor's cousin and once the Kwantung Army's link man with Unit 731, to forward letters and relief parcels to his imprisoned colleagues. Takeda was visiting Moscow for a world skating meeting as president of the Japan Skating League. The Russians, however, refused a request to visit them.[34]

On December 13th, 1956, the Soviet government decided to commute the sentences passed on Japanese war criminals. A proclamation was issued stating that because the state of war had ended between the two countries, and acting on the basis of humanity, the Supreme Soviet had decided to declare that all Japanese citizens be freed and allowed to return home.[35]

The Kwantung Army's former Commander-in-Chief Otozō Yamada, unlike his predecessor Yoshijirō Umezu who died in Sugamo Prison, survived and returned home with the dream of becoming a teacher. But within a week he gave up the hope, fearing he "would not be accepted". He died in 1965, aged eighty-three.

Bacteria factory chief Tomio Karasawa died aboard ship during his homeward passage. His predecessor at Unit 731, former Maj-Gen Kiyoshi Kawashima, survived to attend the detachment's reunions.

The Russian prosecutors, Lev Nicholaevich Smirnov and Mark Raginsky, made spectacular progress in their legal careers. They worked together to produce a book about the Khabarovsk trial from an abridged selection of documents and interrogation reports. It was translated into foreign languages and put into international circulation. The rest of the Khabarovsk records are today kept in the Central Archives of the October Revolution in Moscow. These records unfortunately do not include any documentation from the Second World War about Russian Intelligence estimates of Japanese BW work in Manchuria. As Raginsky observes: "The files of the KGB are not open."

Raginsky became a state prosecutor for the Soviet railways. The Procuracy is the most prestigious component of the Soviet legal system requiring, in the main, membership of the Communist Party, and those qualifications include "the necessary political, professional and moral qualities". Now in his eighties and in retirement in Moscow, Raginsky has recently completed another book which discusses the Khabarovsk trial. Smirnov was even more successful. He reached the pinnacle of Russia's legal system, becoming Chief Justice of the Soviet Union. He died in March 1986, aged eighty-two.

As for Ishii, while the investigations were in progress, his house in Wakamatsu-chō was regularly frequented by many American officers. After the end of 1947, however, his movements became more difficult to trace. In June 1948 he was interviewed in Tokyo by the city's Metropolitan Police Bureau, advising them semi-officially, during the investigation of the mysterious Imperial Bank poisoning case.[36]

In those years, Ishii's daughter Harumi remembers that her father went out frequently. But she does not believe her father was working for the United States Army. She denies he ever visited America. "My father could not get a job in public service," says Harumi. "He was in Wakamatsu-chō mostly, sometimes in Kamo or away elsewhere." She states that it is "absolutely false" that he went to Korea or participated in the alleged American BW project during the Korean War. Harumi, however, does concede that Ishii frequently saw Kobayashi, the manager and treasurer of the Japanese Experimental Animals Laboratories in Saitama Prefecture, the organisation which reportedly supplied vast quantities of animals to America's "J2C 406" during the Korean War period. "Kobayashi was a civilian member of the Unit [731] and he frequently came and saw my father before and after the war," she recalls. "He was a fat guy with a red face."[37]

Ishii, according to his daughter, spent much time in religious study. "He often visited Gekkei-ji temple, Kawada-chō, Shinjuku, just in front of the present Fuji TV, and always had long religious conversations with a priest called Matsuo," she remembers. "Sometimes he came home late from Gekkei-ji but he never stayed there."

Harumi postponed marriage until 1957 because of commitments to her father. Ishii inherited much of the family's property in Kamo village. His two elder brothers Takeo and Mitsuo were childless, unlike Shirō who fathered six children. Takeo, Unit 731's special prison squad leader, eventually died of liver cancer in Kobe, the city whence his second wife had come. Mitsuo, who once supervised the Unit's animal house, outlived his younger brother Shirō but was

245

unable to gain work after the war and lived on the money gained by selling his country property. Mitsuo and Takeo, and their eldest brother Torao, who had been killed in the Russo-Japanese War during Japan's Meiji period, are buried in the Ishii family cemetery at Kamo.

During the 1950s, many ex-members of Unit 731, including Tomosada Masuda, Ryōichi Naitō, pilot Yoshiyasu Masuda, Changteh BW raid leader Kiyoshi Ōta, and Nomonhan suicide squad leader Tsuneshige Ikari, visited their former commander at his Tokyo home. So too, after they were pardoned by the Russians, did Unit 731's training chief Toshihide Nishi and the Kwantung Army's one-time medical administration chief Ryūiji Kajitsuka. Ishii himself went to pay his respects to his former commander Otozō Yamada, after the latter's return from the Soviet Union.[38]

On August 17th, 1958, thirteen years after the end of the war, in the back room of a stonemason's shop called Iwaki-ya near Tama Cemetery, Tokyo, Ishii made his first and apparently only post-war appearance before assembled junior members of his former Unit. He made his farewell speech to twenty former youth trainee technicians who had come from all parts of Japan for the inaugural meeting of the Boyu-kai society of old comrades. He reminisced about the early days of Unit 731. In a speech reportedly still rich in xenophobia and elitism, Ishii described how his unit was to have been the salvation of Japan, a country then encircled by the West, scientifically impoverished yet spiritually rich. He apologised for their sufferings since the end of the war, but urged his audience to remain proud of the memory of Unit 731.

He explained to the assembled group what had been the purpose of the young trainee technicians unit at Pingfan.

> The purpose at the beginning, was to allow those who wanted to study, but who could not because of their family circumstances, to come to Manchuria and study. It was in order that we could have precious human material at the 731 Unit for the saving of the nation. We provided education above middle school level. We believed we could enter them into university. However, we were thwarted by the Department of Education. National circumstances were not permitting. Unfortunately we did not achieve our aims . . .[39]

Harumi, in common with many former members of Unit 731, feels that Ishii has been unjustly condemned. "My father was a very warm-hearted person," she says. "He was so bright that people sometimes could not catch up with the speed of his thinking and made him irritated, and he shouted at them. He was so bright and I am really proud of him."[40]

In the last years of his life, Ishii's medical condition worsened.

One day he took some sample tissue from himself to the University of Tokyo's Faculty of Medicine and asked one of his former subordinates to examine it, without telling him to whom it belonged [recalls Harumi]. When he was told that the tissue was riddled by cancer, he proudly shouted that he had thought so too. No doctor had dared tell him he was suffering from cancer of the throat. He eventually underwent surgery and lost his voice. He was an earnest student of medicine to his last day, taking notes on his physical condition.[41]

He told his old professor Ren Kimura who came to visit him at that time: "It's all over now," writing the message because he could no longer speak. His hero, Admiral Tōgō, the great strategist of the Russo-Japanese War (whose name he had used as a pseudonym) had also been a victim of throat cancer.

"Shortly before his death, he asked to be baptised by the late Dr Herman Heuvers, former President of Sophia University in Tokyo," says Harumi. "Dr Heuvers and my father were acquainted with each other since before the war. My father had much respect for the German people and their culture." Baptised into the Roman Catholic Church, Ishii took the name Joseph. "It seems to me that my father felt relieved somehow," says Harumi.[42] Ishii died on October 9th, 1959, aged sixty-seven.

Although it is said that Unit 731's two commanders had little occasion to meet after the war, Kitano undertook to chair Ishii's funeral committee. The arrangements he made appear to have been elegant.[43] Ishii's grave is in Gekkei-ji temple where he had latterly spent much time in religious reflection. In a religious ritual, part of one of Ishii's bones was buried beneath Unit 731's memorial, the Seikon Tower, in Tokyo's Tama Cemetery.[44] It was done as a mark of respect, a Buddhist custom for someone highly revered.

But what of the marutas, the human beings on whom the Japanese tested their weapons of biological warfare? They died in their hundreds – Chinese, Manchurian and Russian. As for the troops confined at Mukden, those who survived were flown home via Australia, the Philippines and Pearl Harbor, with the British going aboard HMS

Implacable to Canada and on to the United Kingdom, home in time for Christmas 1945.

Many of them have shared certain experiences in the years since. Arthur Christie, in his tiny Post Office in North Wales, says, "Everyone imprisoned by the Japs knows it was an experience that scarred you for life. Only those who've been through it can really understand. A lot of us feel that the world – and the British government for that matter – have tried to forget about us and the sacrifices we made."

Christie's letters to the government have met with a resolute refusal to accept that experiments on Allied PoWs were ever carried out by the Japanese at Mukden as the following extracts from letters from J. C. Robb of the Ministry of Defence (Personnel and Logistics) show:

December 12th, 1986
. . . we still have no evidence to support allegations that the Japanese experimented on Allied PoWs at Mukden, nor any evidence to support the allegation of a conspiracy to conceal the truth about what took place.

March 16th, 1987
. . . we now know that PoWs at Mukden were visited and treated by an outside medical team – possibly from Unit 731, which was based 300 miles away at Pingfan. We know that this treatment, which subsequently helped to reduce the previously high death rate among prisoners, included tests and injections . . . The fact that Unit 731 was engaged on [biological warfare] research at Pingfan is not proof that the same thing was happening at Mukden.

As we write, Mr Christie, and hundreds of others in Britain and the United States, are still seeking compensation for their wartime experiences.

This view was shared by ex-GI Pappy Whelchel, like so many others only too anxious to get back to his home and family at the end of the war. The Japanese supplied no medical records, nor did Pappy seek them out. After "nearly three and a half years in hell" he didn't want to risk delay. He was flown back to the United States. He was checked at Bruns General Hospital, Sante Fe, New Mexico, but he went down with beri beri. He was so ill, he couldn't walk. He was sent back to Bruns General where he stayed for a year and three months. For the rest of his life as a radio technician in Tulsa, he felt he wasn't free of the after-effects of his imprisonment. He was bitter about it. He said: "We had no medical compensation; the Veterans

248

Administration would say: 'Look, Americans don't have beri beri, pellagra or scurvy. You must be mistaken.' They seemed not to believe anything we said . . .''

Pappy Whelchel died in September 1983.

He'd become friendly with another Mukden veteran, Greg Rodriquez. Embittered, he told Rodriquez just before he died, "You know, these government officials – if they weren't there, they don't care."

Rodriquez met Dr Murray Sanders. Of him, he said:

Like Diogenes, I have searched the world for an honest man. I believe in Dr Sanders; he has taken risks with his own reputation in order to speak the truth about Unit 731 and the conspiracy to cover up those war crimes committed by Ishii and his men.

From 1941 on, we Americans have been victims of a series of . . . lies. The truth can now be seen by those who seek it.[45]

Another veteran, Frank James, said he had repeatedly attempted to get included in his health records the diseases from which he suffered during his time as a PoW.

But I always get the same answer from the Army or the VA: *No medical evidence exists!!* So, by God, if there is documentation about the death of an American PoW with the Mukden number 1294, I want help to dig this information out. One thousand two hundred and forty-three days of my life are a void in the official medical records."[46]

On either side of the Atlantic, the survivors of Mukden have fought for financial compensation for what they feel they have endured. As we write, in 1988, the British government are unsympathetic to their petitions.

In the United States, Montana Congressman Pat Williams has taken up their cause and initiated a Congressional inquiry. He said in Washington, on September 17th, 1986, in evidence to the Pensions Sub-committee to the Congressional Committee of Veterans Affairs:

I am submitting the records for Felix Kozakevitch, an American soldier from New York who was imprisoned at one of those experimentation camps. Apart from severe beatings, Kozakevitch was subjected to frostbite experiments, forced to stand at attention in deep snow in sub-zero temperatures.

Felix Kozakevitch never received compensation, never received needed counseling, adequate health care. The country for which he fought, denied his terrible experience. Mr Kozakevitch died a year ago.

Congressman Williams pleaded for belated justice. He had seen the evidence, he believed the truth was leaking out. He added, "These men are victims of a terrible secret, born forty-four years ago deep in Manchuria in Japanese prisoner camps. Theirs perhaps has been the best-kept secret of World War II – long denied by Japan and long concealed by the United States government."[47]

As for General Douglas MacArthur, his overlordship of Japan was to be the pinnacle of his power. His command of the United Nations forces in Korea ended in disgrace, in 1951. He died in 1964.

John Powell? The sedition and treason trials ended his newspaper career, but he never lost interest in America's BW programme. Like his father before him, who had lived to bear witness against his Japanese tormentors at the Tokyo Trial, Powell, Jr, was anxious to set the record straight against those who had persecuted him. In 1977, he left the management of his antique business to his wife and, using the newly-enacted Freedom of Information Act, began tracking through official archives. He wrote hundreds of letters and finally amassed more than 20,000 pages of formerly secret documents.

Finally, in 1980 Powell was able to make his response. In the *Bulletin of Atomic Scientists*, now the *Bulletin of Concerned Asian Scholars*,[48] he used information culled from Fort Detrick and other military archives to reveal the immunity deal done between Unit 731 and the US government – specifically the exchange of memoranda between MacArthur, Willoughby, Legal Section chief Alva Carpenter and the State-War-Navy Co-ordinating Committee. Powell's article also described in detail some of Unit 731's grisly experiments. American press reaction was enormous, forcing official response. "It's very possible and probable that our scientists did get information from the tests," Fort Detrick stated. "We kept everything that was done of an offensive nature under a tight blanket of security – by necessity."[49]

"It was a marvellous feeling," recalls Powell. "I tried to track down Alva Carpenter to confront him with the information. I could remember him screaming across at me during the sedition hearings. But by then he had died."[50]

Across the Pacific on April 7, 1982, in the lower house of the Japanese Parliament the head of the Health and Welfare Ministry's Veteran Relief Bureau Mr Kikuo Moriyama made the first official admission of the existence of Unit 731 and its criminal experiments, and revealed that Ishii had been granted the equivalent of £45,000 as a retirement pension.[51]

Powell's article was accompanied in the same issue of the *Bulletin of Atomic Scientists* by an outraged statement from Bert Röling, the Dutch judge at the Tokyo Trial. Röling lambasted those who had deceived him:

> . . . it is a bitter experience for me to be informed now that centrally ordered Japanese war criminality of the most disgusting kind was kept secret from the Court by the US government.
>
> . . . to use human beings for biological experiments, . . . was among the gravest of war crimes.

Powell's revelations went further. He uncovered his own FBI file which contained a memorandum from Strategic Air Command to FBI Director J Edgar Hoover, dated March 13, 1956, relating to the forthcoming sedition trial. The memorandum stated that American PoWs had been experimented upon with BW agents in Manchuria. It read:

> Mr James J Kelleher, Jr, Office of Special Operations, DoD [Department of Defense] has volunteered further comments to the effect that American Military Forces after occupying Japan, determined that the Japanese actually did experiment with "BW" agents in Manchuria during 1943–44 using American prisoners as test victims. Kelleher stated that such findings were not introduced in subsequent negotiation proceedings on "war crimes" trials as:
>   1) It was felt cases to be presented were strong enough without such information and
>   2) As a political expedient, it was felt that public disclosure of such information would seriously prejudice occupying forces.[52]

Kelleher's memorandum is specific, American PoWs *were* used as test victims. The reasons Kelleher states about why the information was withheld are also new, finding no parallel in any of the other documented debate of the time. Despite requests through official channels no further supportive evidence has yet been forthcoming, although one is left with the conjecture that Kelleher had access to different sources of information. Many records have been destroyed including, in October 1981, more than 80 per cent of Fort Detrick's technical library following a review after the Biological Weapons Convention of 1972.[53]

Powell, however, has been unable to shed much further light on the Korean War BW allegations which remain a web of unverifiable accusations and unverifiable denials.

And Murray Sanders? Dr Sanders returned to his Columbia University in New York as an associate professor, once he had convalesced from tuberculosis. He continued his micro-biological research and, for his work on the investigation of viruses and degenerative diseases of the central nervous system, he was nominated for a Nobel Prize in 1967. In latter years he suffered both cancer and Parkinson's disease and fought both cheerfully and bravely. In his office, part of his long, low, ranch-style house beside the ocean at Delray Beach, Florida, was a hand-written document given a special place among the seventy-six research papers he has presented during his working life. It was the original document, written by Naitō through that long night in Tokyo in 1945. It set out the organisation and activities of Unit 731, a reminder of a game of bluff that Sanders played and won. "Keep it as a souvenir of a job well done," Willoughby had said. And that's precisely what Murray Sanders did.

Looking back, Murray Sanders felt he was used as a pawn, by both sides. By Naitō, because the Japanese concealed the human experimentation from him by telling a deliberate lie. By MacArthur and US Intelligence, because Sanders believes they told him less than the whole truth when sending him out on his mission to investigate Unit 731. He says: "Perhaps they felt that as the only medical doctor on the team, I would have pursued that single line of inquiry to the exclusion of any others if I'd thought the Japanese had been experimenting on human beings . . ."

And perhaps they were right. Towards the end of his life Murray Sanders' eyesight began to fail. He lost the sight in his right eye because of a decision he took in 1942, when he was seeking to beat the outbreak of kerato conjunctivitis, the eye complaint then threatening the US war effort. Sanders, helped by R. C. Alexander and, later, by Phillips Thygeson[54] had isolated the virus. He needed to prove he had done so. The only sure method was to take the virus and "complete the circle" – by attempting to reproduce the disease. He needed a volunteer, a human guinea pig. He chose himself. He took virus that had been passed through six laboratory mice and introduced it into his own eye. "On the sixth day, I was on the way to get a pizza and my eye felt as if I had grains of sand in it – I had caught the disease."

Sanders proved his point and, gradually, lost the sight of that eye. For, once the virus was introduced into the eye's reservoir it never left. But Sanders had needed to be certain – and the only human volunteer he could offer, conscience-free, was himself.

There is no greater contrast with the morality of those Japanese who tampered with, and destroyed, the lives of others in their efforts to produce what they thought, erroneously, would be the ultimate weapon of war. Forty years on, there can at last be no doubt about the full horror of what these men did in the name of science. Ishii's "secret of secrets" can no longer hide behind a sordid deal, struck by men who knew better but who clung to that dangerous adage: the end justifies the means.

APPENDICES

THE NAITŌ DOCUMENT

Private (Secret) Information to Colonel Sanders

1 I felt it is my duty to tell you about BW all I know to help your sincere effort of investigation as a scientist.

The purpose of this information is only to rescue our poor, defeated nation, and to avoid the damage, according to your words, that if we offer the truce [sic truth] as a science, you may help this poor nation with every your effort, but if we keep the matters secret which will be disclosed afterwards, every damages will be added to us. I have no attempt at all to get some private recompense from you, doing this information.

2 I had to do this information earlier, but I had no chance to tell you directly, without any other people. I was compelled to tell you only in some limit, limiting only "defensive".

3 There occurred a big consternation in the circle of higher officers of Japanese Head Quarter when your inquire about BW began (about 10 days ago). A long time disputation was done, whether they should answer to you with the true or not. Almost all members had opinion to offer you the true, because Japan did none of active attack against any enemy in this war; but a few people had another opinion to hide the true (to tell you that Japan did not have even scientific experiment). The latters, the vice chief of general staffs and the chief of Bureau of War-Affairs (Army Ministry), have the fear that the fact that Japan had some laboratories for active BW will bring a big misfortune to the Emperor.

Tenno-heika [Emperor]

Chief of General Staff[1]   Army Minister[2]

[out of this disputation]

× Vice chief of General Staff[3]
  × Chief of Bureau war affairs[4]

○ Vice Minister of Army Ministry[5]
○ Chief of Bureau Medicine Gen Kanbyashi
○ Chief of Section of Sanitation

○ : Opinion to offer the true   × : Opinion to keep them secret

[1]Gen Yoshijirō Umezu
[2]Sadamu Shimomura
[3]Lt-Gen Torashirō Kawabe

[4]Lt-Gen Masao Yoshizumi
[5]Tadakazu Wakamatsu

The chief of Bureau of Medical Affairs had a strong opinion to offer you the true. But in the circumstances now a days, when the War-Ministry yet exists, he must obey to his up-officers (the vice-chief of General Staffs and the chief of Bureau of War-Affairs). General Kanbayashi are doing and continuing every effort to change the opinion of Vice-chief of General Staffs.

I knew this fact through a member of Section of Sanitation. I suppose that all the true shall be offered to you in this 2–3 days from General Kanbayashi, officially. So this information may be a some reference [Vorkenntnis] note book for you to get the true officially.

4 It is true, I dare say, that the Jap. Army had some organisation for BW, not only defensive, but for active offensive. This organisation was as follows.

Tenno-Heika (Emperor)

General Staff		Army Ministry	
2nd Section of War operation	Bureau of War Affairs	Bureau of Medical Affairs	
	Section of Controlling Army Affairs	Section of Foreign Affairs	Section of Sanitation	Section of Medical Affairs
Army Medical College	Kanto (Kwantung) Army	China Army[6]	South Army
Institute of Preventive	Bōeki-Kyū Suibu Harbin	Pepin Nankon Peking Nanking	Canton Kantung	Singapore
(Experiments about offensive BW)				
small	large	none small	none	none ? I don't know exactly

5 Main part of research work concerning BW was done at Harbin. The chief of the organisation was as follows:

1936 ⎫ 1937 ⎪ 1938 ⎪ 1939 ⎬ 1940 ⎪ 1941 ⎭	Col Shirō Ishii
1942 ⎫ 1943 ⎭	Major General Masaji Kitano
1944 ⎫ 1945 ⎭	Lieutenant General Shirō Ishii

[6] China Expeditionary Force

As the former table, Bōeki-Kyūsuibu of Kwantung Army subjecting to the Commander of Kanto (Kwantung) Army, receives indications as follows:

Indications	General and Estimate (Money)	from	Section of Army Affairs (War Ministry)
Indications	detail of research work, mainly on defensive	from	Section of Sanitation Bureau of Medicine War Dept
Indications	research work on offensive	from	2nd Section of (Army) General Staff

6 The Kanto-Army Bōeki-Kyūsuibu (Harbin) had 8 sections as follows:

General Administration
1 Section (Scientific Research)
2 Section (Preparing active offensive)
3 Section (Praxis of Preventive in Kanto-Army district with water supply)
4 Section (Manufacturing preventative products, sera, Propylactics)
Material (Supply and equipment)
Education (training)
Clinik (Hospital)

The chiefs of each section were colonel or major general.

7 The basis of the preparing the offensive research, why Japanese Army had the organisation of BW offensive, was as follows. (This is only my suppose, because I have never been in such position to know the matter.):

a) Soviet-Russia is quite possible to add an attack bacterial to Japan, specially in (at) Manchuria. Indeed, there was some active attack, at North-part of Manchuria (1934 or 1935, on building Peiangchiang – Heihō-Railway, attack with anthrax to horses).

This possibility have existed not only in war-time, but also in peace time, also at beginning of sudden war.

b) Japan, too, should have some preparation for *revenge* for such case, that any enemy use some illegal warfare.

c) The Emperor was know that he do not like the preparation of chemical warfare in Jap. Army or Navy; as the estimate, scale of research for chemical warfare could not be large. The officers of General Head Quarter knew this, as the appointment for Bōeki-Kyūsuibu must not contain officially active attack. The officers of General Head Quarters explained the function of Bōeki-Kyūsuibu purely as defensive.

259

d) General Head Quarter has had no attempt to begin active BW attack to his enemy, before the enemy begin any illegal warfare. As none of the fighting nation (enemy) began such an attack, Japanese Head Quarter had no chance, no reason to use BW.

In addition, the circumstances at last period of this war became very difficult to realise bacterial warfare.

8 The ideas, how to use the BW showed to us, research workers, from general Ishii and other higher officers, were only in the limit of common knowledge.

There was no other idea than the knowledge, which we were able to get from foreign literatures (USA, Germany, Russia, France, Italy).

The idea about measures to carry the warfare is as follows.

Airplane	Bombs
	Direct Dispersing
Artillery	Shells
Spy	(Also with parashute)

In these, the measure with airplane were mainly studies (Harbin).

Which pathogen to use? B.pestis, Vibris cholerae, dysentery, salmonella, anthrax were main problem. None of filtrable viruses were studies, because of difficulties to get them in.

9 Many research-workers were mobilised for this purpose, each having special themes. The results of experiments were not made in press (print), to guard the secret. So, each worker was not able to know the research work of the other. The chieves (chiefs) of each laboratory changed from time to time. In addition, all the experimental-results may be burned in fire, perhaps, at the beginning of Russia's sudden invasion. So, it is impossible I suppose to get any experiment record of Harbin.

However you may be able to know the outline of their experiment-results. If any one of the main members comes back from Korea. If such one come back, General Kanbayashi will immediately devote him to you.

10 In the Army Medical Collage (Tokyo) only some researches were done. But, as the college is very small, and the other works (training of students, manufacturing of sera and prophylactics) were too busy, the research work on active attack could not be done active at Tokyo. In addition, it is very difficult to keep the matter secret, at Tokyo. The research works, which had some reference with BW offensive, were, accordingly to my memory, as follows:

a) Studies on Chespis-flea, its geological studies, with parpone of its defense and tests of insecticides (such as DDT).

b) Studies on mass-production of bacteria, connecting with the immediate mass-production of prophylactic (defensive) at sudden invation of Cholera or Plague epidemy (epidemic).

c) Studies on some poison, hand detective for instance FUGU-toxin, but no success to get pure powder.

d) Studies on keeping bacteria in living state, with "lyophite" process;

but this was not done active, because the equipment (the dryer) were occupied almost always for the sera and human-plasma for transfusion.

In the last period of this for, from August 1944, the college was very busy to avoid the bombardment, to transfer its manufacturing plants to country-side, and at last, in April and May, it is burned up.

11 The purpose of this information is as at first mentioned. I offered my opinion (to let open all these secret) to General Kanbayashi, and he, agreeing to my opinion, did every effort to get the permission from the vice-chief of General Staff, but, till now, he could not get.

12 I have a large fear, that my this act (information) be against our General-staff. So I beg you to fire these papers immediately after you read this. I beg you, by the inquiry to the other officers, not to gustate this information in such a way as

"Information of Liet Col Naitō says, . . ."

"It is evident, according to Dr Naitō's information . . ." I beg you to keep this information secret, not only to General Staffs, but even to General Kanbayashi.

I ask you to understand that I am staking my life doing this Information; I shall be killed if any one knows that I have done this information. My only hope is to rescue this poor, defeated nation.

Here, in this information, must be many discourtesy, because of language difficulty. In such case I ask your large-minded pardon.

(This is from one of the original copies marked RESTRICTED)
Report on Scientific Intelligence Survey in Japan – September–October 1945

Volume V – Biological Warfare

SUMMARY: BIOLOGICAL WARFARE (BW)

1 Responsible officers of both the Army and Navy have freely admitted to an interest in defensive BW.

2 Naval officers maintained that offensive BW had not been investigated.

3 Information has been obtained that from 1936 to 1945 the Japanese Army fostered offensive BW, probably on a large scale. This was apparently done without the knowledge (and possibly contrary to the wishes) of the Emperor. If this was the case, reluctance to give information relative to offensive BW is partially explained.

4 BW seems to have been largely a military activity, with civilian talent excluded in all but minor roles.

5 The initial stimulus for Japanese participation in BW seems to have been twofold:

a) The influence of Lt Gen Shirō Ishii.

b) The conviction that the Russians had practiced [sic] BW in Manchuria in 1935, and that they might use it again. [The Chinese were similarly accused.]

6 The principal BW center was situated in Pingfan, near Harbin, Manchuria. This was a large self-sufficient installation with a garrison of 3,000 in 1939–1940 (reduced to 1,500 in 1945).

7 Intensive efforts were expended to develop BW into a practical weapon, at least eight types of special bombs being tested for large-scale dissemination of bacteria.

8 The most thoroughly investigated munition was the Uji type 50 bomb. More than 2,000 of these bombs were used in field trials.

9 Employing static techniques and drop tests from planes, approximately 4,000 bombs were used in field trials at Pingfan.

10 By 1939, definite progress had been made, but the Japanese at no time were in a position to use BW as a weapon. However, their advances in certain bomb types was such as to warrant the closest scrutiny of the Japanese work.

11 Japanese offensive BW was characterised by a curious mixture of foresight, energy, ingenuity and at the same time, lack of imagination with surprisingly amateurish approaches to some aspects of the work.

12 Organisms which were considered as possible candidates for BW, and which were tested in the laboratory or in the field included:

All types of gastro intestinal bacterial pathogens, P.pestis (plague), B. anthracis (Anthrax) and M.malleomyces (glanders).

13 Japanese defensive BW stresses:

a) Organisations of fixed and mobile preventive medicine units (with emphasis on water purification).

b) An accelerated vaccine production program.

c) A system of BW education of medical officers in all echelons (BW Defensive Intelligence Institute).

14 The principal reasons for the Japanese failure were:

a) Limited or improper selection of BW agents.

b) Denial (even prohibition) of co-operated scientific effort.

c) Lack of co-operation of the various elements of the Army (e.g. ordnance).

d) Exclusion of civilian scientists, thus denying the project the best technical talent in the empire.

e) A policy of retrenchment at a crucial point in the development of the project.

CONCLUSION

It is the opinion of the investigating officer that:

a) If a policy had been followed in 1939 which would have permitted the reasonably generous budget to be strengthened by an organisation with some power in the Japanese military system, and which would have stressed integration of services and co-operation amongst the workers, the Japanese BW project might well have produced a practicable weapon.

b) However, since the Japanese dreaded the United States' capacity for retaliating in kind (i.e. BW) or with Chemical Warfare agents, it is most unlikely that they would have used a BW attack against American troops even if the weapon had been at hand.

c) The Japanese are fully aware of the reasons for their failure in the development of BW. It is extremely unlikely that they would repeat their mistakes.

The report refers to the *Uji* bomb being tested – more than 2,000 of them. The *Ha* bomb, too, was "exploded experimentally".

"Whereas the Uji bomb was an all-purpose munition, the Ha bomb was constructed and produced with only one purpose in mind – the dispersion of anthrax spores. The immediate effect was gained by shrapnel bursts with secondary considerations given to ground contamination. The statement has been made that a scratch wound from a single piece of shrapnel was sufficient to produce illness and death in 50–90% of the horses, and in 90–100% of sheep exposed in experiments. More than 500 sheep were used in such field trials and estimates of horses similarly expended vary from 100 (App 29-F-a) to 200 (App 20-E-b)."

Attached to the report as "Supplement 1a" was a map indicating that the Japanese Army had water purification units attached to their 18th, 31st, 33rd, 49th, 53rd, 54th, 55th and 56th Divisions stationed in Burma, with larger fixed field water purification units at Rangoon and Mandalay.

APPENDIX C

THE THOMPSON REPORT

CONCLUSIONS

It is the opinion of the investigating officer that:

1 The information regarding Japanese BW activities obtained from presumably independent sources was consistent to the point where it seems that the informants had been instructed as to the amount and nature of information that was to be divulged under interrogation.

2 All information was presumably furnished from memory since all records are said to have been destroyed in accordance with directives of the Japanese Army. Yet, some of the information, especially sketches of the bombs, was in such detail as to question the contention that all documentary evidence had been destroyed.

3 It was evident throughout the interrogations that it was the desire of the Japanese to minimize the extent of their activities in BW, especially the effort devoted to offensive research and development.

4 Failure to fully utilize Japanese scientific capability by restriction of BW research and development to the military with lack of co-operation between the military services precluded progress toward development of BW into a practical weapon.

5 Had a practical BW weapon been achieved, it is unlikely that Japan would have resorted to its use because of fear of retaliation by means of chemical warfare. Insofar as could be learned, Japan had no information of American activity in BW.

APPENDIX D

THE INGLIS REPORT

Summary of the assessment on Japan made by the report by Rear Admiral Thomas B. Inglis, *Naval Aspects biological warfare*, August 1947. The quotations are from the report.

The report was unequivocal:

"Research extended to the use of human beings as subjects – the only admitted occurrence of this kind . . . Further the Kwantung Army launched actual BW attacks against the Chinese . . ."

Crucially, the report averred that "Chinese claims have been verified by the admissions of Japanese BW personnel and by American investigators." It then gave a comprehensive summary of the scale of the Japanese effort in BW.

Boeki Kyusui BU had engaged in research on the instigation and prevention of anthrax, typhoid, plague, cholera, "Songo" fever, and other diseases. The work on vaccines had been extensive, 20 million dosages being produced annually. The life-span of numerous strains of micro-organisms had been investigated as had bacterial clouds, plant pathogens, and animal diseases. Ground-contaminating and wound infecting bombs had been developed and given field trials, in some instances against human beings. Experiments with cholera, plague, and anthrax had been carried out on Manchurian criminals who had been sentenced to death.

The reason that the Japanese BW campaign had been only "a limited success" had been two-fold. First the munitions designers and the biologists had failed to co-operate closely enough, so the weapons has not been truly efficient. Secondly, only the anthrax experiments had been truly effective. Thirdly there had been "the personal objections of the Emperor" – though no further evidence or comment was made on this point.

The assessment was confirmation of what the United States already knew: The Japanese had gone further, achieved more in germ warfare than any other nation. Inglis' report ruminated on the lessons for the future: "Had they [the Japanese] been able to provoke one or more full-scale epidemics, as contrasted with the isolated outbreaks that were started, the Japanese would have had a powerful weapon for use in their theatre of war where sanitation is at a low level.

"As for the future, should vigilant supervision over scientific research be relaxed, Japan could continue its pursuit of BW knowledge; and, if so desired, could probably wage effective biological warfare within five years after the removal of Allied control . . ."

266

NOTES

Chapter 1

1 Matsumura, Takao, "Documents on Experiments for Chemical and Biological Weapons by Unit 731", *Journal of Historical Studies (Rekishi Gaku Kenkyū)*, Aoki Publishing Company, Tokyo; February 1985, pp 56–64.

Chapter 2

1 Thompson, Lt-Col Arvo T., "Report on Japanese Biological Warfare" (hereinafter Thompson), Army Service Forces, Camp Detrick, Frederick, Maryland, May 31, 1946, pp 2–3, RG 330, MFB, WNA.

2 "Japanese Military Water Supply Equipment", Chief Engineer, GHQ, AFPAC, in BIOS/JAP/PR/1592, April 1946, p 126, WO 208/2235, UKPRO.

3 Smith, 1st Lt Neal R., "Report on Case 330: Motoji Yamaguchi . . . Shirō Ishii, alias Hajime Tōgō", Investigation Division, Legal Section, SCAP, April 4, 1947, p 2, RG 331, MFB, WNA.

4 Tsuneishi, Kei'ichi, and Tomizo Asano, *The Bacteriological Warfare Unit and the Suicide of Two Physicians (Saikinsen Butai to Jiketsu Ita Futari no Igakusha)* (hereinafter Asano), Shincho-Sha, Tokyo, 1982, Section: "The Bereaved Family".

5 Schindler, Detrich, and Jiri Toman, *The Laws of Armed Conflict: A Collection of Conventions*, Resolutions and other Documents, Sijthoff, Leiden, 1973, pp 109–19.

6 Asano, Section: "The Ishii Bacteriological Warfare Unit".

7 Thompson, p 2.

8 *Materials on the Trial of Former Servicemen of the Japanese Army Charged with Manufacturing and Employing Bacteriological Weapons* (hereinafter Khabarovsk), Foreign Languages Publishing House, Moscow, 1950, p 295.

9 Sanders, Lt-Col Murray, "Report on Scientific Intelligence Survey in Japan" (hereinafter Sanders), Scientific and Technical Advisory Section, GHQ, AFPAC, Vol 5, September and October 1945, Section 3, BIOS/JAP/PR/746, UKPRO.

10 Tsuneishi, Kei'ichi, *The Biological Warfare Unit that Disappeared (Kieta Saikinsen Butai)* (hereinafter Tsuneishi), Kaimei-Sha, Tokyo, 1981, pp 23–5.

11 Khabarovsk, p 295.

12 *Ibid.*, pp 292–6.

13 *Japanese Army Medical Journal*, No 52 (1914), pp 449–68; Kei'ichi

Tsuneishi, "C. Koizumi: as a Promoter of the Ministry of Health and Welfare and an Originator of the BCW Research Programme", *Historia Scientarium*, No 26 (1984), The History of Science Society of Japan, Tokyo, 1984.

14 Asano, Section: "Poison Gas Masks".

15 *Fifty Year History of the Army Medical School, (Rikugun Gun'i-Gakkō Gojū-Nen Shi)*, Tokyo, 1936; Asano, Section: "Poison Gas Masks".

16 Harris, Robert, and Jeremy Paxman, *A Higher Form of Killing* (hereinafter Harris and Paxman), Chatto & Windus, London, 1982, xiv.

17 Tsuneishi, p 25.

18 Asano, Section: "The Ishii Bacteriological Warfare Unit".

19 *Ibid.*

20 Morimura, Seiichi, *The Devil's Gluttony Part I (Akuma no Hoshoku)* (hereinafter Morimura I), Kadokawa Shoten, Tokyo, 1983, Section: "The Kagura-Zaka Millionaire".

21 Tsuneishi, pp 39–40.

Chapter 3

1 The Foreign Affairs Association of Japan, *Japan Year Book 1935*, Kenkyūsha Press, Tokyo, 1935, pp 1202–3.

2 Asano, Section: "The Bereaved Family".

3 Morton, T. R., *Today in Manchuria*, Student Christian Movement Press, London, 1939, pp 65–104; F. C. Jones, *Manchuria Since 1931*, Royal Institute of International Affairs, London, 1949, pp 212–15; *Japan Year Book 1935*, p 1207.

4 Tsuneishi, pp 98–9.

5 Khabarovsk, p 114.

6 *Fifty Year History of the Army Medical School*, op. cit., Asano, Section: "The Bacteriological Warfare Unit".

7 Endō, Saburō, *The Fifteen Years War Between Japan and I*, Niccho Shorin, Tokyo, 1974, p 162; Asano, Section: "The Ishii Bacteriological Warfare Unit".

8 Morton, T. R., *Today in Manchuria*, op. cit., pp 65–104; F. C. Jones, *Manchuria Since 1931*, op. cit., pp 212–15.

9 Khabarovsk, p 104.

10 Asano, Sections: "The Ishii Bacteriological Warfare Unit" and "Physicians".

11 Tsuneishi, pp 47–51.

12 Khabarovsk, pp 250–1.

13 Akiyama, Hiroshi, *Special Unit 731 (Tokushu Butai Nana-San-Ichi)*, San-Ichi Shobo, Tokyo, 1956; Tsuneishi, p 73.

14 Khabarovsk, pp 113 and 105.

15 *Ibid.*, p 105.

16 Perry Robinson, Julian, *The Problem of Chemical and Biological Warfare, Vol II, CB Weapons Today* (hereinafter SIPRI II), Stockholm International Peace Research Institute, Stockholm, 1973, pp 67–8.

17 Morimura I, Section: "The Bacteria Factory Ghost".

18 Khabarovsk, pp 266–7.
19 Khabarovsk, p 101.
20 Tsuneishi, p 214.
21 "Plague – the vector", *Encyclopaedia Britannica*, William Benton, London, 1964, p 993.
22 Khabarovsk, p 255.
23 Khabarovsk, p 129.
24 *Ibid.*, pp 374–5.
25 Thompson, p 15.
26 Khabarovsk, pp 98–9.
27 Morimura, Seiichi, *The Devil's Gluttony – A Sequel, (Akuma no Hoshoku)* (hereinafter Morimura II), Kadokawa Shoten, Tokyo, 1983, Section: "Bacterial Spraying Bombs". See also Sanders, "Summary of Findings", No 8.
28 Khabarovsk, p 259.
29 Sanders, "Summary of Findings", No 5.
30 Thompson, pp 10–16.
31 Khabarovsk, p 102.
32 *Ibid.*, p 417.
33 *Ibid.*; "Bacteriological Warfare", *Sunday Mainichi*, January 27, 1952; *Report of the International Scientific Commission for the Investigation of the Facts Concerning Bacterial Warfare in China and Korea*, (hereinafter ISC), Peking, 1952, pp 285–6.
34 ISC, p 286.
35 Hill, Dr Edwin, and Dr Joseph Victor, "Summary Report on BW Investigations" (hereinafter Hill and Victor), to Gen Alden C. Waitt, Chief Chemical Corps, December 12, 1947, Table S, Fort Detrick archives.

Chapter 4
1 Endō, Saburō, *The Fifteen Years War Between Japan and China and I*, op. cit., p 162; Asano, Section: "Ishii Bacteriological Warfare Unit".
2 *Ibid.*
3 *Ibid.*
4 Khabarovsk, p 114.
5 *Ibid.*, p 127.
6 "Statement of Major Tomio Karasawa", undated (but given early 1946), ATIS document 9306, RG 331, Allied Operational and Occupation Headquarters, World War II, SCAP, Legal Section, Administrative Division, Investigative Reports, MFB, WNA.
7 Tsuneishi, p 243.
8 *Ibid.*
9 Khabarovsk, pp 235–7.
10 *Ibid.*, pp 149–50.
11 *Ibid.*, pp 165–7.
12 *Ibid.*, p 165.
13 Morimura II, Ch 1, Section: "The 'logs' supply route".
14 Khabarovsk, p 20.

15 Conversation with Naokata Ishibashi, Atami, Japan, December 1984.
16 Ryōhei Sakaki, "Bacteriological Warfare", *Sunday Mainichi*, No 1682, January 27, 1952.
17 Conversation with Dr Sueo Akimoto, Yokohama, Japan, December 1984.
18 Conversation with Dr Shirō Kasahara, Tokyo, February 1985.
19 Yutu, Jian, Li Zhongduo and Song Guangchang, "Seroepidemiologic Study of EHF with Renal Syndrome", *Chinese Medical Journal*, No 94(4), 1981, pp 221–8.
20 Conversation with Dr Yasuo Tokoro, Atami, Japan, February 1985.
21 Ishii, Shirō *et al*, "Research on So-Called Songo Fever", *Japanese Army Medical Journal*, No 327, 1940.
22 Conversation with Dr Shirō Kasahara, Tokyo, February 1985.
23 Masaji Kitano, "Epidemic Prevention Confidential Anecdotes" ("*Bōeki Hiwa*"), *Japan Medical Affairs Bulletin (Nihon-I-Ji Shinpo)*, No 1947, 1961; Tsuneishi, p 146.
24 Conversation with Dr Shirō Kasahara, Tokyo, February 1985.
25 "Epidemic Haemorrhagic Fever", *Department of the Army (United States) Technical Bulletin*, TB MED 240, May 5, 1953, pp 1–22.
26 Kitano *et al*, "Entscheidung des Erregers des Epidemischen Haemorrhagischen Fiebers", *Journal of the Japanese Pathological Society*, No 33, 1943, pp 476–7.
27 Khabarovsk, pp 355–6.
28 Morimura 1, Section: "What the young trainees saw".
29 Khabarovsk, pp 62–3.
30 "Japanese Experiments in Resistance to Cold", GHQ, FEC, Military Intelligence Section, Technical Intelligence Detachment, March 15, 1949, RG 331, MFB, WNA.
31 Khabarovsk, p 358.
32 *Ibid.*, p 289.
33 *Ibid.*, p 367.
34 Conversation with Naoji Uezono, Tokyo, February 1985.
35 Yoshimura, Hisato, "On Frostbite", Special Lecture at the Harbin Branch of the 15th Manchurian Medical Conference, October 26, 1941, Japanese Archive of Government Documents (Kobunshokan-Zo); Tsuneishi, pp 160–76, *passim*.
36 Tsuneishi, Kei'chi, "The Research Guarded by Military Secrecy – the Isolation of the EHF Virus in the Japanese Biological Warfare Unit", *Historia Scientiarum*, The History of Science Society of Japan, Spring 1986.
37 *History of CW Research*, Ministry of Health and Welfare, Tokyo, 1956, preface.
38 SIPRI II, pp 50–2.
39 Matsumura, Takao, "Documents on Experiments for Chemical and Biological Weapons by Unit 731", *Journal of Historical Studies (Rekishi Gaku Kenkyū)*, Aoki Shoten, Tokyo, February 1985, pp 56–64.
40 Morimura II, Sections: "Death Box", and "The 37 Year Wake".
41 Conversation, February 1985.

42 Asano, Section: "Malnutrition on the Front".
43 Conversation with Naokata Ishibashi, Atami, December 1984.
44 Khabarovsk, p 116.
45 Conversation with Masakuni Kurumizawa, March 1985.
46 Kitano Masaji, *et al*, "Determining the Pathogen(s) of EHF", *Bulletin of Japan Pathology Academy* (*Nihon Byōri Gakkai Kaishi*), Vol 34, 1944.
47 Kitano, Masaji, "Army Health History", Jieitai Eisei Gakkō, Tokyo, Vol 7, 1971.
48 Morimura I, Section: "The Operation Vikings".
49 Raginsky, Mark, M. Rozenblit, and Lev N. Smirnov, *Bacteriological Warfare: The Criminal Weapons of Imperialist Aggression* (hereinafter Raginsky), Soviet Academy of Sciences, Moscow, 1950, Ch 3.
50 Morimura II, Section: "Disinfect and Kill".
51 *Ibid.*, Section: "A Conspectus of the Devil's Research Menu".
52 Khabarovsk, p 268.

Chapter 5
1 All interviews quoted in the chapter carried out by authors for Television South, 1985.
2 Monthly report, Japanese PoW Intelligence Bureau, May 1943.
3 Exhibit 3114, Tokyo War Crimes trial, Report on Malnutrition in Mukden PoW Camp, February 17, 1943, by Nagayama, chief of Medical Section.
4 Report to Geneva by Red Cross representative Pestallocchi, November 1943.

Chapter 6
1 Sanders, 29-E-d-1.
2 "Transcript of secret document presented to Col Murray Sanders by Ryōichi Naitō", (hereinafter Naitō), September 1945, given by Dr Sanders to authors.
3 *History of Army Health and Sanitation During the Greater East Asia War* (*Dai-Tōa Sensō Rikugun Eisei-Shi*), Chapter: "The Activities of the Water Supply Unit during the Nomonhan Incident", Japan Ground Self Defence Force Health and Sanitation School (Rikujō Jieitai Eisei Gakkō), Tokyo, 1968–71, Vols I–VII; Tsuneishi, pp 59–62.
4 Khabarovsk, p 288.
5 "Ishii Commendation", *Tokyo Asahi Shinbun*, May 23, 1940; Tsuneishi, p 58.
6 Conversation with Naokata Ishibashi, Atami, December 1984.
7 Khabarovsk, pp 203–4.
8 Conversation with Naokata Ishibashi, Atami, December 1984.
9 Khabarovsk, p 270.
10 *Ibid.*, p 262.
11 *Ibid.*, pp 287–8.
12 *Ibid.*, p 253.
13 *Ibid.*, p 116.
14 *Ibid.*, p 260; and Dr P. Z. King, "Japanese Attempts at Bacterial Warfare in China", Director General of the Chinese National Health

Administration, March 31, 1942, RG 319, MFB, WNA.

15 *Japanese Army Medical Journal*, No 344; Kei'ichi Tsuneishi, *Target: Ishii*, Nagasaki University, Nagasaki, 1985, p 22.

16 Khabarovsk, pp 260–2.

17 Submission made by Dr Wen-kwei Chen, Report of the International Scientific Commission for the Investigation of Facts Concerning Bacterial Warfare in Korea and China, Peking, 1952, pp 213–16.

18 "Japanese Preparations for Bacteriological Warfare in China", PoW interrogation report, HQ, USAF, China Theater, Office of the AC of S, G-2, December 12, 1944, RG 319, MFB, WNA.

19 WNA document uncovered by Prof. Kentarō Awaya, Rikkyō University, Tokyo.

20 Khabarovsk, p 355.

21 *Ibid.*, p 58.

22 "Transcript of Interrogation of Lt-Gen Masaji Kitano in Tokyo by Lt-Col A. T. Thompson", February 6, 1946, Fort Detrick ref 013.

23 Tsuneishi, p 220.

24 Raginsky, Ch 3.

25 Thompson, p 3.

26 "Stenographic Transcript of Interrogation of Lt-Gen Shirō Ishii, in Tokyo by Lt-Col A. T. Thompson", February 5 and 8, 1946, Fort Detrick ref 013.

27 Morimura I, Section: "The Medium for Corrosion".

28 Tsuneishi, pp 238–41, *passim*.

29 Asano, Section: "The Ishii Bacteriological Warfare Unit".

30 "Underground Factory of Death", *Akahata*, February 8, 1950; Raginsky, Ch 3.

31 Masuda, Tomosada, "The Bacteriological Warfare", Army Medical Colonel, Instructor, Army Medical College, December 15, 1942, Fort Detrick ref 004.

32 Asano, Section: "Physicians".

33 *Ibid.*, Section: "The Health and Welfare Minister Knows Defeat in War".

34 Sakuyama, Motoharu, "On the Preservation of Rickettsiae Outside the Live Body", *Japanese Army Medical Journal*, No 355; Tsuneishi, pp 179–82.

35 Sanders, 29-E-a-5.

36 *Ibid.*

37 *Ibid.*, 29-F-b-2.

38 *Ibid.*, 29-E-d-3.

39 "Current Events Titbits" (*Jiji Henpen*), Group News Column, Military Surgeon Group Magazine, No 311, April 1939; Tsuneishi, pp 130–1.

40 Sanders, 29-A-a-1.

41 Viewed by author.

42 Sanders, 29-A-a-1.

43 Khabarovsk, *passim*.

44 *Ibid.*, pp 315–16 and 76.

45 *Ibid.*, pp 120–1.
46 *Ibid.*, p 80.
47 *Ibid.*, pp 316–18.
48 Naitō, and Khabarovsk, *passim*.
49 Khabarovsk, p 53.
50 *Ibid.*, p 372.
51 *Ibid.*, p 53.
52 *Ibid.*, p. 283.
53 Conversation with Tadashi Yamashita, Chiba Prefecture, December 1984.
54 Mikasa-no-miya, Takahito, *Ancient Orient and I (Kodai Oriento-Shi To Watakushi)*, Gakusei Sha, Tokyo, 1984, pp 16–17.
55 Khabarovsk, pp 138 and 124.
56 *Ibid.*, pp 137–8.
57 *Ibid.*, p 127.
58 Conversation with Naoji Uezono, Tokyo, December 1984.
59 *Ibid.*
60 "Emperor Article Upsets Ministry", *Daily Yomiuri*, October 24, 1982.
61 Sanders, 29-D-a-1; Thompson, pp 11 and 19.
62 Shin'ichi, Fujii, *The Constitution of Japan: A Historical Survey*, Kokushikan University, Tokyo, 1965, pp 297–300.

Chapter 7
1 Correspondence with Prof Tsuneishi, Nagasaki University, December 14, 1985.
2 *Ibid.*
3 Khabarovsk, pp 97, 133 and 281.
4 "Daughter's Eye View of Lt-Gen Ishii, Chief of Devil's Brigade", (hereinafter Daughter's Eye View), *The Japan Times*, August 29, 1982.
5 Khabarovsk, p 135.
6 *Ibid.*, pp 115–16.
7 *Ibid.*, p 138.
8 *Ibid.*, p 372.
9 Asano, Section: "The Ishii Bacteriological Warfare Unit".
10 Conversation with Naoji Uezono, Tokyo, February 1985.
11 *Ibid.*
12 Asano, Sections: "Return to Japan", and "From Gas to Bacteriological Warfare".
13 Daughter's Eye View.
14 "Death Centre", *Hsinhua*, as reported in *Isvestia*, February 15, 1950.
15 Tsuneishi, p 227.
16 Conversation with Naoji Uezono,Tokyo, November 1984.
17 Daughter's Eye View.
18 Morimura I, Section: "The Truth about the Massacre of the Logs".
19 Asano, Section: "The Bacteriological Warfare Unit".
20 Morimural I, Section: 'Defend the Unit's Secrets to the Death".
21 "Death Centre", *Hsinhua*, as reported in *Isvestia*, February 15, 1950.

22 Khabarovsk, pp 382–3.
23 *Overall Summary View of Army Combat Weapons* (*Rikugun Heiki Sōran*), Tosho Shuppansha, Tokyo, 1977; Tsuneishi, p 213.
24 Asano, Section: "Human Experimentation".
25 *Report of the International Scientific Commission for the Investigation of the Facts Concerning Bacterial Warfare in Korea and China*, Peking, 1952 p 14.
26 Morimura II, Sections: "Post War Headquarters of the 731", and "The Unit which Carried the Burden of a Black Past".
27 Morimura II, Section: "*Fu* and Food Supplies Depot 1".
28 "Underground Factory of Death", *Akahata*, February 8, 1950.
29 Morimura II, Section: "*Fu* and Food Supplies Depot 1".
30 Asano, Section: "One Month After Surrender".

Chapter 8
1 "Japanese Attempts to Secure Virulent Strains of Yellow Fever Virus", War Department, Military Intelligence Division, G-2, January 27, 1941, RG 112, MFB, WNA.
2 *Ibid.*
3 "Japanese Attempts to Secure Virulent Strains of Yellow Fever Virus", G-2 to Office of the Surgeon General, February 3, 1941, RG 112, MFB, WNA.
4 "Digest of Information Regarding Axis Activities in the Field of Bacteriological Warfare", Federal Security Agency, January 8, 1943, RG 319, MFB, WNA.
5 "Intelligence Regarding Biological Warfare", Office of Chief of Naval Operations for Joint Intelligence Staff, January 28, 1944, RG 319, MFB, WNA.
6 Clendinin, Richard M., *Science and Technology at Fort Detrick, 1943–68* (hereinafter Clendinin), Fort Detrick Technical Information Division, Frederick, Maryland, 1968, p 5.
7 *Ibid.*, preface.
8 *Ibid.*
9 Thompson, p 4.
10 Clendinin, preface and pp 1–5.
11 Statement on June 6, 1942, WRO 193/712, UKPRO.
12 Clendinin, p 10.
13 Hill and Victor, Appendix F.
14 "Digest of Information Regarding Axis Activities in the Field of Bacteriological Warfare", *loc. cit.*
15 *Ibid.*
16 "Intelligence Regarding Biological Warfare", *loc. cit.*
17 Chen, Dr Wen-kwei, "Report on Plague in Changteh, Hunan", WO 188/680, 58986, UKPRO.
18 King, Dr P. Z., "Allegations of Japanese Bacterial Warfare in China", Director General Chinese National Health Administration, RG 319, MFB, WNA.

19 Minutes of Sub-Committee on Bacteriological Warfare, November 17, 1936, WO 188/648, 58986, UKPRO.

20 *Ibid.*, January 22, 1937.

21 Sub-Committee on Bacteriological Warfare Report, March 17, 1937, WO 188/648, 58986, UKPRO.

22 *Ibid.*

23 Notes on Conversation between Maj-Gen H. M. J. Perry AMD-7 and Capt D. C. Evans, MI 10, on Bacteriological Warfare, December 22, 1939, WO 188/648, 58985, UKPRO.

24 Hankey, Lord (Paymaster General's Office) "Bacteriological Warfare" to Prime Minister, December 6, 1941, CAB 120/782, 58921, UKPRO.

25 Smith, C. E. Gordon, "Research Establishments in Europe: 69 – The Microbiological Research Establishment, Porton", *Chemistry and Industry*, March 4, 1967, p 339.

26 Hankey, Lord (Paymaster General's Office), *loc. cit.*

27 Harris and Paxman, p 111.

28 Letter, A. Landsborough Thomson (Medical Research Council) to Henry Everett (Offices of the War Cabinet), January 6, 1942, WO 188/680, 58986, UKPRO.

29 Letter, Dr Paul Fildes (Porton) to Henry Everett (Offices of the War Cabinet), January 10, 1942, WO 188/680, 58986, UKPRO.

30 "The Alleged BW Incident at Changteh", Biology Section, Experimental Station, Porton, March 23, 1942, WO 188/680, 58986, UKPRO.

31 Fildes, Dr Paul, "Paragraph for BW Intelligence Summary No 1", WO 188/690, 58986, UKPRO.

32 Correspondence between Gen H. L. Ismay and the Hon Sir Alexander Cadogan, Foreign Office, July 20, 1942 (and related memoranda), CAB 120/775, 58921, UKPRO.

33 "Japanese Attempts at Bacteriological Warfare in China", initialled as agreed for circulation by Churchill, July 9, 1942, PREM 3/65, UKPRO.

34 Extract from Joint Intelligence Chiefs Memo, Ref 986-1 (JIC 156/M) for Cols Smith and Pettigrew, January 22, 1944, RG 319, MFB, WNA.

35 "Biological Warfare", War Department to CnC South West Pacific Area, the Commanding Generals, Theatres of Operations, Eastern and Caribbean Defence Commands, Alaskan Department, Separate Base Commands, February 14, 1944, RG 338, MFB, WNA.

36 Special Projects Periodic Intelligence Reports (various during 1944) (hereinafter Special Digest) WO 188/690, 58986.

37 *Ibid.*

38 *Ibid.*

39 *Ibid.*

40 *Ibid.*

41 *Ibid.*

42 *Ibid.*

43 *Ibid.*

44 *Ibid.*

45 *Ibid.*

46 Report of Chemical Warfare Conference held under the direction of Maj-Gen J. L. Frink, US Army Services of Supply, South-West Pacific Area, October 10–13, 1944, RG 319, MFB, WNA.
47 "BW Intelligence Received to Date on Japan", undated (but after September 1944), MFB, WNA.
48 Notes on Japanese Photostats, by Rev Moule, March 26, 1945, WO 188/690, 58986, UKPRO.
49 Special Digest, *loc. cit.*
50 "Japanese Bacteriological Warfare in China", PoW interrogation, China G-2, December 12, 1944, RG 319, MFB, WNA.
51 Washington to GHQ, SWPA, January 3, 1945, RG 338, MFB, WNA.
52 "Condensed Minutes of Ninth Service Command BW Meeting", March 9–10, 1945, RG 112, MFB, WNA.
53 "Tropical Assignment", broadcast in English from Singapore, May 24, 1945, MFB, WNA.
54 "BW Information – Source: Captured Personnel and Material Branch", War Department, Military Intelligence Service, April 6, 1945, RG 319, MFB, WNA.
55 War Diary, Medical Directorate (Admin), HQ, ALFSEA, by Maj-Gen W. E. Tyndall, September 1–30, 1945, WO 177/222, 80124, UKPRO.
56 Letter, Dr Leonard Short to Robert Whymant, *Guardian* Tokyo correspondent, undated but evidently written in the aftermath of article by John W. Powell. There were in fact two articles by Powell: *Bulletin of Concerned Asian Scholars*, "Japan's Germ Warfare: The US Cover-up of a War Crime", 1980, 12(4); and *Bulletin of Atomic Scientists*, "Japan's Biological Weapons 1930–45", October 1981.

Chapter 9
1 Hunt, Frazier, *The Untold Story of Douglas MacArthur*, Robert Hale, London 1955.
2 Cable to Chief of Staff George C. Marshall.
3 "The authority of the Emperor and the Japanese Government to rule the state is subordinate to you as Supreme Commander for the Allied Powers. You will exercise your authority as you deem proper to carry out your mission. Our relations with Japan do not rest on a contractual basis but on an unconditional surrender. Since your authority is supreme, you will not entertain any question on the part of the Japanese as to its scope." US Joint Chiefs of Staff to MacArthur, September 6, 1945, State Department Publication No 2671, Occupation of Japan: Policy and Progress, Appendix 16.
4 Address, Allied Council for Japan, April 5, 1946.
5 *Ibid.*
6 Hunt, *op. cit.*
7 "Beware most strictly any outbursts of emotion which may engender needless complications . . ." Extract, Emperor Hirohito's speech to his people, August 14, 1945.
8 Kawai, Kasuo, *Japan's American Interlude*, University of Chicago Press, Chicago, 1960.

9 Dr John Pritchard, conversation with authors, 1985.

10 Willoughby, Maj-Gen Charles A. and Jon Chamberlain, *MacArthur 1941–51*, Heinemann, London, 1956.

11 *Ibid.*

12 Hunt, *op. cit.*

Chapter 10

1 Clendinin.

2 According to Clendinin, one experienced investigator who had long worked with *Bacillus anthracis* complained to the Scientific Director, Dr Baldwin, saying that the safety regulations were an unnecessary interference with his work; he was quite willing to take any personal risks that might result from by-passing the rules. Dr Baldwin refused to permit any relaxation of the safety rules that, as he emphasised, were designed as much for the protection of the community as for safeguarding the health of the researchers. No accident affecting the local community ever occurred. There were "only 60 cases of accidental infection that required treatment and another 159 cases of exposure to pathogens wherein prompt treatment prevented infection".

3 Pledge to secrecy.

4 All the quotations from Murray Sanders in this Chapter are from conversations with the authors, Delray Beach, Florida, 1985.

5 J. P. Marquand was the author of the Mr Moto stories in the *Saturday Evening Post*, portraying a fictional Japanese character. Good as these might have been, Marquand's lectures on intelligence, according to Murray Sanders, did not impress the assembled scientists at Camp Detrick.

6 Conversation with authors, Pompano, Florida, 1986. Col Fellowes, who had been working on vaccines for Merck, Sharpe and Dohme before joining Camp Detrick, left in 1952 to help set up veterinary research laboratories at Plum Island, off Long Island, New York. Plum Island was a fort in the Spanish–American war. It had a hospital, therefore, and living accommodation and the animals on which experiments were and are carried out were kept in the old gun galleries underground. The cattle came from a single ranch on the Virginia–Tennessee border. Plum Island was run jointly by the War Department and the Department of Agriculture. Fellowes remembers: "It had its own navy, its own transport and, because we borrowed trucks from the atomic energy people it led to rumours that we were in the nuclear business." Plum Island is unique. Nothing that is taken on to the quarantine area of the island is ever taken off. Personnel who work there may take their lunch sandwiches with them – but may never take the wrapping back home. They must remove everything, including wedding rings, before donning protective clothing to enter the restricted area. Fellowes remembers "taking twenty showers a day. I even had two sets of spectacles – one for the Island, the other for the rest of my life."

7 Henderson was a microbiologist, seconded from Porton.

8 Ironically, this was the disease that Ishii had chosen to study early in his germ warfare researches. Sanders was later to warn that it had a "mortality

rate of over 50 per cent and could remain virulent for three weeks or more, if freeze dried".

9 The envelope of the balloon was made of four or five pieces of mulberry paper about the thickness of cigarette paper and bonded with a cellulose cement that made the resulting paper an excellent balloon material. Many segments of paper were cemented together to form an almost perfect sphere 30 to 33 feet in diameter with a lifting capacity of about half a ton at sea level and about 300 pounds at 30,000 feet when filled with hydrogen. A metal valve with a rubber diaphragm maintained a pressure of about one ounce per square inch and prevented the balloon from exploding if it should rise above pressure height. On balloons found in the early months of the enemy's campaign there was a capsule of flash powder attached to the envelope with a fuse connecting it to the ballast release gear. This was designed to ignite the envelope when the balloon had dropped its load or in case something went wrong with the mechanism, but these capsules were not found on later balloons.

The load was carried on 19 shroud lines about 40 feet long, made from manilla hemp.

An ingenious device was employed to drop increments of ballast and bombs at the proper time. It consisted of a cast aluminium wheel shaped device with seventy-two holes in the periphery into which explosive plugs were inserted – two to each increment of ballast or bomb. The sandbags or bombs were fastened to T hooks so that even though one plug failed the ballast was dropped. Above the ballast ring there was a switch or jack ring with seventy-two switches held open by explosive jacks and connected to the ballast ring with delay fuses. Above the jack ring was a wooden box that housed four aneroids, one of which controlled the balloon; the others were used only if the master aneroid failed to operate. A battery surmounted the whole mechanism – a wet-celled two-volt battery housed in a succession of plastic cases, one of which contained a solution of calcium chloride, probably to prevent excesses of temperature from affecting the operation of the battery.

The ballast usually consisted of thirty-two increments, probably sandbags although the interception of signals similar to those of a radiosonde indicated the possibility of radio gear being substituted for one increment. The pay load consisted of up to four incendiary bombs of about 10 pounds apiece and one bomb, either incendiary or high explosive anti-personnel of about 30 pounds.

10 Top secret abridged account of meeting.

11 Sir Philip Ewen Mitchell, Governor and Commander-in-Chief of Kenya Colony 1945.

12 Text of cable:

TO KENYA (Sir P. Mitchell)

FROM Secretary of State for the Colonies

Sent 8th June 1945 21.30 hrs

Following Top Secret and Personal from Creasy. Begins.

Secretary of State's telegram no 361
Smith has already warned Daubney about these experiments in his secret letter of the 22nd March. For your own and Daubney's information, experiments are connected with possibility that Japanese might attempt to introduce rinderpest into North America by means of balloons. US and Canadian authorities are most anxious that these experiments are being carried out. They particularly ask therefore that connection of work (a) with biological warfare and (b) with North America should be concealed. Suggestion is made in Smith's letter that in order to provide cover the two officers might be described as visitors studying work on diseases or stock being carried out in Kenya. If, however, you think that a better cover could be provided, authorities concerned here would be grateful for any suggestions to this end. No doubt you will be prepared to give laboratory facilities, etc. free of cost; any extra cost should be charged to Imperial Government. Ends.

13 Text of cable:
FROM KENYA (Sir P. Mitchell)
TO Secretary of State, Colonies

R 11th June 1945 16.00 hrs
(No 414 Top Secret)
Your top secret telegram No 361
New vaccine for rinderpest
Your paragraph 2 noted.
Your paragraph 3. Following in Daubney's advice on the three points. Begins.

(1) and (2). Can arrange with twenty animals in each case.

(3) Will arrange additional test in paddocks with about forty animals. Field trial with 10,000 animals to follow after arrival of party and discussion with them. Daubney confirms that 10,000 (repeat 10,000) would be suitable number. Ends.

2. Your paragraph 5. Mid-July convenient. Given advance notice of seven days before arrival of vaccine, arrangements for immediate action will be made.

3. Your paragraph 6. Noted.
14 Text of cable
FROM KENYA (Sir P. Mitchell)
TO Secretary of State, Colonies

Received 11th June 1945 16.35 hrs
Not numbered. Top Secret
Following personal for Creasy. Begins.

Your Top Secret and Personal telegram of 9th March.
Rinderpest.
Noted. Daubney suggests best cover would be US Agricultural, etc. Mission

in Abyssinia. If party has own aircraft and came via Addis Ababa cover would be specially good. If not, one at least should go there and both should pretend to be engaged in the interests of the Abyssinian Government for the purpose of conversation with local technical staff and the general public.

2. One risk, since rinderpest is of such wide interest throughout East Africa, would be curiosity in other territories. I have, accordingly, told the Governors of Tanganyika and Uganda and the Chief Secretary of the Governors' Conference in strict personal secrecy.

3. Needless to say, the fact that the new (repeat new) vaccine is being tried must be kept top secret. Object of visit would be to study the application of existing vaccines to the problem of Abyssinia. New (repeat new) rinderpest vaccine would be headline news from here to Cape Town.
Ends.
15 Text of cable:
FROM KENYA (Acting Governor)
TO Secretary of State, Colonies

Received 24th October 1945 09.20 hrs
(No 875 Top Secret)

Following from Daubney for General [Tommy] Kelser.

Six controlled trials and two large field trials satisfactory to date. Leaving Kabets on or before 25th October.
16 This was only one such example of co-operation between the US and Britain. In 1948 Dr E. A. Perren, a British scientist from Porton Down, recommended a 25–30 square mile site near Benin, Nigeria as suitable to test chemical and biological weapons in "hot, humid conditions" (letter, Ministry of Supply to L. H. Gorsuch, Colonial Office, October 28, 1948). Arrangements for supplies of small animals "for research" were approved, including mice and rats "bred at the Rockefeller Yellow Fever Institute, Yaba, Lagos . . ."
17 Conversation with Seiichi Niizuma, Tokyo, July 1986.

Chapter 11
1 *Pacific Stars and Stripes*, January 6, 1946.
2 "Report to the Secretary of War by Mr George W. Merck", January 3, 1946, Fort Detrick.
3 *Exhibition on Bacteriological War Crimes Committed by the Government of the United States of America*, The Chinese People's Committee for World Peace, Peking, 1952, p 5.
4 "Stenographic Transcript of Interrogation of Lt-Gen Masaji Kitano in Tokyo by Col S. E. Whitesides and Col A. H. Schwichtenberg", January 11, 1946, Fort Detrick ref 013.
5 Case 330, "Motoji Yamaguchi alias Honji Yamaguchi, Yujirō Wakamatsu . . . Shirō Ishii, alias Hajime Tōgō" (hereinafter Smith),

Investigation Division, Legal Section, GHQ, SCAP, April 4, 1947, RG 331, MFB, WNA.

6 Thompson, summary p i.

7 Daughter's Eye View.

8 "Stenographic Transcription of Interrogation of Lt-Gen Shirō Ishii in Tokyo by Lt-Col A. T. Thompson", February 5, 1946, Fort Detrick ref 013.

9 "Transcript of Interrogation of Lt-Gen Masaji Kitano in Tokyo, Japan, by Lt-Col A. T. Thompson", February 6, 1946, Fort Detrick ref 013.

10 "Stenographic Transcript of Interrogation of Lt-Gen Shirō Ishii in Tokyo by Lt-Col A. T. Thompson," February 8, 1946, Fort Detrick ref 013.

11 "Japanese attempts to secure virulent strains of yellow fever virus", War Department General Staff, Military Intelligence Division, G-2, Washington, February 3, 1941, RG 112, MFB, WNA.

12 Conversations with Kiyoshi Fijino, Tokyo, December 1984, and February 1985.

13 *Pacific Stars and Stripes*, February 27, 1946.

14 "Transcript of Interrogation of Maj Yoshiyasu Masuda in Tokyo, Japan, by Lt-Col A. T. Thompson", February 9, 1946, Fort Detrick ref 013.

15 "Transcript of Interrogation of Lt-Col Yoshitaka Sasaki in Kyoto, Japan, by Lt-Col A. T. Thompson", February 20, 1946, Fort Detrick ref 013.

16 Thompson, pp 17 and 19.

17 Tsuneishi, pp 138–9 and 160–1.

18 Morimura I, Ch 10.

19 Asano, Section: "Human Experimentation".

20 SIPRI I, p 316.

21 *Ibid.*

22 Conversation with Dr Riley Housewright, April 1986.

23 DCIGS to CIGS, August 14, 1946, WO 216/570, 80333, UKPRO.

Chapter 12

1 Pritchard, R. John, and Sonia M. Zaide (eds), *Proceedings of the International Military Tribunal for the Far East*, (hereinafter IMTFE), Garland, New York, 1981, Vol 1, p. 21.

2 Nuremberg Charter text in "International Conference on Military Trials", Department of State Publication No 3080, US Govt Printing Office, Washington, 1949, pp 422–8.

3 *Judgement and Annexes*. IMTFE, Vol 20, Annex A-1.

4 Watt, Donald Cameron, "Historical Introduction", IMTFE, Vol 1, vii–xix *passim*.

5 Department of State to British Ambassador, Washington, October 18, 1945, FO 371/51049, UKPRO.

6 *Ibid.*, enclosed memorandum FEAC 7: "Policy of the United States in regard to the apprehension and punishment of war criminals in the Far East".

7 Watt, Donald Cameron, *Foreign Relations of the United States*, US

Department of State, US Govt Printing Office, Washington, 1945, Vol VI, p 926.

8 Pritchard, R. John "An Overview of the Historical Importance of the Tokyo Trial", unpublished ms, published in abbreviated form in *The Tokyo War Crimes Trial: An International Symposium*, ed. by Hosoya, *et al*, Kōdansha, Tokyo, 1986, pp 89–97; letter Robert Donihi to Pritchard, May 13, 1977.

9 *New York Times*, December 9, 1954, p 33; *Time*, May 20, 1946; Richard H. Minear, *Victors' Justice, The Tokyo War Crimes Trial*, Charles E. Tuttle, Tokyo, 1982, p 40.

10 U 6563/6/73, "Far Eastern Commission, Committee No 5: War Criminals, Transcript of the Special Meeting of Committee No 5, held in Main Conference Room, 2516 Massachusetts Avenue, NW", June 25, 1946, p 1, FO 371/57432, UKPRO.

11 Pritchard ms, and Donihi letter, *loc. cit.*

12 "Memorandum of Staff Meeting in Room 510, Meiji Building at 10 a.m.", December 10, 1945.

13 Watt, *op. cit.* Pritchard ms, *loc. cit.*; IMTFE, Vol 1, Pre-Trial Documents.

14 Humphreys, Christmas, *Via Tokyo*, Hutchinson, London, 1948, pp 9–10; U 4480/5/73 (file), March–April 1946, FO 371/57426, UKPRO.

15 Watt, *op. cit.*; U 790/5/73, telegram 44, British Mission, Tokyo, to Foreign Office, January 18, 1946, FO 371/57422, UKPRO.

16 Watt, *op. cit.*; U 1620/5/73, telegram 137, British Mission, Tokyo, to Foreign Office, February 8, 1946, FO 371/57422, UKPRO.

17 Watt, *op. cit.*

18 *Ibid.*

19 Pritchard ms, *loc. cit.*

20 Watt, *op. cit.*

21 Pritchard ms, *loc. cit.*; Humphreys, *op. cit.*, pp 76–85.

22 IMTFE, Vol 1, The Indictment and Appendices.

23 Pritchard ms, *loc. cit.*

24 U 4332/5/73 (file), February–April 1946, FO 371/57426, UKPRO; Pritchard ms and Watt, *loc. cit.*

25 Col Thomas H. Morrow to Joseph B. Keenan, "Sino-Japanese War", March 2, 1946, WNA.

26 "Minutes of the Meeting of the Executive Committee", March 4, 1946.

27 Humphreys, *op. cit.*, pp 84–5.

28 "Report Assignment B", GHQ, SCAP, IPS, Col Thomas Morrow to Joseph B. Keenan, March 8, 1946, WNA.

29 "Minutes of Meeting of Associate Prosecutors", April 17, 1946.

30 IMTFE, Vol 2, Record of the Proceedings for August 29, 1946, pp 4546–4552.

31 Document received from Prof Kentarō Awaya, Rikkyō University, Tokyo.

32 Memorandum "General Suggestions Paper No 6", from David Nelson Sutton to all IPS attorneys, April 14, 1947; R. John Pritchard, *Vol 5, Index*

and Guide, Tokyo War Crimes Trial, Garland Publishing, New York; 1981.
33 Mendelsohn, John, "The Preservation of Japanese War Crimes Trials Records in the US National Archives", *Committee on East Asian Libraries Bulletin*, Association for Asian Studies, February/June 1983, No 70/71.
34 *Time*, September 17, 1945; *Reports of Gen MacArthur, MacArthur in Japan; The Occupation: Military Phase, Vol 1 Supplement*, prepared by his General Staff, US Government Printing Office, Washington, 1967, p. 108.
35 "Infectious Disease Research Laboratory", Investigation Division, Legal Section, GHQ, SCAP, January 31, 1947, RG 331, MFB, WNA.

Chapter 13
1 Jones, F. C., *Manchuria Since 1931*, Royal Institute of International Affairs, London 1949, p 225.
2 *The Times*, September 11, 1945; F. C. Jones, *op. cit.*, p 224.
3 "Subject: Bacteriological Warfare Experiments by Japanese", to A C of S, G-2, FEC, GHQ, FEC, Military Intelligence Section, General Staff, January 17, 1947, RG 331, MFB, WNA.
4 Khabarovsk, p 191.
5 Raginsky, pp 73–4.
6 Khabarovsk, pp 159–60.
7 *Ibid.*, pp 211–13.
8 *Ibid.*, pp 165–7.
9 *Ibid.*, pp 183–6.
10 *Ibid.*, pp 426–7.
11 Conversation with Dr Shirō Kasahara, Tokyo, February 1985.
12 Khabarovsk, p 516.
13 "Statement of Maj Tomio Karasawa", undated, ATIS, Document 9306, RG 331, MFB, WNA.
14 "Questionnaire – PoW – The former chief medical officer of the First Army Group of the Kwantung Army, Maj-Gen Kiyoshi Kawashima, at Khabarovsk on September 12, 1946", ATIS, Document 9305, RG 331, MFB, WNA.
15 *Ibid.*, ATIS, Document 9309, RG 331, MFB WNA.
16 Conversation with Dr Raginsky, Moscow, December 1985.
17 C-in-C FE, Tokyo, Japan (Carpenter, Legal Section, SCAP) to War (WDSCA, WC), June 7, 1947, RG 153, MFB, WNA.
18 As cited in C-in-C FE, Tokyo, Japan, to War Department for WDSCA, February 10, 1947, RG 331, MFB, WNA.
19 "Interrogation of Dr Kiyoshi Ōta, re – bacteriological warfare", GHQ, US Army Forces, Pacific, Office of Chief Chemical Officer, December 2, 1946, RG 319 ACSI, ID Files, MFB, WNA.
20 Memorandum, Maj-Gen Vasiliev to Maj-Gen Willoughby through IPS, January 9, 1947, RG 331, MFB, WNA.
21 "Bacterial Warfare Experiments by the Japanese", Lt-Col R. McQuail to A C of S, G-2, January 17, 1947, RG 331, MFB, WNA.
22 *Ibid.*
23 *Ibid.*

24 "Allied Operation and Occupational Headquarters World War II, SCAP, Civil Property Custodian Section. Memorandum for Record: Russian Request to Interrogate Japanese on Bacteriological Warfare", Outgoing Message, CnC FE to WDSCA, February 7, 1947.

25 "Memorandum for Record, Subject: USSR Request to Interrogate and Arrest Japanese Bacteriological Warfare Experts", To: Chief of Staff, March 27, 1947, RG 331, MFB, WNA.

26 From: Washington (JCS), To: CnC FE (MacArthur), W 94446, March 21, 1947, RG 331, MFB, WNA.

27 Memorandum To Lt-Gen Kusma Derevyanko, Member for USSR, Allied Council for Japan, Memo No 1087, March 7, 1947, RG 331, MFB, WNA.

Chapter 14

1 "Conference with Dr Kan'ichirō Kamei", April 21, 1947, Fort Detrick ref 006 (hereinafter 006).

2 "Interrogation of Tomosada Masuda", April 22, 1947, 006.

3 "Conference with Kan'ichirō Kamei", April 24, 1947, 006.

4 "New copies of questionnaire", April 30, 1947, documents released to author under the US Freedom of Information Act (FOIA) from Dept of Army custody.

5 "Interrogations of Hitoshi Kikuchi", May 1, 2 and 5, 1947, 006.

6 *Ibid.*, May 2 and 5, 1947, 006.

7 Radio C-52423, CnC FE, Tokyo, Japan, to War Department for WDGID (pass to CCMLC) MID pass to Maj-Gen Alden Waitt, May 6, 1947, RG 331, MFB, WNA.

8 "Interrogations of Shirō Ishii", May 8 and 9, 1947, 006.

9 Conversation with Dr Sanders, January 1986.

10 "Interrogations of Shirō Ishii", May 8 and 9, 1947, 006.

11 "Conversation with Dr Kan'ichirō Kamei", May 7, 1947, 006.

12 Interrogations of Takashi Murakami, Kiyoshi Ōta, Tsuneshige Ikari, on May 10 and Yujrō Wakamatsu on May 29, 1947, 006.

13 Conversation with Dr Raginsky, Moscow, December 25, 1985.

14 Daughter's Eye View.

15 Letter, Dr Norbert H. Fell to Brig-Gen C. A. Willoughby, August 14, 1947, document released under FOIA from Dept of Army custody.

16 Letter, Lt-Col Robert McQuail to Dr Norbert H. Fell, July 2, 1947, document released under FOIA from Dept of Army custody.

17 Conversation with Mr William Covert, Chief, Public Affairs, Fort Detrick, January 1986.

18 Letter, Lt-Col Robert McQuail to Dr Norbert H. Fell, July 2, 1947, document released under FOIA from Dept of Army custody.

19 Letter, Maj W. M. Drake to Dr Norbert H. Fell, August 12, 1947, document released under FOIA from Dept of Army custody.

Chapter 15

1 Smith, April 18, 1947, RG 331, MFB, WNA.

2 *Ibid.*, April 4, 1947.

3 Khabarovsk, p 384.

4 Smith, *loc. cit.*

5 *Ibid.*

6 *Ibid.*

7 *Ibid.*

8 *Ibid.*

9 War Crimes Branch to SCAP, Tokyo, for Carpenter, Legal Section, June 2, 1947, RG 153, MFB, WNA.

10 CnC FE to War Dept (WDSCA WC), June 7, 1947, RG 153, MFB, WNA.

11 WDSCA WC to CnC FE, June 21, 1947, RG 153, MFB, WNA.

12 CnC FE to WDSCA, June 23, 1947, RG 153, MFB, WNA.

13 CnC FE to WDSCA WC, June 27, 1947, RG 153, MFB, WNA.

14 SFE 188/2, State-War-Navy Co-ordinating Sub-Committee for the Far East, August 1, 1947, RG 153, MFB, WNA.

15 *Ibid.*

16 *Ibid.*

17 *Ibid.*

18 *Ibid.*

19 SFE 188/2, State-War-Navy Co-ordinating Sub Committee for the Far East, August 1, 1947, RG 153, MFB,WNA.

20 *Ibid.*

21 Letter, McQuail to Fell, July 2, 1947, document released under FOIA from Dept of Army custody.

22 Letter, Willoughby to Fell, July 22, 1947, document released under FOIA from Dept of Army custody.

23 Letter, Fell to Willoughby, August 14, 1947, document released under FOIA from Dept of Army custody.

24 Hill and Victor, *loc. cit.*

25 *Ibid.*

26 *Ibid.*

27 SFE 188/5, State-Army-Navy-Air Force Co-ordinating Sub-Committee for the Far East, March 4, 1948, RG 153, MFB, WNA.

28 SANACC 351/3, State-Army-Navy-Air Force Co-ordinating Committee, March 11, 1948.

29 IMTFE, Vol 12, T 28110 and T 28239–44.

30 *Ibid.*, T 4545–7.

31 IMTFE, Exhibit 3100 (Defence Document 2470), "Sworn Testimony of Tsuneo Yasuda", September 2, 1947.

32 Webb, "Separate Opinion", p 17; Richard H. Minear, *op. cit.*, p 162.

33 Whitney Courtney, *MacArthur*, New York, Knopf, 1956, pp 281–2; Minear, *op. cit.*, pp 166–7.

34 United Nations War Crimes Commission, Far Eastern and Pacific Sub Commission, List of War Criminals and Material Witnesses, List No 7, October 1945, FO 371/51052, 80283, UKPRO.

Chapter 16
1 An edited transcript of the trial is contained in materials on the *Trial of Former Servicemen of the Japanese Army, charged with manufacturing and employing Bacteriological Weapons*, published by Foreign Language Publishing House, Moscow, 1950.
2 Public Record Office FO 371 76254 8033.
3 *Ibid.*
4 *Ibid.*
5 *Ibid.*
6 *Ibid.*
7 *Ibid.*
8 Except, of course, by comparison with the Murray Sanders, Arvo Thompson and Hill and Victor reports, in US hands since 1945 and 1947.
9 New York Times Library
10 Conversation with Dr Raginsky, Moscow, December 1985.
11 "Hirsch Report–Part 1", US Department of Defense, undated.

Chapter 17
1 (Chapter 12, Note 4.) Watt, *op. cit.*
2 "US Backed Japan's Germ Tests on Mentally Sick", *Observer*, August 21, 1983.
3 Tsuneishi, p 146.
4 Asano, Section: "The Bereaved Family".
5 *Ibid.*
6 "US Backed Japan's Germ Tests on Mentally Sick", *Observer*, August 21, 1983.
7 *Ibid.*, and *Who's Who*.
8 *Ibid.*, and *Who's Who of Contemporary Japanese*, 1963.
9 *Who's Who*.
10 Asano, Section: "The Central China Anti-Epidemic Water Supply Unit".
11 *Ibid.*
12 "US Backed Japan's Germ Tests on Mentally Sick", *Observer*, August 21, 1983.
13 *Ibid.*
14 Document, Fort Detrick Ref 007.
15 Asano, Section: "The Central China Anti-Epidemic Water Supply Unit".
16 Document, Fort Detrick Ref 007.
17 *Who's Who*.
18 Conversation with Professor Kei'ichi Tsuneishi, Nagasaki, Japan, November 1984.
19 Asano, Section: "The Central China Anti-Epidemic Water Supply Unit".
20 TBS Television documentary, November 2, 1976.
21 Conversation with Professor Kei'ichi Tsuneishi, Nagasaki, Japan, November 1984.

22 Khabarovsk, p 103.
23 Conversation with Dr Sueo Akimoto, Yokohama, Japan, December 1984.
24 "Hirohito Personally Approved Germ Warfare Unit", *Guardian*, September 17, 1982.
25 Conversation with Dr Seiichi Niizuma, Tokyo, Japan, July 1986.
26 "Personality Profile", *Japan Times*, April 22, 1964.
27 "Let Me Have My Say", *Japan Times*, March 2, 1963.
28 "Personality Profile", *Japan Times*, April 22, 1964.
29 Conversation with Professor Kei'ichi Tsuneishi, Nagasaki, Japan, November 1984.
30 Alpha Therapeutic Corporation prospectus, and *Who's Who*.
31 "'Japan's Green Cross Troubled By Events", *Asian Wall Street Journal*, December 3, 1982.
32 Alpha Therapeutic Corporation prospectus and *Who's Who*.
33 Ikeda, Naeo, "Infection Experiments with the flea and lice of epidemic haemorrhagic fever", *Japan Infectious Diseases Society Journal* (*Nihon Densenbyō Gakkai Zasshi*), August 20, 1968, Vol 42, No 5.
34 Tsuneishi, p 113.
35 "Otozō Yamada, 83, Former General", *New York Times*, July 20, 1965.
36 Triplett, William, *Flowering of the Bamboo*, Woodbine House, Kensington, Maryland; 1985, pp 149–51.
37 Conversation with Harumi Ishii, Tokyo, Japan, April 1987.
38 *Ibid.*
39 *Boyu* (magazine published occasionally by ex-members of Unit 731), Vol 2, No 6; Morimura I, Section: "Let's Be Proud of the 731".
40 Conversation with Harumi Ishii, Tokyo, Japan, April 1987.
41 Daughter's Eye View.
42 *Ibid.*
43 Asano, Section: "The Ishii Bacteriological Warfare Unit".
44 Conversation with Harumi Ishii, Tokyo, Japan, April 1987.
45 Evidence to Committee on Veteran Affairs, September 1986.
46 *Ibid.*
47 *Ibid.*
48 See Ch 8, Note 56.
49 "Report claims Americans killed in Germ-War Tests", *The Oregonian*, October 31, 1981.
50 Conversation with John Powell, April 1987.
51 "Japan admits Germ War tests killed PoW Guinea Pigs", *Daily Telegraph*, April 8, 1982.
52 SAC, SFO to Director FBI "John William Powell, Internal Security-R-Ch Sedition", March 13, 1956, document held at Fort Detrick.
53 Conversation with Norman Covert, Chief, Public Affairs (historian), Fort Detrick, April 1987.
54 Sanders, Murray and R. D. Alexander, "Epidemic Kerato Conjunctivitis, Isolation and Identification of a Filterable Virus", *Journal of Experimental Medicine*, Vol 77, No 1943, pp 71–96.

INDEX

940.5413 Williams, Peter,
WIL   1933-

         Unit 731

                                    22.95

         $22.95

DATE		

© THE BAKER & TAYLOR CO.